THE DYNAMICS OF NORTH AMERICAN
TRADE AND INVESTMENT

CONTRIBUTORS

Gerardo Bueno

Richard E. Caves

Alan V. Deardorff

Morley Gunderson

Daniel S. Hamermesh

Richard G. Harris

Alain Ize

Yehuda Kotowitz

Mauricio de María y Campos

Charles E. McLure, Jr.

Clark W. Reynolds

A. E. Safarian

Fernando Sánchez Ugarte

Jeffrey J. Schott

Murray G. Smith

Robert M. Stern

Saúl Trejo Reyes

Leonard Waverman

Sidney Weintraub

Sponsored by the Project on
North American Relations

The Dynamics of
North American Trade
and Investment

CANADA, MEXICO, AND THE UNITED STATES

Edited by
Clark W. Reynolds, Leonard Waverman,
and Gerardo Bueno

Stanford University Press, Stanford, California

The Dynamics of North American Trade and Investment: Canada, Mexico, and the United States is sponsored by the Project on North American Relations. It represents the first of several books with a focus on North American Relations in the continuing series *U. S.–Mexico Relations*, published by Stanford University Press.

"Global Implications of the Canada-U.S. Free Trade Agreement," by Jeffrey J. Schott, is reprinted with permission of the Institute for International Economics, Washington, D.C.

Stanford University Press, Stanford, California
© 1991 by the Board of Trustees of the
Leland Stanford Junior University
Printed in the United States of America

CIP data appear at the end of the book

Preface

T HIS VOLUME is the first published under the auspices of the Project on North American Relations, an outgrowth of the U.S.-Mexico Relations Project begun in 1979. The North American Project brings together Canadian, Mexican, and U.S. scholars and decision-makers from the private and public sectors in workshops, seminars, and conferences whose aim is to stimulate and share research on changing economic and social relations among the three economies of North America. It grew out of an experiment in which Canadian participants were invited to join members of the U.S.-Mexico Project in a series of workshops on comparative energy policy analysis. The success of this experiment made it evident that considerable benefits could arise from the comparative analysis of a wide range of policy problems facing the three countries, independent of their commitment to formal regional integration.

The trinational group that sponsored this volume first met in the spring of 1985 to organize a conference that took place in Mérida, Yucatán, on "Industrial Organization, Trade, and Investment in North America: United States, Canada, and Mexico" in December of that year. That conference produced a number of papers and considerable discussion among specialists in trade and industrial organization analysis, macroeconomic policy, and applied industrial research on particular industries. In addition, these specialists were joined by top policy analysts from the three countries concerned. The interaction of scholars and policymakers brought the best of contemporary theory and applied research to bear on practical problems confronting a region facing increasing trade and economic integration.

The Mérida studies demonstrated that changing trade and economic relations among the three countries call for new conceptual approaches to integration among economies with very different structures of production and productivity, social relations, and history, values, and institu-

tions. A compilation of papers from that conference is forthcoming as
two issues of *The North American Review of Economics and Finance*
(1990/1991) under the titles *Essays on Comparative Advantage in North
America: Theory and Policy,* and *Case Studies of Dynamic Comparative
Advantage in North America.*

The success of the Mérida conference caused the organizers to work
toward a follow-up session to be held in Canada. While plans were under
way, several important changes occurred. Events from 1985 to 1988 confirmed a major increase in trade between Canada and the United States
and the United States and Mexico. The process of trade growth reflected
a more complex underlying network of production-sharing and market-
sharing in which economic decisions were being made on an increasingly
binational and even trinational basis. And the very asymmetries among
the three countries provided incentives for decision-makers to increase
regional trade and investment in order to realize potential gains. Meanwhile, debates surrounding the Canada-U.S. Free Trade Agreement and
U.S.-Mexico negotiations on trade, investment, technology transfer, and
migration made the issues discussed far more than academic.

The North American Project launched its conference in Toronto on
"The Dynamics of North American Trade and Economic Relations" just
one week before the June 1988 Summit of OECD leaders in the same
city, in an effort to contribute to the framing of a new trinational policy
agenda. The essays in this volume are based on papers delivered at that
conference, a forum that also benefited from additional verbal presenta-
tions and discussion by top policymakers and scholars from the three
countries. The organizers, Gerardo Bueno of El Colegio de México,
Clark Reynolds of Stanford University, and Leonard Waverman of the
University of Toronto, were founding directors of the North American
Project and joint coordinators of the earlier Mérida conference.

Since 1988 the process of regional integration has been moving forward at a faster pace than either formal analysis or policy coordination.
The speed of change in North America has been exceeded only by that of
its competitors in Europe and Asia. As a result of the Toronto conference,
the coordinators and their colleagues have determined to build the framework for trinational policy research on alternative economic and social
interdependencies among the North American nations. To this end, two
workshops were held in 1989—one in Cocoyóc, Mexico, in July, and the
other at Stanford in November—to prepare an agenda for consortium-
based research and analysis. The initial coordinating institutions for this
agenda will be the Centre for International Studies of the University of
Toronto, the Americas Program of Stanford University, and El Colegio

de México, in cooperation with other institutions and specialists from the private and public sectors.

All activities of the North American Project are conceptualized, coordinated, researched, and funded on a trinational basis. The essays in this volume are not circumscribed by any preconceived model of regional integration, though each author was encouraged to consider the interaction of economic and social relations and their political consequences to the extent possible given the nature of the subject and the limitations of space and time.

Appreciation is expressed to the William and Flora Hewlett Foundation, the Tinker Foundation, the Donner Canadian Foundation, and the governments of Canada and Mexico for support of activities leading to the publication of this volume. The editorial assistance of Julie Carlson has been indispensable, along with the efforts of Jessica Sylla, Sylvia Martinez, and the staff at Stanford, Toronto, and El Colegio de México. The editors wish to acknowledge the valuable role of Professor John Wirth of Stanford and Grant Barnes, Director of Stanford University Press, in providing advice and assistance at all stages of production.

Clark W. Reynolds
Leonard Waverman
Gerardo Bueno

Contents

Contributors

GERARDO BUENO is Director of The Instituto de Capacitación e Investigación para el Desarrollo in Nacional Financiera and professor at El Colegio de México. He has been Project and Industrial Programming Manager in Nacional Financiera; Director General of the Consejo Nacional de Ciencia y Tecnologia; Ambassador to the European Economic Community, Belgium, and Luxemburg; and professor of monetary theory and international economics. He has recently coauthored the book *Toward Renewed Economic Growth in Latin America* (1986).

RICHARD E. CAVES is Professor of Economics and Business Administration at Harvard University, from which he received his Ph.D. His main field of interest is applied industrial organization, with special reference to its international aspects. His books include *Competition in the Open Economy* (1980); *Multinational Enterprise and Economic Analysis* (1982); *Britain's Productivity Gap* (1987); and *Efficiency in U.S. Manufacturing Industries* (1990).

ALAN V. DEARDORFF is Professor of Economics and Public Policy in the Department of Economics and Institute of Public Policy Studies at The University of Michigan. He received his Ph.D. from Cornell University. He specializes in international trade theory and policy. His publications include a number of papers on aspects of the theory of comparative advantage, and he is coauthor, with Robert M. Stern, of *The Michigan Model of World Production and Trade* (1986).

MORLEY GUNDERSON is Director of the Centre for Industrial Relations and a Professor in the Department of Economics at the University of Toronto. He earned his Ph.D. from the University of Wisconsin, Madison and has published extensively on such topics as sex discrimination and pay and employment equity; pensions, the aging work force and mandatory retirement; public-sector wages and employment; the determinants and impact of immigration; labor-market adjustment policies; and issues related to poverty and income distribution. His books include *Labour Market Economics: Theory, Evidence, and Policy in Canada* (1988); *Economics of Poverty and Income Distribution* (1983); *Union-Management Relations in Canada* (1989); and *Women and Labour Market Poverty* (1990).

DANIEL S. HAMERMESH is Professor of Economics at Michigan State University and Research Associate of the National Bureau of Economic Research. He received his Ph.D. at Yale University and specializes in labor economics. He is the author of *Jobless Pay and the Economy* (1977) and of numerous journal articles in the areas of labor demand and labor-market programs, and coauthor of *The Economics of Work and Pay* (1988).

RICHARD G. HARRIS is Professor of Economics at Queen's University and Simon Fraser University, and is Director of the John Deutsch Institute at Queen's. He obtained his Ph.D. in Economics at the University of British Columbia and specializes in international trade and general equilibrium theory. He is a Fellow of the Royal Society of Canada, has served as a consultant to various government and international agencies, and was the winner of the Queen's University Research Award in 1988. Some of his popular publications include *Trade, Industrial Policy, and Canadian Manufacturing* (1984) and journal articles such as "The New Protectionism Revisited" (*Canadian Journal of Economics*); "Trade Liberalization and Industrial Organization: Some Estimates for Canada" (*Journal of Political Economy*); and "Applied General Equilibrium Analysis of Small Open Economies with Scale Economies and Imperfect Competition" (*American Economic Review*).

ALAIN IZE is Senior Economist in the Fiscal Affairs department of the International Monetary Fund. He earned his Ph.D. from Stanford University and has published in the fields of international finance, public economics, and macroeconomics of developing economies, with a particular emphasis on issues related to the Mexican economy.

YEHUDA KOTOWITZ is Professor of Economics at the University of Toronto. He received his Ph.D. from the University of Chicago, and specializes in economic theory. Some of his more popular authored and co-authored articles include "Positive Industrial Policy: The Implications for R & D" (Ontario Economic Council, 1985); "Patent Policy in an Open Economy" (*Canadian Journal of Economics,* 1982); "Optimal R & D Processes and Market Structure" (*Economica,* 1985).

MAURICIO DE MARÍA Y CAMPOS is Executive Vice President of Banco Mexicano SOMEX and an adviser to UNIDO. He received his Lic. in economics from the National Autonomous University in Mexico (UNAM) and an M.A. in economic development from Sussex University. At the time of the conference in June 1988, he was Undersecretary for Industry in the Secretariat of Commerce and Industrial Development (SECOFI); prior to that time he worked in the finance industry on fiscal incentives. One of his more recent publications is "Mexico Facing the Challenges of the New Technological Revolution," featured in *Comercio Exterior* (Dec. 1988).

CHARLES E. MCLURE, JR. is a Senior Fellow at the Hoover Institution at Stanford University. Having received his Ph.D. in economics from Princeton University, he is an expert in tax policy. Among his recent publications are *State Corporation Income Tax: Issues in Worldwide Unitary Combination* (1984); *The Value-Added Tax: Key to Deficit Reduction* (1987); *Economic Perspectives on State Taxation of Multijurisdictional Corporations* (1987); and *The Taxation of Income from Business and Capital in Colombia* (1989).

CLARK W. REYNOLDS has been Professor of Economics at the Food Research Institute at Stanford University since 1967. In 1980, he became founding director of the Americas Program, an interdisciplinary program which sponsors research on the social, economic, and political aspects of development, and regional and international exchange. Professor Reynolds is the author of numerous publications and is currently writing the sequel to the 1970 volume, *The Mexican Economy: Twentieth Century Structure and Growth,* to be entitled *The Mexican Economy: Managing Interdependence.*

A. E. SAFARIAN is Professor Emeritus of Economics and Professor of Business Economics at the University of Toronto. In recent years, his research has focused on policies toward multinational firms in the industrial countries. His publications include: *Foreign Ownership of Ca-*

nadian Industry (1966); *Canadian Federalism and Economic Integration* (1974); and *Governments and Multinationals: Policies in the Industrial Countries* (1983).

FERNANDO SÁNCHEZ UGARTE has occupied several different positions in the Mexican Ministry of Finance, including Adviser to the General Director of Fiscal Economic Studies (1976), Director of the Income Tax Office (1978–79), General Subdirector of the Tax Policy Office (1980), and General Director of the Tax Policy Office (1986–88). From 1983 to 1986 he worked as a staff member of the Tax Policy Division at the Fiscal Affairs Department of the International Monetary Fund. He is presently the Undersecretary of Industry and Foreign Investment. He has taught public finance and economics, and in 1983 received the Banamex National Award in Economics.

JEFFREY J. SCHOTT is a research fellow at the Institute for International Economics in Washington, D.C., and has concurrently been Adjunct Professor of International Business Diplomacy at Georgetown University in the School of Foreign Service. Formerly a Senior Associate at the Carnegie Endowment for International Peace and an official of the U.S. Treasury Department from 1974 to 1982 in the areas of international trade and energy policy, Mr. Schott was a member of the U.S. delegation that negotiated the GATT Subsidies Code during the Tokyo Round of multilateral trade negotiations in the GATT. Two of his latest endeavors are a new study, "More Free Trade Areas?," and a 1988 monograph on the Canada-U.S. Free Trade Agreement. He holds an M.A. in international relations from the Johns Hopkins University School of Advanced International Studies.

MURRAY G. SMITH is Director of the International Economics Program at the Institute for Research on Public Policy. He studied economics at the Universities of British Columbia and Michigan. During the Tokyo Round of multilateral negotiations, Mr. Smith was Director of International Economic Relations for the government of British Columbia and represented this province in national and international meetings. Currently, he serves on the panel that resolves disputes under Chapter 18 of the Canada-U.S. Free Trade Agreement. His most recent publication is *Canada, the Pacific and Global Trade* (1989), which examines current proposals for cooperation among Pacific economies.

ROBERT M. STERN is Professor of Economics and Public Policy in the Department of Economics and Institute of Public Policy Studies at The University of Michigan. He received his Ph.D. from Columbia University. He has published numerous articles and books in the last three decades dealing with a variety of empirical and policy related issues in international trade and finance.

SAÚL TREJO REYES is currently Special Advisor to the Secretary of Programming and Budget in Mexico. He received his Ph.D. from Yale University and has worked in the fields of industrial policy, employment, and international economics. He is the author of *Industrialization and Employment in Mexico* (1973), *The Future of Industrial Policy in Mexico* (1987), and *Employment for All: The Challenge and the Means* (1988), published in Mexico. He has held a number of government positions and has been Senior Research Fellow at El Colegio de México.

LEONARD WAVERMAN is Professor of Economics and Director of the Centre for International Studies at the University of Toronto. In 1991 he will be a Visiting Professor at INSEAD in Fontainebleau. His research interests are in industrial organization, energy economics, and productivity analyses. Forthcoming publications include an examination, coauthored with Melvyn Fuss, of costs and productivity in the U.S., Canadian, Japanese, and German auto industries, and an analysis of import-substitution policies in the Mexican, Argentinean, and Korean auto industries.

SIDNEY WEINTRAUB is Dean Rusk Professor, Lyndon B. Johnson School of Public Affairs, University of Texas at Austin, and Distinguished Visiting Scholar at the Center for Strategic and International Studies in Washington, D.C. He earned his Ph.D. at the American University. He has written extensively on international trade and finance. His most recent book is *A Marriage of Convenience: Relations Between Mexico and the United States* (1990).

THE DYNAMICS OF NORTH AMERICAN
TRADE AND INVESTMENT

Introduction

Clark W. Reynolds, Leonard Waverman, and Gerardo Bueno

NORTH AMERICAN trade and economic relations are changing faster than anyone could have predicted three years ago. The essays in this volume, original versions of which were presented at a conference in Toronto in June 1988, have proven prescient. The issues discussed affect all three countries of North America: Canada, Mexico, and the United States. They reflect a watershed in the development of the regional economy, just after U.S. ratification of the Canada-U.S. Free Trade Agreement (FTA) and before its hotly contested endorsement by general election in Canada. The atmosphere at Toronto was charged, as supporters and opponents debated the advantages and disadvantages of free trade between the two northern neighbors, a debate that has intensified as Mexican incorporation into the North American market has become increasingly probable. For the first time, Mexican academics were beginning to signal that regional free trade was on the agenda.

The papers address a new set of issues: given the endorsement of the FTA, how might the Canada-U.S. agreement affect Mexican trade and economic relations? How might Canada be affected by the recent (1987) signing of a Framework Agreement for the discussion of trade and economic relations between the United States and Mexico? And what effect might General Agreement on Tariffs and Trade (GATT) negotiations for increased global free trade have on North American economic integration? One certain implication is dawning on all three countries: given the large and growing amount of exchange between Canada and the United States, and between the United States and Mexico, Mexico is bound to have a major impact on the North American economy with or without a formal North American free trade agreement, both directly through bilateral exchange and indirectly as changing relations with one northern neighbor affect the other through the FTA.

With 23 percent of the region's population and only 3 percent of its GNP, Mexico represents an economy whose scope for participation in the regional market is virtually untapped. Per capita income differentials of ten to one between the United States and Canada (almost equal at $19,000) and Mexico ($1,900) offer major opportunities for shared development. With continued liberalization of regional trade and investment, and improvements in economic and social infrastructure among the three countries, the pattern of divergence in productivity and income between Mexico and its northern neighbors in the 1980s could be reversed in the 1990s. If this widening of the economic gap in North America could be reversed, with Mexico's productivity rising even faster than that of Canada and the United States, there would be enormous gains from increased trade and investment between the two countries, notwithstanding the adjustment costs involved. And with Mexico catching up, Canada and the United States would have the opportunity to become even more competitive in global markets by restructuring their output in the direction of higher productivity goods and services.

The three nations of North America are already larger than the European Community in terms of combined population and GDP. Together they provide scope for economies of scale, product and process innovations, entrepreneurship, and gains from the removal of market barriers that will be of critical importance to their welfare in a time of expanding global trade and competitiveness. Significant GATT progress notwithstanding, in practice international integration is proceeding in stepwise fashion, with regional blocs providing the building blocks for greater harmonization of fiscal and financial policies, legal, institutional, and regulatory measures, and the reduction of nontariff barriers on which the gains from trade and investment depend.

The economic, social, and political problems associated with North American integration remain enormous. Major questions are already being raised in terms of national security, sovereignty, the ownership and control of productive resources, the treatment of labor, and the ability to reconcile divergent social programs especially in terms of public and private costs, as well as political agendas that differ markedly among the three countries. What are the estimated benefits and costs that would result from alternative patterns of regional exchange under such circumstances? And how might such gains and losses be apportioned among the countries involved, given their current disparities in productivity and income, not to mention differences in values, institutions, social structure, and power relations?

These issues constitute an imposing agenda for research and policy analysis, with implications that are bound to modify the climate for regional investment, employment, and politics for years to come, and thereby profoundly affect the international system. As this volume goes to press, the movement toward regionalism is being increasingly debated in all three countries, and especially in Canada and Mexico. Such pressures assure that the agreements reached to date will be subject to considerable modification over time as policymakers have to deal with the kind of issues introduced in these papers.

RECENT AGREEMENTS

The Canada-U.S. Free Trade Agreement, already signed by the chief executives of both countries at the end of 1987, was ratified by the U.S. Congress and endorsed by a Canadian national election in the fall of 1988. A Framework Agreement between Mexico and the United States was signed in the fall of 1987, following Mexico's entry into GATT the previous year. Subsequently, sectoral discussions have taken place between the United States and Mexico, including a major commitment by Presidents Bush and Salinas de Gortari in the fall of 1989 to work within the framework of GATT toward significant increases in bilateral trade and investment, as well as toward technology transfer and the exchange of services.

In January 1990, the Seventh Meeting of the Canada-Mexico Joint Ministerial Committee was held in Ottawa. Agreement was reached on the need for considerable expansion of Canada-Mexico trade, closer cooperation in global and regional economic forums, and joint efforts toward solving the debt problems of the developing countries and improving the international economy. This meeting was followed by a visit by Prime Minister Mulroney of Canada to Mexico in March, at the invitation of President Salinas de Gortari, for the purpose of signing a Canada-Mexico Framework Agreement on bilateral trade and economic relations. Another major step was taken in late February 1990, at a meeting in Washington between top-level officials of Mexico and the United States where the decision was made to explore the possibility of a bilateral trade and investment agreement. All of these activities will substantially affect the future world position of the three countries of North America.

THE PRESENT VOLUME

The book is divided into five parts. The initial one, titled "What Have We Learned from the Past?," explores movements toward the Canada-U.S. Free Trade Agreement in terms of the impact of prior liberalization policies at both the macro- and the microeconomic levels. Part two, "Multilateral Trade Negotiations," relates the Canada-U.S. regional integration process to global trade discussions, including implications for the possible incorporation of Mexico into a North American free trade area. The third part, "Investment Strategies and Fiscal Harmonization," deals with the implications of regionalism for national policies affecting investment, taxation, and intellectual property. Part four, "Intellectual Property and Technology Transfer," examines the consequences of the new information technologies for trade and investment liberalization between developed and developing countries. Part five, "Labor Markets and Adjustment Assistance," deals with the impact of increased regional trade and investment on employment, wages, and working conditions in Canada, the United States, and Mexico. The final part, "Bilateral Trade Agreements and the Future of North American Economic Relations," provides views from Canada and the United States on the prospects for North American integration, given the challenges of world trade and the opportunities presented by a new regionalism. Highlights from each part follow.

Part I explores the question, How much has global liberalization affected economies of the region? According to a model of world production and trade, Deardorff and Stern argue that the GATT Tokyo Round has had little *net* impact on employment in either Canada or the United States, despite important reallocation of resources among sectors of the two economies. The authors show that increased competition from imports was at least partially offset for each country by gains in exports in response to GATT liberalization. The trade balance is a result of net capital flows in response to macroeconomic policy rather than tariff changes. Indeed, in today's world of increasing economic interdependence, macroeconomic linkages seem to matter much more than tariff policy.

Trade liberalization increases efficiency and competitiveness in previously sheltered industries, according to Caves, favoring trade growth in both directions (increased exports and imports of similar products for a given sector in each country). His approach differs from that of Deardorff and Stern (who assume pure competition) by introducing the possibility of oligopoly. As industries dominated by one or a few firms experience pressure from increased imports brought about by tariff reductions, such firms are induced to cut costs and improve quality, taking advantage of increasing returns from a larger scale of production. Such results are possible since liberalization widens the market even as it overcomes barriers to entry. This is substantiated by Caves from Canadian evidence. As imports rise, so does investment in the threatened (oligopolistic) industries, with attendant increases in exports and productivity.

The findings of Part I have important implications for Canada and Mexico, both of which are experiencing a rapid rise in the trade share of GNP, two-thirds of which is with the United States. As each country is becoming more vulnerable to swings in the U.S. economy, macroeconomic linkages are of as much concern as additional tariff cuts, and the more trade barriers are reduced, the greater this sensitivity becomes. And with the growth of trade and investment linkages, all three North American countries face increasing pressures to reach agreements that limit the ability of any single partner to unilaterally affect the others.

Caves' point about the positive effects of trade liberalization on productivity for economies subject to previously protected oligopolies has particular relevance for Mexico. Its recent policies of increased openness may be expected to induce a response to competitive pressures in many of its major industries, permitting the most forward-looking firms to take advantage of scale economies and lower costs made possible by opening to a wider international market, beginning with the United States and Canada.

Macroeconomic policy in Mexico has proved important in providing the stability needed for effective integration of its economy into the international market. Jaime Serra, then Mexico's Undersecretary of Finance (and now Minister of Trade and Industry), gave a verbal presentation at the Toronto conference describing his country's unique Economic Solidarity Pact, introduced at the end of 1987. The Pact, born at a time of unprecedented inflation, capital flight, and stock market collapse, called for trade liberalization, fiscal tightening, voluntary restraints on wages and prices, and a temporary freezing of public sector prices and the exchange rate, to be followed by a process of slow preannounced devaluation. The agreement among business, labor, and the state attempted to lower inflationary expectations (the so-called "inertial" causes of inflation that led to self-fulfilling wage and price hikes) by convincing the public that all major interest groups had committed themselves to stability.

Serra provided evidence of the Pact's success in its early months, as inflation plummeted from a monthly rate of more than 14 percent in November 1987 to under 2 percent in May 1988. Now, two years later (spring 1990), the annual rate of inflation has stabilized at around 20 percent. While it was recognized that the deflationary policies of the Pact involved a trade-off in terms of slower growth and unemployment, the argument was made that such costs are necessary to create the stability needed for medium-term recovery and growth. Serra noted that the Pact's success was helped by the fact that in June 1988 Mexico enjoyed the highest level of foreign-exchange reserves in history (about $15 billion).[1]

[1] Mexican inflation stabilized at under 2 percent per month between mid-1988 and spring 1990, undoubtedly owing to the influence of the Pact (and imports) on wages and prices, along with tight fiscal measures. However the slow rate of devaluation has caused

Part II sets regional integration in the context of multilateral trade negotiations. Jeffrey Schott examines the broad implications of the FTA for the GATT system and sees the two as mutually complementary. He argues that both countries' larger trade interests will lead them in the direction of a multilateral system. Indeed in several respects, the Canada-U.S. Free Trade Agreement is seen to boost the GATT: it counters a worldwide protectionist trend; it is fully consistent with GATT requirements for bilateral free trade areas regarding trade coverage, trade creation, and the absence of new trade restrictions; and it contains provisions on dispute settlement, services, and investment that could serve as models for prospective multilateral GATT accords because current GATT provisions in these areas are vague.

While the large degree of interdependence between the United States and Canada makes the FTA a special case, the political, economic, and social benefits of such an accord might eventually justify the extension of discriminatory preferences to Mexico, despite the problems of attempting to reconcile Mexico's policies with Canadian-U.S. goals. Mexico's role in the regional economy is bound to increase. Notwithstanding the many obstacles in both directions, Schott believes that "only the degree of liberalization and the context in which such reforms would be implemented" remain to be determined.

Murray Smith considers the tension between bilateralism and multilateralism in the approaches of Canada, the United States, and Mexico toward the FTA and the Uruguay Round of GATT. All three countries face common external challenges and have similar interests in a liberalized multilateral trading system, though their approaches have been different. The fact that each nation is an international debtor, with the United States in the lead, will ultimately affect both regional and international trade flows. Because the United States will be obliged by mount-

---

the peso to gradually rise against the dollar, tending to offset the benefits to exports from earlier devaluation and to add to a surge in imports from trade liberalization. There is a risk that continued balance-of-payments pressures could offset improved expectations from macroeconomic stability, counteracting the positive effect of the Pact, unless domestic and foreign investors inject new capital. The Baker Plan debt agreement signed in February 1990 was almost certain to improve expectations, as was the announcement of discussions about a free trade agreement in March, and a bill to reprivatize the banking system in May. Indeed prospects for the economy's recovery and growth are improving.

Though per capita income levels remained below 1981, and foreign investment has been less than expected, the year 1989 was the first since the Pact was introduced to show a turnaround from negative to slightly positive rates of growth in output per capita. Under the circumstances a new strategy of formal opening to the North American market is understandable. It offers prospects for growth with price stability beyond the short-term measures of the Pact by hopefully inducing an inflow of foreign direct investment and a return of flight capital.

ing foreign debt-service requirements to continue its efforts to reduce the trade deficit, Canada and Mexico must look to third markets for growing export opportunities.

With respect to the Canada-U.S. Free Trade Agreement, Smith agrees with Schott that its architecture is compatible with the goals of a multilateral system. The bilateral agreement establishes a free trade area, not a customs union. And since the FTA is much closer to a rule-based than a power-based system for resolving trade issues, it is likely to encourage a strengthening of dispute-settlement procedures in the Uruguay Round. As for Mexico, the FTA impact is likely to favor trade creation over trade diversion. Given the obstacles in the path of a truly multilateral trading system, Smith proposes that major developing countries such as Mexico be brought more fully into the dialogue, so that attention to their concerns may increase the potential for global liberalization.

Part III deals with the problems of macroeconomic policy coordination in North America, given the pressures for integration that currently exist. Alain Ize sees a regional approach as a way to restart Mexico's economic growth after several years of stagflation. But he argues that even though the country has gone a long way to meet the conditions for stable, efficient growth, new tax policies are needed to reduce the government's financial deficit and free savings for productive investment. Deficit reduction through cutbacks in government expenditure has reached a limit, in his view, since any further squeezing of public investment in economic and social infrastructure will work against both economic growth and political stability. A simulation model is employed to illustrate how broadening the tax base (beyond its current heavy dependence on petroleum) could expand public savings in a way that would complement private savings by permitting the domestic debt to be reduced. This would release private savings for productive investment, rather than debt service, thereby improving the potential for growth with stability.

Claiming that the rate of private investment is much lower than its potential in terms of domestic resource availability, Ize argues that Mexico enjoys a "savings surplus" rather than a "savings gap" and points to capital flight and the accumulation of offshore reserves to make his point. An agenda aimed at the eventual creation of a North American free-trade zone would provide the necessary assurance to investors by limiting Mexico's remaining uncertainties about future commercial and exchange-rate policies, especially if it complemented a program of reduction in the domestic and foreign debt.[2]

---

[2] Two years after the Ize presentation, the situation described still exists. The extent to which private investment can mobilize the resources made available by fiscal adjustment

Exploring the implications of increasing economic interdependence for tax policy, Charles McLure, Jr., demonstrates that unless countries harmonize their fiscal regimes, gaps and overlaps will occur—especially when taxing income from foreign investment. The country of source usually gets first crack at income generated from a new product or innovation, while residence countries must adapt. In a world of increased capital movement and treaty-shopping by investors, the pressure for fiscal harmonization is bound to grow. He calls for greater emphasis on consumption-based rather than income-based taxation, so as to eliminate fiscal distortions that favor current consumption over investment (for future consumption).

In McLure's view, U.S. tax policies tend to encourage outflows of capital that would otherwise have been available for domestic investment, a goal, according to Ize, that is central to Mexican growth. The present situation creates problems for all three countries of North America. For Canada and Mexico a possibility exists that domestically owned portfolio capital will be invested in the United States rather than at home. For the United States there is the risk of tax evasion by residents using foreign addresses to invest at home. These policies give rise to a distortion in regional patterns of investment and resource allocation.

A. E. Safarian investigates what Canada is likely to gain and lose with regard to foreign direct investment under the Canada-U.S. Free Trade Agreement and predicts that even though Canada made larger concessions than the United States in this area, much of the little change that will occur will be positive for Canada. He argues that Canada made few concessions in terms of its current policies on foreign direct investment, while winning more assured access to the United States for its own investors.

One fear in Canada regarding the FTA is that it will doom efforts to attract investment once protection is reduced or eliminated. Safarian sees such concerns as unfounded, given the positive aspects of the agreement which tend to encourage global investment in Canadian natural resources and primary manufacturing, improve the climate for competition, and favor investment by third-country firms in Canadian manufacturing owing to the assured access to the U.S. market which the FTA provides. He

and foreign lending will determine whether Mexico can recover, restructure, and grow beyond the limits imposed by its (lower) domestic and foreign debt. The ability to more fully utilize existing resources (potential "savings surplus") in turn depends on whether investors can be reassured about future profit potential and political stability. This can only be accomplished, according to Ize, if Mexico accumulates foreign reserves, stabilizes (or indexes) its key macroeconomic prices, permanently resolves the debt crisis, and defines an ambitious agenda for trade with the United States.

cautions, however, that some sectors and workers will be facing considerable adjustment pressures. "One of the more important tests of the economic desirability and political feasibility of free trade," he concludes, "is precisely whether convincing arrangements exist to assist people in coping with the changes that will come with it."

Fernando Sánchez Ugarte offers a Mexican perspective on some of the key issues addressed in this section, by comparing his own country's tax policies with those of the United States and Canada in terms of their effect on investment and regional capital flows. His analysis comes at a time of pressures for tax reform in the three countries, along with recognition that such policies be viewed from a regional perspective if restructuring of the North American economy is to occur with minimal distortions and if capital is once again to flow from north to south rather than the reverse (as during the period of debt crisis and adjustment of the 1980s).

Along with Ize, Sánchez Ugarte points out that Mexico must foster a major increase in foreign direct investment to complement domestic savings, now that private international lending has dried up. He also argues, however, that developing countries such as Mexico have a limited role to play in promoting foreign investment and should not undertake to attract foreign capital through tax policy, but should only use tax rates to encourage the reinvestment of profits. In his view, the limited fiscal leverage of capital-importing countries contrasts sharply with the ability of capital-exporting countries to promote or discourage foreign investment through tax policies. Both foreign tax credits and tax deferrals assist the flow of investment to developing countries and result in a fair distribution of revenue between the home and host countries. Sánchez Ugarte joins the other authors in this section in advocating that tax policies be harmonized among Mexico, the United States, and Canada. In his words, "Each nation should recognize the right of the country where income is generated to tax that income. This policy will not only provide for a fair distribution of tax jurisdictions, but will also allow an economically efficient flow of capital between countries."

Part IV deals with intellectual property and technology transfer—the new source of positive sum gains from international trade and investment—in the context of the North American system. Yehuda Kotowitz addresses the interests of innovators and their home country vis-a-vis those of consumers and countries where the innovations are applied. Different degrees of protection among countries as well as different tax policies and degrees of market competition will influence the locus of research and development. Although the Canada-U.S. Free Trade Agreement is expected to rationalize production, differential patent protection might disrupt this process. Furthermore, even if rationalization does occur because of the agreement, will it resolve some of the conflicts associated with patent policy? Since free riding will still exist, the situation must be resolved through negotiations. Kotowitz argues that because small countries benefit more than large countries from both free riding and free trade agreements, resolution through discussion seems possible; it is clearly in the interest of all countries to set patent protection at some globally optimal level, while allowing for a more equitable distribution of innovation rents.

This point coincides with the position of Mauricio de María y Campos that Mexico has the option of pursuing policies that reconcile the need to protect intellectual property with the desire to share in its benefits. The information revolution is seen to threaten developing countries by reducing the demand for traditional raw materials and labor while increasing the need for scarce technological skills. He fears that in this period of growing high-tech competition, multinational corporations will use their influence to limit developing country access to the new technologies, pressing for much stronger intellectual property protection, exporting goods rather than licensing their production, and demanding full ownership of capital in order to command the returns to research and development. In his view Mexico must overcome its traditional passivity toward technology and pursue a fresh strategy of cooperation between business and government, including not only support for local research and development but for training in administration, marketing, and informatics. For María y Campos, the proper approach to achieving these goals is through sector agreements rather than general trade liberalization, given the asymmetries between Mexico and its northern neighbors. He calls for a complementary inflow of human and financial resources to strengthen science and technology, said to be a precondition for the much greater convergence of development on which a North American Common Market must ultimately rest.

Part V deals with the impact of regional trade liberalization on the labor markets of the three countries in terms of the costs and benefits to workers. Morley Gunderson and Daniel Hamermesh discuss the potential impact of the FTA on labor in Canada and the United States and show that most of the burden of adjustment falls on labor. The cost to those affected by the FTA averages 10 to 15 percent of wage income. Furthermore, many who bear the brunt of dislocation are already disadvantaged in terms of wages, race, gender, industry, or region. Efficiency losses also occur, because of the negative externalities from loss of income by those workers forced to bear the burden of adjustment. Since it is also harder for labor than capital to diversify against the risk of trade shocks, in both equity and efficiency terms the losers deserve compensation for the adverse consequences of policies that make the rest of society better off.

Given Canada's much larger trade share of GDP (30 percent, compared to 10 percent for the U.S.) and its higher rate of unionization (40 percent of the work force, compared to 19 percent in the U.S.), the issues are more volatile there. Moreover there are fewer cushions for labor during the adjustment process when the shocks come from the external market (the North American case) than from within the enterprise (as in Japan). The problems raised by the FTA are certain to increase manyfold as the Canada-U.S. labor market becomes increasingly integrated with that of Mexico.

Yet the analysis by Saúl Trejo Reyes shows that it is essential to bring Mexican labor much more fully into the North American market, through trade if not migration, if wages are to recover and growth to be restored in his country. To illustrate the magnitude of the problem, the FTA is estimated to create 250,000 new jobs, net of adjustment, according to figures cited by Gunderson and Hamermesh, while Mexico adds over three times that many to its work force each year.

Trejo views the economic relationship between Mexico and the United States and Canada in terms of an interdependent region-wide labor market in which demand and supply overlap. Given this relationship, each country faces one of two alternatives. The first is not to give special consideration to others in the North American region. This would leave Mexico with a worsening employment problem even under the most favorable conditions, and with increasing migration from the countryside to already overcrowded cities and from both rural and urban areas to the United States. Competitive pressures would cause the United States to increase protection against imports, including in particular those from Mexico.

The alternative, which Trejo sees as in the best interest of all three countries, is to look at the possibilities for North American regional co-operation on all fronts. Mexico's 1988 labor force of 28 million (twice the size of the Canadian labor force) has more than tripled in the past 38 years, accompanying a rapid growth in urban population. While the drastic fall in Mexico's real wages over the past eight years is probably over, says Trejo, there is no likelihood that migration pressures will decline over the next decade.

Promotion of "best sector" activities such as tourism, assembly plants, and labor-intensive agriculture (especially fruits and vegetables) would help Mexico in the medium term, according to the author. Although a

North American free trade zone might be unacceptable to the United States if it were to include substantial freedom of labor to migrate, Trejo argues that a general shift in policies in both countries in the direction of a "North American labor-trade agreement" could allow Mexico to pursue its employment and growth objectives by taking advantage of a region-wide market. While no estimate is made of the implications to U.S. and Canadian workers of fuller Mexican entry into the North American economy, the adjustment costs will be considerable on all sides, leading to much greater pressures for compensation than those accompanying the FTA.

The final section, Part VI, looks at the future of North American economic relations in the context of the global system. Richard Harris itemizes the changes likely to accompany increased trade resulting from the Canada-U.S. Free Trade Agreement. Investment flows are expected to expand in both directions, since exports of complex services and manufacturing call for expenditures on distribution as well as production. Real wages are expected to rise by 10 to 12 percent in Canada relative to the United States over the long run, raising the capital intensity of production in Canada and, on balance, lessening the incentive for labor to move from Canada to the United States. Indeed, there may be some reverse migration northward given differential tax/public goods packages available between certain U.S. states and Canadian provinces.

Will the FTA force a harmonization of labor market and social policies between Canada and the United States? Harris feels that the agreement itself provides no cause to change Canada's broad social or labor-market policies, despite claims by business that their costs are too high. He accepts the argument that where labor is immobile, social policy differences tend to be reflected in the bilateral exchange rate. In fact, given the differentials in state versus private social programs between Canada and the United States, some of the gain in real wages might be taken out in the form of increased expenditure on social policies.

The negotiation of a free trade accord among Mexico, the United States, and Canada is seen to depend on the degree to which the world trading system forms into large regional blocs. Harris points to the danger that a trinational accord could lead to substantial trade diversion from the rest of the world to the North American region, with gains for Mexico as a source of low-cost labor, and—together with Canada—as a source of energy for the United States: "We would certainly see most basic industries revitalize in North America, although many of these would end up in Mexico." A preferable approach would be to see the Canada-U.S. Free Trade Agreement as a stage in the transition to greater multilateral trade liberalization, particularly along Europe-North

America-Pacific Rim lines. This approach would reduce the significance of the United States to both Canada and Mexico and diminish the "one-sided nature" of their trade. However, the failure of GATT to make significant progress on non-tariff barriers and continued international macroeconomic imbalances make the formation of regional trade blocs "a highly plausible scenario."

Asking "Where do we go from here?," Sidney Weintraub speculates about the future of North American trade policy from a U.S. perspective. Noting the perennial tension in the United States between liberalization and protection, he sees recent trade and current-account deficits to be increasing the popularity of protection among U.S. politicians. Vulnerable countries such as Mexico and Canada, which send over two-thirds of their exports to the United States, have factored this into their policy-making. Bilateralism, the other tendency in U.S. trade policy, is a path to either trade liberalization or restriction. With or without the inclusion of Mexico, the FTA is likely to produce dynamic effects that will benefit third countries even as it shifts U.S. policy away from the unconditional most-favored-nation goal held up as the cornerstone of GATT.

For Weintraub, though Mexico's economy is still far from open, it has come a long distance in a short time: "A half-century of internal development is being jettisoned." Trade debate in Mexico centers on whether its opening is going too fast, endangering many previously protected industries. Mexican policymakers are also concerned about whether the Canada-U.S. agreement will lead to a diversion of exports away from Mexico and its impact on GATT. Mexico does not want to be left out of a North American trading bloc, but it does not feel ready to join because of its economic unpreparedness and the political sensitivity of entering a free trade agreement with the powerful United States. The evolution of Mexico's trade policy will depend on the success of the current opening strategy. If nonpetroleum exports continue to grow, Weintraub expects the fears in Mexico about North American free trade to diminish, allowing it to begin the important task of positioning itself for free-trade negotiations with the United States and Canada, an opportunity Weintraub believes might arise "in the not-too-distant future."[3]

CONCLUSIONS

The relentless process of regional integration under way in Europe, Asia, and elsewhere assures a different international economy in the 1990s. All bets are off, and the only certainty is that no region, much less

[3] These remarks were prophetic. On March 27, 1990, the *Wall Street Journal* announced: "U.S. and Mexico Agree to Seek Free Trade Pact," an article confirmed by both governments.

North America, will be spared by the force of global change. No nation, however powerful, can stand still in today's world without falling behind. Whether or not a formal trade agreement is reached for the region as a whole, the essays concur that economic interdependence in North America has brought overlapping problems and opportunities.

Even though there is no Monet-like North American vision to guide the three nations, each is attempting to prevent global imbalances from threatening existing relations. Within the region, each country recognizes its growing de facto interdependence, asymmetrical as it may be. Bilateral relations between Canada and the United States and between Mexico and the United States have a long history and have been the subject of analysis by academics and policymakers. Canada already shares with the United States the largest bilateral trade relation in the world, and has felt the threat of rising U.S. protectionism. Both Canada and the United States meanwhile face growing competition in many of their most important economic activities (in agriculture, industry, and services). Mexico sees the United States, its major trading and investment partner, as having a market that is fundamental to the success of its new openness strategy, which will be affected greatly by the Canada-U.S. Free Trade Agreement. By the same token, possible links between the United States and Mexico are of increasing concern to Canada.

The ability of each country to respond to domestic and international pressures by improving the competitiveness of its production, raising the educational levels of its youth, and improving the technical skills of its population depends increasingly on relations with its continental neighbors. These essays illustrate that whatever the outcome of specific regional trade, investment, and employment negotiations, a comprehensive approach to North American economic interdependence—one that includes Mexico—is long overdue. This volume appears on the threshold of a new era in North American economic relations.

PART I
What Have We Learned from the Past?

Impact of the Tokyo Round and U.S. Macroeconomic Adjustments on North American Trade

Alan V. Deardorff and Robert M. Stern

T HE WORLD ECONOMY has experienced disturbances of unprecedented magnitudes in the past fifteen years as the result of the oil
shocks of 1973–74 and 1979–80 and the macroeconomic and trade imbalances arising from U.S. monetary contraction and fiscal expansion in
the first half of the 1980s. It is remarkable that during this period of
economic turmoil the major industrialized countries were able to enter
into in 1973 and conclude in 1979 the seventh (Tokyo) round of multilateral trade negotiations under the auspices of the General Agreement
on Tariffs and Trade (GATT).

The Tokyo Round negotiations resulted in the reduction of existing
tariffs by as much as one-third (with exceptions for certain sensitive sectors) and agreement on a series of codes relating to a variety of nontariff
measures—antidumping procedures, subsidies and countervailing duties,
standards, government procurement, customs valuation, and import licensing—designed to bring about greater transparency and harmonization in the use of these measures among the major industrialized countries. The Tokyo Round tariff reductions were phased in between 1980
and 1987; meanwhile, implementation and operation of the nontariff
codes have become an integral part of the GATT process.

Given that the GATT member countries embarked in September 1986
on the eighth (Uruguay) round of multilateral trade negotiations (which
are scheduled to be completed at the end of 1990), it may be instructive
to assess the effects of the Tokyo Round negotiations. For this purpose,
we have adapted the Michigan Model of World Production and Trade to

determine how sectoral trade and employment in the United States and Canada may have been affected by their tariff reductions and those implemented by other industrialized countries as the result of the Tokyo Round negotiations.[1]

Because tariffs had been reduced significantly in previous GATT negotiations, the Tokyo Round reductions were bound to have a comparatively small impact. This is all the more true when the effects induced by the U.S. macroeconomic imbalances of the 1980s are taken into consideration. To illustrate this relative impact, we used the Michigan model to calculate the sectoral trade and employment effects of two different types of macroscenarios. The first scenario involves an assumed autonomous change in U.S. capital inflows equal to 1 percent of U.S. gross domestic product (GDP). This scenario is designed to mimic the effects of a U.S. policy of monetary contraction that, by increasing the U.S. rate of interest relative to foreign rates, would lead to a capital inflow, a matching trade deficit, and an appreciation of the dollar. The second scenario involves an assumed exogenous increase in U.S. aggregate expenditure equal to 1 percent of GDP, accompanied by an equal capital inflow. This scenario is intended to reflect a U.S. fiscal expansion that, by increasing demand for all tradable and nontradable goods, requires a shift toward foreign tradable goods to equilibrate markets especially for nontradable goods. The resulting increase in U.S. imports and the trade deficit will necessitate an appreciation of the dollar.

These two scenarios cannot capture the full complexity of the international financial effects and dynamic processes involved. They may nonetheless provide some insight into the magnitudes and composition of the sectoral adjustments that may have been necessitated by changes in U.S. macroeconomic policies in the first half of the 1980s.

Our paper proceeds as follows. In section 2, we present a brief overview of some salient economic developments that have taken place in the North American economies since the 1970s. The results of our computational experiments are presented in sections 3 and 4, and we make some concluding remarks in section 5.

AN OVERVIEW OF ECONOMIC DEVELOPMENTS IN THE NORTH AMERICAN ECONOMIES SINCE THE 1970S

Some selected economic data covering 1973 to early 1988 for the United States, Canada, and Mexico are presented in Table 1. The nominal effective exchange rate of the U.S. dollar has appreciated by 50 per-

[1] Alan V. Deardorff and Robert M. Stern, *The Michigan Model of World Production and Trade: Theory and Applications* (Cambridge, Mass., 1986).

TABLE I

Selected Economic Data for the United States, Canada, and Mexico, 1973–1988, II

Year	Effective exchange rate (1980 = 100)	Trade balance		Current account balance		Government deficit	
		Billions of U.S. $	Pct. of GNP	Billions of U.S. $	Pct. of GNP	Billions of U.S. $	Pct. of GNP
UNITED STATES							
1973	106.8	0.91	0.07	7.07	0.52	−16.23	1.19
1980	100.0	−25.50	1.02	1.84	0.06	−76.18	2.79
1981	112.7	−27.97	1.02	6.87	0.22	−78.74	2.58
1982	125.9	−36.45	1.15	−8.64	0.27	−125.69	3.97
1983	133.2	−67.08	1.97	−46.28	1.36	−202.52	5.95
1984	143.7	−112.51	2.99	−107.09	2.84	−178.26	4.73
1985	150.2	−122.15	3.05	−116.43	2.90	−212.10	5.29
1986	122.5	−144.54	3.41	−138.84	3.27	−212.60	5.02
1987	108.0	−160.28	3.57	−153.95	3.43	−156.00	3.48
1988.I	100.5	−130.12		−140.04			
1988.II	99.7						
CANADA							
1973	120.3	2.99	2.42	0.11	0.09	−1.70	1.38
1980	100.0	8.00	3.14	−0.95	0.37	−8.72	3.42
1981	102.9	6.58	2.29	−5.11	1.78	−7.03	2.44
1982	104.9	14.99	5.11	2.23	0.76	−16.87	5.75
1983	108.3	14.97	4.68	2.49	0.78	−20.42	6.38
1984	106.3	16.56	4.96	2.57	0.77	−22.29	6.68
1985	102.7	13.17	3.87	−0.88	0.26	−21.00	6.17
1986	92.6	8.08	2.28	−6.66	1.88	−14.76	4.16
1987	92.3	8.76	2.16	−7.24	1.79		
1988.I	94.1						
1988.II	96.8						
MEXICO							
1973	181.8	−1.52	2.79	−1.42	2.61	−2.19	4.02
1980	100.0	−2.83	1.56	−8.16	4.49	−5.84	3.22
1981	93.2	−4.10	1.77	−13.90	6.00	−16.01	6.91
1982	40.9	6.80	4.30	−6.22	3.94	−25.77	16.32
1983	18.9	13.76	10.26	5.42	4.04	−11.35	8.47
1984	13.6	12.94	8.03	4.24	2.63	−12.48	7.75
1985	8.9	8.45	5.10	1.24	0.75	−15.49	9.34
1986	3.6	4.60		−1.67			
1987	1.6	8.43		3.89			

SOURCE: All data are taken from the International Monetary Fund, *International Financial Statistics*: lines am x for the U.S. and Canadian effective exchange rates measured in terms of U.S. dollars per unit of national currency, line wf for Mexico's exchange rate (U.S. dollars per peso), lines 77 ac d and 77 az d for the trade and current account balances measured on an annualized balance-of-payments basis, and line 8o for the (central) government deficit. Data for the government deficit and GNP for Canada and Mexico were converted into U.S. dollars.

NOTE: The data for recent years were estimated in part for Canada and Mexico. An increase in the exchange-rate index signifies an appreciation of the currency and a decrease signifies a depreciation.

cent between 1980 and 1985, and by the second quarter of 1988 returned to its 1980 level. Because U.S. domestic prices did not diverge materially from those in the other industrialized countries during this period, the index provides a reasonable guide to the real exchange-rate movement of the dollar. The nominal trade deficit of the United States (measured on a balance-of-payments basis) rose from $25.5 billion in 1980 to $122.2 billion in 1985, and increased to $160.3 billion between 1985 and 1987. The U.S. current account showed a small surplus in 1980 and 1981, and thereafter moved into a deficit of roughly the same size as the trade deficit from 1984 to 1987. The U.S. trade and current-account deficits exceeded 3 percent of GNP in 1985–1987. The nominal U.S. government deficit increased markedly after 1981. It averaged around 5 percent of GNP in 1983–1986 and declined to 3.5 percent of GNP in 1987, which was about the same size as the trade and current-account deficits.

Canada's nominal effective exchange rate appreciated by less than 10 percent between 1980 and 1983, depreciated from 1983 to 1987, and has appreciated thereafter. Canada had a nominal trade surplus in each of the years indicated, ranging from 2 to 4 percent of GNP, whereas it had a current account deficit in 1980–81 and 1985–1987. Canada had a nominal government deficit in all years shown. It was around 6 percent or more of GNP from 1982 to 1985 and declined to about 4 percent of GNP in 1986. It is interesting to note that despite the relative importance of Canada's government deficit, it has not experienced the sizable trade and current-account deficits that have been recorded for the United States. Canadian domestic savings have thus been the primary source for financing Canada's government budget deficit, whereas the U.S. government budget deficit has been financed in large measure by foreign savings and capital inflows.

The very sizable and accelerating depreciation of the Mexican peso is evident in Table 1. Mexico had a nominal trade deficit in 1980–81 and a surplus thereafter. Its current account, which was in deficit from 1980 to 1982, moved into surplus from 1983 to 1985, and recorded a small deficit in 1986. Mexico's nominal government budget deficit exceeded 16 percent of GNP in 1982 and since has been in the 7 to 9 percent range. The Mexican data for 1988 reflect the impact of the domestic stabilization measures introduced in late 1987 that were designed to reduce inflationary pressures and reverse the depreciation of the peso.

The data in Table 1 thus document the wide swing in the U.S.-dollar exchange rate that has occurred in the 1980s, together with the coincidence of the historically unprecedented increases in the U.S. nominal government deficit and the deficits in trade and current account. The U.S.

record is not necessarily typical, however, as the Canadian experience suggests. In contrast to its North American neighbors, Mexico has been trying to deal with inflation, a rapidly depreciating currency, and a sizable government budget deficit, and at the same time generate trade and current-account surpluses so it can continue to pay its foreign debts.

Changes in Bilateral and Global Trade, 1973–1986

Let us now look in more detail at the changes that have occurred in U.S. and Canadian bilateral and global merchandise exports, imports, and trade balances. Table 2 shows that more than 20 percent of total U.S. exports went to Canada, and Canada supplied about 17 percent of total U.S. imports in 1986 (down from its 24 percent share in 1973). The United States had a $23.9 billion merchandise trade deficit with Canada in 1986 and a $176.7 trade deficit globally. The comparable deficits in 1973 were both around $3 billion. The bilateral trade deficit with Canada comprised chiefly raw materials, fuels, semi-manufactures, almost all varieties of engineering products, and consumer manufactures.

The United States accounted for 77 percent of Canada's exports in 1986 as compared to 68 percent in 1973. The United States supplied 68 percent of Canada's imports in 1986 as compared to 71 percent in 1973.[2] While Canada's global net trade roughly mirrors its bilateral net trade with the United States, it had larger global net imports of engineering products and consumer manufactures.

In the absence of comparable information on U.S.-Canadian bilateral trade with Mexico, if we combine the global data in Table 2 with data reported in the Economist Intelligence Unit Ltd., U.S. exports to Mexico were around 6 percent of total U.S. exports in 1986, and its imports from Mexico were 4.5 percent of total U.S. imports in that year.[3] According to the Economist Intelligence Unit Ltd., the United States accounted for 63 percent of Mexico's total exports and supplied 59 percent of Mexico's total imports in 1972.[4] This compares to 67 percent and 65 percent for the U.S. shares of Mexico's total exports and imports in 1986. Nearly half of U.S. imports from Mexico in 1972 consisted of primary products; machinery and related products accounted for about an additional 20 percent. In 1986, U.S. imports of raw materials were 37 percent and U.S. imports of machinery and related products were 31 percent of total im-

---

[2] It will be noted that the bilateral U.S.-Canadian exports, imports, and trade balances recorded in Table 2 do not match because U.S. imports are valued at cost plus insurance plus freight. There may also be some differences in classifications of the bilateral trade flows and some underreporting of bilateral trade, especially in road motor vehicles.

[3] Economist Intelligence Unit Ltd., *Quarterly Economic Review of Mexico,* 1987.

[4] Economist Intelligence Unit Ltd., *Quarterly Economic Review of Mexico,* 1973.

TABLE 2

U.S. and Canadian Bilateral and Global Merchandise Exports, Imports, and Trade Balances, 1973 and 1986

(Billions of U.S. Dollars)

Commodity group	Year	U.S./Canada Exports	U.S./Canada Imports	U.S./Canada Balance	U.S./World Exports	U.S./World Imports	U.S./World Balance	Canada/U.S. Exports	Canada/U.S. Imports	Canada/U.S. Balance	Canada/World Exports	Canada/World Imports	Canada/World Balance
Primary products, total	1973	2.08	6.91	(4.83)	24.73	27.21	(2.48)	7.10	2.26	4.84	13.10	4.78	8.32
	1986	4.60	18.08	(13.48)	48.11	85.65	(37.54)	18.01	6.76	11.25	30.73	12.33	18.40
Food	1973	.94	.99	(.05)	16.58	10.28	6.30	1.02	1.08	(.06)	3.57	2.08	1.49
	1986	1.48	3.20	(1.72)	25.78	27.25	(1.47)	3.15	2.56	.59	7.79	4.92	2.87
Raw materials	1973	.38	2.21	(1.83)	3.95	3.45	.50	2.10	.43	1.67	3.00	.58	2.42
	1986	.70	4.91	(4.21)	8.76	7.75	1.01	4.91	1.07	3.84	7.70	1.40	6.30
Ores & other minerals	1973	.19	.77	(.58)	1.47	1.84	(.37)	.76	.25	.51	2.40	.43	1.97
	1986	.52	.94	(.42)	3.60	2.91	.69	1.02	1.09	(.07)	3.89	1.44	2.45
Fuels	1973	.36	2.07	(1.71)	1.67	9.15	(7.48)	2.29	.26	2.03	2.47	1.32	1.15
	1986	1.39	6.53	5.14	8.13	39.77	31.64	6.70	1.43	5.27	8.12	3.76	4.36
Nonferrous metals	1973	.21	.87	(.66)	1.06	2.49	(1.43)	.93	.24	.69	1.66	.37	1.29
	1986	.51	2.50	(1.99)	1.84	7.97	(6.13)	2.23	.61	1.62	3.23	.81	2.42
Semi-manufactures, total	1973	1.98	2.54	(.56)	9.88	10.73	(.85)	2.41	2.01	.40	3.26	2.89	.37
	1986	4.58	10.69	(6.11)	31.43	46.16	(14.73)	10.66	6.10	4.56	13.27	9.50	3.77
Iron & steel	1973	.44	.26	.18	1.30	3.34	(2.04)	.37	.37	—	.49	.67	(.18)
	1986	.32	1.28	(.96)	1.08	9.56	(8.48)	1.54	.59	.95	1.74	1.39	.35
Chemicals	1973	.89	.58	.31	6.20	2.74	3.46	.52	1.01	(.49)	.78	1.34	(.56)
	1986	2.73	2.92	(.19)	23.82	17.35	6.47	2.89	3.79	(.90)	4.24	5.46	(1.22)
Other semi-manufactures	1973	.65	1.70	(1.05)	2.38	4.65	(2.27)	1.52	.63	.89	1.99	.88	1.11
	1986	1.53	6.49	(4.96)	6.53	19.25	(12.72)	6.23	1.72	4.51	7.29	2.65	4.64
Engineering products, total	1973	9.44	7.45	1.99	30.39	25.39	5.00	7.17	10.86	(3.69)	8.21	13.03	(4.82)
	1986	27.28	31.67	(4.39)	105.40	182.29	(76.89)	33.80	37.46	(3.66)	37.35	48.82	(11.47)
Machinery, specialized	1973	2.00	.75	1.25	7.78	3.16	4.62	.71	2.17	(1.46)	.88	2.68	(1.80)
	1986	3.73	2.33	1.40	17.63	22.99	(5.36)	2.34	5.28	(2.94)	3.03	7.84	(4.81)

TABLE 2 (*continued*)
(*Billions of U.S. Dollars*)

Commodity group	Year	U.S./Canada			U.S./World			Canada/U.S.			Canada/World		
		Exports	Imports	Balance	Exports	Imports	Balance	Exports	Imports	Balance	Exports	Imports	Balance
Engineering products, total													
Office & telecom. equipment	1973	.54	.22	.32	3.99	2.45	1.54	.32	.72	(.40)	.53	.93	(.40)
	1986	2.76	1.78	.98	23.93	28.16	(4.23)	1.89	4.07	(2.18)	2.44	4.97	(2.53)
Road motor vehicles	1973	4.12	4.92	(.80)	6.03	10.59	(4.56)	4.65	4.82	(.17)	4.81	5.35	(.54)
	1986	13.86	20.88	(7.02)	18.51	69.42	(50.91)	23.38	18.28	5.10	23.94	21.82	2.12
Other mach. & transp. equipment	1973	2.45	1.48	.97	11.52	5.85	5.67	1.43	2.76	(1.33)	1.90	3.34	(1.44)
	1986	6.32	6.36	(.04)	42.78	40.16	2.62	5.30	8.70	(3.40)	6.80	11.32	(4.52)
Household appliances	1973	.33	.08	.25	1.07	3.34	(2.27)	.06	.39	(.33)	.09	.73	(.64)
	1986	.61	.32	.29	2.55	21.56	(19.01)	.89	1.13	(.24)	1.14	2.87	(1.73)
Consumer manufactures, total	1973	.89	.45	.44	3.42	8.70	(5.28)	.38	1.16	(.78)	.58	2.35	(1.77)
	1986	2.12	2.87	(.75)	10.48	58.02	(47.54)	2.11	3.08	(.97)	2.49	7.65	(5.16)
Textiles	1973	.30	.04	.26	1.22	1.70	(.48)	.06	.36	(.30)	.15	.78	(.63)
	1986	.50	.24	.26	2.56	5.83	(3.27)	.25	.76	(.51)	.40	1.78	(1.38)
Clothing	1973	.03	.06	(.03)	.29	2.31	(2.02)	.09	.06	.03	.12	.33	(.21)
	1986	.04	.23	(.19)	.88	18.70	(17.82)	.25	.09	.16	.30	1.53	(1.23)
Other consumer goods	1973	.56	.35	.21	1.91	4.69	(2.78)	.23	.74	(.51)	.31	1.24	(.93)
	1986	1.58	2.40	(.82)	7.04	33.49	(26.45)	1.61	2.23	(.62)	1.79	4.34	(2.55)
Total manufactures	1973	12.31	10.44	1.87	43.69	44.82	(1.13)	9.96	14.03	(4.07)	12.05	18.27	(6.22)
	1986	33.98	45.23	(11.25)	147.31	286.47	(139.16)	46.57	46.64	(.07)	53.11	65.97	(12.86)
Total	1973	14.83	17.97	(3.14)	70.25	73.60	(3.35)	17.12	16.51	.61	25.21	23.32	1.89
	1986	42.35	66.22	(23.87)	204.65	381.86	(176.71)	64.92	54.58	10.34	84.25	79.84	4.41

SOURCE: GATT, *International Trade*, 1986–87 and 1981–82.
NOTE: United States: exports, f.o.b., and imports, c.i.f.; Canada: exports and imports, f.o.b. Total exports and imports include commodities not classified according to kind.

ports from Mexico. U.S. imports of petroleum and related products were about 1 percent of total imports from Mexico in 1972 as compared to 22 percent in 1986. U.S. exports of chemicals and capital goods to Mexico were about 60 percent of the total in 1972 as compared to 66 percent in 1986.

It is thus evident that the United States currently accounts for about two-thirds of Mexico's total exports and imports and Mexico accounts for about 5 percent of total U.S. exports and imports. While Mexico has relatively large exports of primary products to the United States, its exports to the United States of machinery and related products are important as well. Mexico's imports from the United States consist chiefly of chemicals and capital goods.

Having examined some aggregate data as well as some detailed trade data for the United States, Canada, and Mexico, let us turn now to our computational analyses of the effects of the Tokyo Round tariff reductions and changes in U.S. macroeconomic policies.

COMPUTATIONAL ANALYSIS OF TOKYO ROUND TARIFF REDUCTIONS

As already mentioned, the Tokyo Round negotiations, which concluded in 1979, resulted in tariff reductions by as much as one-third. An indication of the average percentage reductions for the major industrialized countries is given in Table 3. The weighted average reduction for the United States was 34.1 percent and for Canada, 29.1 percent. The lower percentage for Canada reflects some unilateral reductions made prior to 1979, which are not included in the rates used to calculate the average reduction noted in the table. There are no developing countries listed in Table 3 since none of them opted to reduce their tariffs or other barriers in the Tokyo Round.

We have had occasion to analyze the economic effects of the Tokyo Round negotiations.[5] For this purpose, we used the Michigan Model of World Production and Trade, which is a general equilibrium computational model that includes the 18 major industrialized countries, the 16 major developing countries, and the rest of the world in the aggregate. There are 22 tradable and 7 nontradable sectors in each country.

We will investigate how trade and employment for the United States and Canada may have been affected by their own and each other's tariff reductions as well as by the tariff reductions of the remaining industrialized countries. It should be noted in this connection that the actual tariff

[5] Deardorff and Stern, *The Michigan Model of World Production and Trade: Theory and Applications,* 52–61. This will hereafter be cited by a shortened form of the title only.

TABLE 3

*Average Post-Kennedy Round Base Rate Tariffs on Industrial Products.
Tokyo Round Offer Rate Tariffs, and Percentage Depth of Cut
for the Major Industrialized Countries in the Tokyo Round
(Weighted by Own-Country Total Imports)*

Country	(1) Average post-Kennedy Round base rate (%)	(2) Tokyo Round offer rate (%)	(3) Average cut (%)
Australia[a]	17.0	16.5	2.8
Austria	15.4	12.1	21.5
Canada[a]	7.3	5.2	29.1
European Economic Community			
Belgium-Luxembourg	8.2	5.9	28.3
Denmark	9.0	6.6	25.8
France	8.3	6.0	27.8
German Federal Republic	8.7	6.3	27.1
Ireland	9.4	6.9	26.7
Italy	7.3	5.4	27.0
Netherlands	9.2	6.8	26.7
United Kingdom	7.3	5.2	27.7
Finland	9.6	7.1	25.2
Japan[a]	3.9	2.9	25.3
New Zealand	18.9	16.7	11.8
Norway	6.9	5.2	24.8
Sweden	6.4	5.0	23.0
Switzerland	3.9	3.1	21.2
United States	6.5	4.3	34.1
All countries	7.8	5.8	26.4

SOURCE: Based on data supplied by Office of U.S. Trade Representative.
[a]Based on prevailing rates, which include unilateral reductions in the Post-Kennedy Round tariffs.

reductions negotiated in the Tokyo Round were phased in annually from January 1980 to January 1987. However, because our model deals with comparative statics, we assumed that the negotiated tariff reductions were implemented all at one time.[6] The model was then solved for per-

[6]The detailed sectoral tariff reductions used for computational purposes are given in *Michigan Model*, 50–51. Certain minor modifications in agricultural nontariff barriers (NTBs) were negotiated in the Tokyo Round as well as the various NTB codes mentioned above. Although some of the NTB codes may have resulted in greater transparency and harmonization of national procedures and policies and reductions in the costs of international trade, their effects are not readily measurable in quantitative terms and are therefore not included in our calculations. For an assessment of the Tokyo Round codes, see Robert M. Stern, John H. Jackson, and Bernard M. Hoekman, "An Assessment of the Implementation and Operation of the Tokyo Round Codes," Seminar Discussion Paper 174, Research Seminars in International Economics (Ann Arbor, University of Michigan, May 1986).

centage changes in the endogenous variables, and absolute changes were found by multiplying the percentage changes by initial 1976 levels (which serve as the benchmark for all calculations based on the model). In this experiment, aggregate expenditure in each of the industrialized countries was permitted to vary so as to keep the level of employment unchanged. The results thus permit us to analyze the intersectoral adjustments of a given labor force to tariff changes.

Our model yields information on changes in a variety of endogenous variables, including exports, imports, employment, output, value-added, exchange rates, and prices. We have chosen to focus here on the net percentage changes in employment in Canada and the United States that may be attributed to the Tokyo Round multilateral tariff reductions.[7] The results are given in Tables 4 and 5. The first column in each table indicates the net percentage changes in employment by sector in the country due to the tariff reductions of all Tokyo Round industrialized countries taken together. The next four columns decompose these changes according to tariff reductions implemented by all other industrialized countries excluding the United States and Canada.

The last four columns of the tables provide some indication of the relative importance of own-country and cross-country tariff reductions. Each reports a ratio of two of the earlier columns, converted to a percentage, in order to indicate the fraction of the effect on the country that can be attributed to particular tariff reductions. For example, the column headed "U.S. & Canada as pct. of all developed" reports column 3 as a fraction of column 1—the fraction of the employment effect due to all countries' tariff reductions that can be attributed to the tariff reductions of the United States and Canada. In the first row of Table 4, therefore, we find that while all countries' tariff reductions together increase Canadian agricultural employment by 0.49 percent, more than half of that increase—0.26 percent, which is 52 percent of 0.49—is due to the tariff reductions of the United States and Canada alone. Similarly, the last column in Table 4 compares column 5 with column 3, and thus reports the share of this latter number due to Canadian tariff reductions.

With this interpretation, the signs of the entries in these columns indi-

---

[7] In interpreting the employment results, it should be noted that they reflect the multilateral adjustments involved rather than the bilateral effects. In our model, we assume that goods are perfect substitutes in world markets, but that there is imperfect substitution between imports and home goods. If, instead, it were assumed that goods could be distinguished by country of origin, bilateral effects could be analyzed directly. See John Whalley, *Trade Liberalization among Major World Trading Areas* (Cambridge, Mass., 1984) and Drusilla K. Brown, "A Computational Analysis of the Effects of the Tokyo Round Negotiations on Preferential Trading Arrangements," *Journal of International Economic Integration* (Seoul, 1988).

cate whether own and cross effects of tariff reductions are reinforcing or offsetting. Looking again at the first row of Table 4, for example, the negative sign in the next to last column indicates that entries in columns 3 and 4 have a positive sign; thus U.S. tariff reductions have the opposite effect on Canadian agricultural employment than the effects of Canada's own tariff reductions. Similarly, negative signs in the third to last columns in both tables indicate sectors in which tariff reductions outside the United States and Canada tend to offset employment effects of the tariff reductions in the two countries.

The principal results, then, are as follows.[8] First, the employment effects are comparatively small in all sectors of the United States and in almost all sectors of Canada. This is to be expected because the tariff changes themselves are small and since a variety of general equilibrium interactions also dampen the effects of individual tariff reductions, as we have discussed in our 1986 study.[9]

Second, the own-country results show both negative and positive effects across sectors because total employment is held constant. The negative effects occur in the sectors with the deepest tariff cuts. For Canada, these include rubber products, electric machinery, metal products, printing and publishing, and glass and glass products. For the United States, the negative effects occur in miscellaneous manufactures, nonmetallic mineral products, wearing apparel, wood products, glass and glass products, rubber products, and furniture and fixtures. Most of the nontradable sectors in both countries also have negative effects, which reflect the substitution in favor of tradables resulting from the tariff reductions.

Third, the own-country effects are much larger than the cross-country effects. This would be expected in any case, since tariffs here are multilateral rather than bilateral. However, the weakening of cross-country effects may be enhanced in our model, where one country's tariffs affect another's trade only indirectly through world prices.

Fourth, the cross-country effects tend to be opposite in sign to, and thus to some extent tend to offset, the own-country effects. The apparent reason for this offsetting is that the patterns of tariff reductions by the industrialized countries were fairly similar. Thus, sectors with the deepest tariff reductions in a given country will experience the largest increases

[8] The calculated effects of the tariff reductions on Mexico and the other major developing countries are too small to be reported here. The main reasons for the small results stem from the fact that existing NTBs, which affect many of these countries, remain in place and the trade of these countries affected by the tariff reductions is of minor importance compared to the trade of the industrialized countries. The detailed results are reported in *Michigan Model*, 53–59.

[9] Ibid.

TABLE 4

Net Percentage Changes in Employment in Canada Due to Tariff Reductions in the U.S., Canada, and Other Developed Countries

		Percentage employment change due to tariff cut in					Percentage shares of employment effects			
		All developed	Developed, less U.S. & Canada	U.S. & Canada	U.S.	Canada	U.S. & Canada as pct. of all developed	Developed, less U.S. & Canada, as pct. of all developed	U.S. as pct. of U.S. & Canada	Canada as pct. of U.S. & Canada
Traded goods										
Agr., for., & fishing	(1)	0.49	0.23	0.26	−0.02	0.28	52	47	−8	108
Food, bev., & tobacco	(310)	0.11	−0.07	0.18	−0.02	0.20	169	−69	−11	111
Textiles	(321)	−0.09	−0.09	−0.00	0.00	−0.00	4	96	−39	142
Wearing apparel	(322)	0.19	0.02	0.17	0.04	0.13	89	11	23	77
Leather products	(323)	3.70	−1.83	5.63	−1.89	7.67	152	−50	−34	136
Footwear	(324)	0.60	−0.52	1.12	−0.03	1.15	187	−86	−2	102
Wood products	(331)	0.97	−0.05	1.02	0.02	1.00	105	−5	2	98
Furniture & fixtures	(332)	0.34	0.16	0.18	0.20	−0.02	53	47	113	−13
Paper & paper products	(341)	0.76	−0.30	1.07	−0.24	1.31	140	−40	−23	123
Printing & publishing	(342)	−1.32	−0.07	−1.26	−0.02	−1.24	95	5	2	98
Chemicals	(35A)	0.90	0.35	0.55	0.15	0.39	61	39	28	72
Petrol. & rel. prod.	(35B)	−0.12	0.46	−0.57	−0.65	0.08	489	−391	114	−15
Rubber products	(355)	−3.31	0.07	−3.37	0.27	−3.63	102	−2	−8	108
Nonmetallic min. prod.	(36A)	−0.21	−0.13	−0.08	0.28	−0.36	39	61	−335	434
Glass & glass products	(362)	−1.16	−0.13	−1.03	0.16	−1.19	89	11	−15	115
Iron & steel	(371)	0.81	−0.74	1.56	0.21	1.35	194	−92	14	86
Nonferrous metals	(372)	4.30	−1.12	5.48	−0.86	6.40	127	−26	−16	117
Metal products	(381)	−1.53	0.25	−1.77	0.16	−1.93	116	−16	−9	109
Nonelectric machinery	(382)	1.82	−0.25	2.08	−0.05	2.13	114	−14	−2	102
Electric machinery	(383)	−2.01	0.04	−2.05	0.08	−2.13	102	−2	−4	104
Transportation equip.	(384)	1.38	0.15	1.23	0.16	1.07	89	11	13	87
Miscellaneous manufac.	(38A)	3.08	0.29	2.77	1.23	1.53	90	10	44	55
Total traded		0.37	0.01	0.37	0.04	0.33	99	2	10	90

TABLE 4 (*continued*)

		Percentage employment change due to tariff cut in					Percentage shares of employment effects			
		All developed	Developed, less U.S. & Canada	U.S. & Canada	U.S.	Canada	U.S. & Canada as pct. of all developed	Developed, less U.S. & Canada, as pct. of all developed	U.S. as pct. of U.S. & Canada	Canada as pct. of U.S. & Canada
Nontraded goods										
Mining & quarrying	(2)	0.46	0.06	0.40	-0.50	0.90	87	13	-123	224
Electric, gas & water	(4)	-0.07	-0.04	-0.04	0.00	-0.04	51	49	-6	106
Construction	(5)	0.14	-0.00	0.14	-0.01	0.15	102	-2	-6	106
Wholesale & ret. trade	(6)	-0.14	-0.01	-0.13	0.00	-0.13	93	7	-0	100
Transp., stor. & com.	(7)	-0.02	-0.01	-0.01	-0.00	-0.01	60	40	10	90
Fin., ins. & real est.	(8)	-0.12	0.01	-0.13	-0.00	-0.13	105	-5	0	100
Comm., soc. & pers. serv.	(9)	-0.23	0.00	-0.23	-0.00	-0.23	100	-0	2	98
Total nontraded		-0.13	-0.00	-0.13	-0.01	-0.11	99	2	10	90
Total all industries		0.00	0.00	0.00	0.00	0.00			10	90

TABLE 5

Net Percentage Changes in Employment in the United States Due to Tariff Reductions
in the U.S., Canada, and Other Developed Countries

		Percentage employment change due to tariff cut in					Percentage shares of employment effects			
		All developed	Developed, less U.S. & Canada	U.S. & Canada	U.S.	Canada	U.S. & Canada as pct. of all developed	Developed, less U.S. & Canada, as pct. of all developed	U.S. as pct. of U.S. & Canada	Canada as pct. of U.S. & Canada
Traded goods										
Agr., for., & fishing	(1)	0.41	0.26	0.15	0.15	0.00	36	64	98	2
Food, bev., & tobacco	(310)	-0.03	-0.07	0.04	0.05	-0.01	-166	265	114	-14
Textiles	(321)	0.12	-0.41	0.53	0.51	0.02	459	-357	96	4
Wearing apparel	(322)	-0.18	-0.03	-0.15	-0.16	0.01	85	15	104	-4
Leather products	(323)	0.74	-1.64	2.43	2.51	-0.08	326	-221	103	-3
Footwear	(324)	0.17	-0.15	0.32	0.32	0.00	191	-91	100	0
Wood products	(331)	-0.17	-0.06	-0.12	-0.07	-0.04	67	33	63	37
Furniture & fixtures	(332)	-0.12	0.03	-0.15	-0.16	0.01	123	-23	106	-6
Paper & paper products	(341)	0.12	-0.12	0.24	0.28	-0.04	199	-98	118	-17
Printing & publishing	(342)	0.04	-0.01	0.06	0.03	0.03	134	-34	54	46
Chemicals	(35A)	0.18	0.05	0.13	0.12	0.01	73	27	96	4
Petrol. & rel. prod.	(35B)	0.34	-0.08	0.43	0.41	0.01	124	-24	97	3
Rubber products	(355)	-0.15	-0.04	-0.11	-0.21	0.10	72	28	189	-89
Nonmetallic min. prod.	(36A)	-0.48	-0.05	-0.42	-0.43	0.01	89	11	102	-2
Glass & glass products	(362)	-0.17	-0.09	-0.08	-0.10	0.02	46	54	125	-25
Iron & steel	(371)	0.02	-0.15	0.17	0.15	0.02	959	-857	91	9
Nonferrous metals	(372)	0.05	-0.21	0.26	0.34	-0.08	515	-414	132	-32
Metal products	(381)	0.02	0.07	-0.05	-0.10	0.05	-328	429	187	-87
Nonelectric machinery	(382)	0.21	-0.15	0.36	0.37	-0.01	171	-71	102	-2
Electric machinery	(383)	0.17	-0.00	0.18	0.11	0.07	102	-2	61	39
Transportation equip.	(384)	0.13	0.01	0.11	0.13	-0.02	88	12	116	-16
Miscellaneous manufac.	(38A)	-0.66	0.00	-0.66	-0.68	0.02	101	-1	102	-2
Total traded		0.07	-0.02	0.09	0.08	0.01	131	-31	90	10

TABLE 5 (continued)

		Percentage employment change due to tariff cut in					Percentage shares of employment effects			
		All developed	Developed, less U.S. & Canada	U.S. & Canada	U.S.	Canada	U.S. & Canada as pct. of all developed	Developed, less U.S. & Canada, as pct. of all developed	U.S. as pct. of U.S. & Canada	Canada as pct. of U.S. & Canada
Nontraded goods										
Mining & quarrying	(2)	0.25	-0.11	0.36	0.35	0.00	144	-44	99	1
Electric, gas & water	(4)	-0.04	-0.01	-0.04	-0.03	-0.01	89	12	87	13
Construction	(5)	0.03	0.01	0.01	0.02	-0.00	48	52	124	-24
Wholesale & ret. trade	(6)	-0.03	0.01	-0.04	-0.03	-0.00	119	-19	91	9
Transp., stor. & com.	(7)	-0.01	-0.01	-0.01	-0.00	-0.00	48	52	76	25
Fin., ins. & real est.	(8)	-0.03	0.01	-0.04	-0.04	-0.00	133	-33	92	8
Comm., soc. & pers. serv.	(9)	-0.03	0.01	-0.04	-0.04	-0.00	138	-38	93	7
Total nontraded		-0.02	0.01	-0.03	-0.03	-0.00	131	-31	90	10
Total all industries		0.00	0.0	0.00	0.00	0.00	0.0			

in imports, and thus decreases in employment. If these same sectors have the deepest tariff reductions in other countries as well, however, then the foreign tariff reductions will stimulate the home country's exports and thus increase employment. Conversely, those sectors with the smallest tariff reductions both at home and abroad will have employment diverted toward them by the larger own-country tariff reductions in other sectors, but away from them by the larger tariff reductions in other sectors abroad.

Our analysis of the Tokyo Round thus suggests that the multilateral tariff reductions may have dampened possible dislocation effects of a country's own tariff reductions. As just mentioned, this conclusion reflects the similarity of tariff reductions among the industrialized countries. It would be interesting in this light to investigate how individual countries would be affected in cases where there were important dissimilarities in sectoral levels and tariff-reduction patterns.[10]

COMPUTATIONAL ANALYSIS OF CHANGES IN U.S. MACROECONOMIC POLICIES

Although the Michigan model was designed mainly to analyze sectoral effects of changes in trade and related policies, we have on occasion used it to analyze the effects of changes in exchange rates and macroeconomic policies. The model is not particularly well suited for macroanalysis, however, since it does not include interest rates and other financial influences; it treats the capital account as exogenous.

Granting these limitations, we thought it might nonetheless be of some interest to investigate what insights the model might offer with respect to the possible sectoral impacts of U.S. macroeconomic policies in the first half of the 1980s. For this purpose, we carried out two experiments. The first attempts to mimic a policy of monetary contraction, such as that which occured in 1981–82, by assuming an exogenous increase in U.S. capital inflows equal to 1 percent of U.S. GDP. A contractionary monetary policy would presumably increase the U.S. rate of interest relative to foreign rates, thus leading to capital inflow, appreciation of the U.S. dollar, and a corresponding trade deficit. The second experiment involves an assumed fiscal expansion, such as that which occurred after 1982, financed by a capital inflow. Again, we assume that U.S. aggregate expen-

[10] See Alan V. Deardorff and Robert M. Stern, "Alternative Scenarios for Trade Liberalization," in David Audretsch and Michael P. Claudon, eds., *The Internationalization of U.S. Markets* (New York, 1990) for a computational analysis of different negotiating options in the Uruguay Round, including the possible elimination of existing tariffs in the major industrialized and developing countries and the elimination of nontariff restrictions in agriculture, textiles and apparel, automobiles, and other sectors.

diture increases by 1 percent of U.S. GDP, and that there is an accompanying exogenous capital inflow of the same amount. The increase in expenditure would increase the demand for both tradables and nontradables. Greater expenditure on tradables would require a shift toward foreign goods induced by an appreciation of the dollar. There would be a capital inflow and a corresponding trade deficit.

The two experiments were run on the alternative assumptions of fixed-money and flexible wages. In the case of fixed-money wages, we allow unemployment to occur, whereas the labor market is permitted to clear when wages are assumed to be flexible.

The sectoral percentage trade and employment effects for each of the two cases of both experiments are shown for the United States in Tables 6 and 7. In addition, the calculated changes in the U.S. effective exchange rates are shown at the bottom of Table 7. It is noticeable, first, that the sectoral effects on both trade and employment are not at all sensitive to which scenario is run. That is, there is very little variation across the rows in either of these tables, except for the final row reporting effective exchange rates.

This consistency can be understood as follows. Consider the effects of a capital inflow itself, whether or not it is accompanied by an increase in expenditure. A capital inflow requires three kinds of adjustment in order to restore equilibrium. First, an overall trade deficit equal to the capital inflow must be induced, requiring that the country's nominal expenditure exceed its nominal income by the amount of the capital inflow. Second, relative prices of domestically produced versus imported goods must adjust to assure that overall demand for domestic goods not exceed their supply, as they otherwise would given the aforementioned rise in expenditure relative to income. And third, relative prices of the individual sectors must adjust to equilibrium, to the extent that individual supplies and demands are affected differently by overall changes in expenditure, price levels, and exchange rates. The first two of these adjustments are accomplished in somewhat different ways depending on whether the capital inflow is accompanied by a rise in nominal expenditure, but these differences have little to do with the intersectoral effects. It is only in the third of these adjustments that sectors are affected, and here the different scenarios are pretty much the same.

To illustrate the different kinds of adjustment, note that a capital inflow by itself causes an appreciation of the currency, which both lowers domestic prices so as to decrease the nominal value of income relative to the given nominal expenditure and cheapens imported goods relative to domestic goods so as to divert this expenditure away from domestic goods.

TABLE 6
Sectoral Percentage Trade Effects in the United States Due to an Increase in the U.S. Trade Deficit by 1 Percent of GDP Under Alternative Assumptions

	Exports				Imports			
	Capital inflow alone		Expenditure increase with capital inflow		Capital inflow alone		Expenditure increase with capital inflow	
	Flex. wage	Fixed wage	Flex. wage	Fixed wage	Flex. wage	Fixed wage	Flex. wage	Fixed wage
Traded goods								
Agr., for., & fishing (1)	-1.28	-1.20	-1.26	-1.25	2.85	1.89	2.79	3.04
Food, bev., & tobacco (310)	-12.01	-11.56	-12.10	-12.27	1.79	1.50	1.80	1.90
Textiles (321)	-26.18	-26.94	-26.14	-25.97	0.53	0.21	0.52	0.63
Wearing apparel (322)	-43.91	-47.07	-44.56	-44.28	3.12	3.18	3.17	3.23
Leather products (323)	-34.44	-35.92	-35.05	-34.77	1.73	1.19	1.74	1.93
Footwear (324)	-35.39	-38.78	-36.17	-35.94	3.05	3.05	3.12	3.21
Wood products (331)	-7.65	-7.71	-7.63	-7.58	3.05	2.36	3.04	3.26
Furniture & fixtures (332)	-21.94	-23.23	-22.05	-21.78	8.45	8.24	8.49	8.63
Paper & paper products (341)	-19.55	-20.65	-19.49	-19.09	2.52	2.15	2.51	2.63
Printing & publishing (342)	-14.27	-15.15	-14.25	-13.95	2.95	2.85	2.95	2.98
Chemicals (35A)	-8.02	-8.26	-7.91	-7.79	4.86	4.23	4.78	4.97
Petrol. & rel. prod. (35B)	-36.98	-36.28	-36.95	-37.24	1.32	1.07	1.32	1.41
Rubber products (355)	-12.21	-13.04	-12.15	-11.89	12.15	12.04	12.09	12.14
Nonmetallic min. prod. (36A)	-12.50	-13.25	-12.46	-12.21	7.29	6.92	7.26	7.39
Glass & glass products (362)	-12.84	-13.86	-12.80	-12.49	3.74	3.50	3.73	3.83
Iron & steel (371)	-25.30	-26.48	-25.13	-24.71	1.81	1.46	1.80	1.92
Nonferrous metals (372)	-26.62	-27.48	-26.50	-26.00	0.44	-0.04	0.44	0.59
Metal products (381)	-13.11	-14.12	-13.09	-12.80	7.98	7.88	7.97	8.05
Nonelectric machinery (382)	-9.43	-10.03	-9.33	-9.14	2.33	1.86	2.31	2.47
Electric machinery (383)	-10.12	-10.75	-10.00	-9.79	4.22	3.81	4.17	4.31
Transportation equip. (384)	-4.77	-5.05	-4.74	-4.64	7.23	6.62	7.19	7.39
Miscellaneous manufac. (38A)	-4.94	-5.36	-4.94	-4.83	3.82	3.33	3.82	4.01
Total traded	-9.93	-10.28	-9.88	-9.77	3.24	2.83	3.23	3.37

TABLE 7

*Sectoral Percentage Employment Effects in the United States
and Change in Effective Exchange Rate Due to an Increase
in the U.S. Trade Deficit by 1 Percent of GDP Under Alternative Assumptions*

		Capital inflow alone		Expenditure increase with capital inflow	
		Flex. wage	Fixed wage	Flex. wage	Fixed wage
Traded goods					
Agr., for., & fishing	(1)	−1.22	−2.16	−1.20	−0.84
Food, bev., & tobacco	(310)	0.43	−0.26	0.42	0.65
Textiles	(321)	−4.53	−5.26	−4.53	−4.31
Wearing apparel	(322)	−0.77	−1.60	−0.81	−0.57
Leather products	(323)	−15.35	−16.48	−15.67	−15.41
Footwear	(324)	0.17	−0.66	0.14	0.39
Wood products	(331)	−2.04	−2.73	−2.04	−1.79
Furniture & fixtures	(332)	−0.00	−0.70	−0.01	0.22
Paper & paper products	(341)	−2.59	−3.34	−2.58	−2.32
Printing & publishing	(342)	−0.06	−0.70	−0.06	0.16
Chemicals	(35A)	−3.01	−3.76	−2.98	−2.72
Petrol. & rel. prod.	(35B)	−5.55	−6.49	−5.55	−5.24
Rubber products	(355)	−2.65	−3.49	−2.63	−2.35
Nonmetallic min. prod.	(36A)	−0.94	−1.74	−0.94	−0.67
Glass & glass products	(362)	−1.73	−2.43	−1.72	−1.48
Iron & steel	(371)	−2.80	−3.48	−2.77	−2.54
Nonferrous metals	(372)	−4.52	−5.24	−4.50	−4.22
Metal products	(381)	−1.26	−1.95	−1.26	−1.02
Nonelectric machinery	(382)	−2.53	−3.21	−2.50	−2.27
Electric machinery	(383)	−1.61	−2.25	−1.59	−1.37
Transportation equip.	(384)	−1.08	−1.63	−1.07	−0.89
Miscellaneous manufac.	(38A)	−2.75	−3.67	−2.75	−2.45
Total traded		−1.75	−2.50	−1.75	−1.49
Nontraded goods					
Mining & quarrying	(2)	−5.10	−6.37	−5.09	−4.66
Electric, gas & water	(4)	0.50	−1.03	0.50	1.02
Construction	(5)	0.87	0.20	0.86	1.09
Wholesale & ret. trade	(6)	0.69	−0.20	0.69	0.99
Transp., stor. & com.	(7)	0.09	−0.72	0.09	0.37
Fin., ins. & real est.	(8)	0.73	−0.53	0.73	1.17
Comm., soc. & pers. serv.	(9)	0.72	0.03	0.71	0.95
Total nontraded		0.61	−0.23	0.61	0.90
Total all industries		0.01	−0.81	0.01	0.29
Change in effective exchange rate		4.31	3.63	2.78	2.97

If, on the other hand, the capital inflow is accompanied by an increase in nominal expenditure, then a portion of the expenditure adjustment is accomplished directly, domestic prices can rise, and a smaller appreciation is needed for both purposes. This trend is evident in the exchange-rate results for the two scenarios reported in Table 7. The difference between the results is largely nominal, in that the nominal exchange rate appreciates less and the overall level of prices (not reported in the table) rises more when nominal expenditure rises. However, relative prices across sectors are not very sensitive to these nominal differences, and thus the intersectoral adjustments required in both cases are mostly the same.

There is also some difference in the exchange-rate results depending on whether wages are fixed or flexible, but again the intersectoral results are not affected much by this distinction. If wages are flexible, then they can adjust along with nominal expenditure, prices, and exchange rates, and the effects just described occur unhindered. If wages are fixed, however, then changes in these other nominal variables cause some changes in real wages and hence in outputs. As a result, a portion of the drop in nominal expenditure is brought about by a drop in outputs, and there is less need for adjustment of nominal variables. This change appears in Table 7, where the changes in effective (nominal) exchange rates across the two experiments are shown to be somewhat more similar with fixed wages than with flexible wages.

Although there is not much variation across scenarios in these sectoral effects, considerable variation exists within each scenario across the sectors themselves. The main determinants of the sectoral effects of a change in the exchange rate or a change in expenditure include (1) the elasticity of an industry's supply and share of exports in total production, (2) the share of imports in total demand and the elasticity of substitution between imports and home goods, (3) industry shares of world supply and demand, (4) industry shares of final demand and labor shares of value-added, and (5) the size and direction of expenditure changes.[11]

It is evident from Table 6 that there are sizable percentage increases in imports and even larger declines in exports. The larger changes in exports reflect the fact that export supplies tend to be substantially more price elastic than import demands. Table 7 shows the net percentage declines in employment across practically all tradable industries. Employment increases in the nontradable sectors, except for mining and quarrying. It is noteworthy that these results do not differ a great deal between the two experiments or when wages are assumed to be fixed or flexible.

We noted in Table 1 that the dollar appreciated significantly after

[11] *Michigan Model*, 139–51.

1980. We show an appreciation of about 3 to 4 percent for the various experiments in the last line of Table 7, but the size of the appreciations is obviously very much smaller than what actually occurred. We may therefore be underestimating possible sectoral impacts, although there is no clear way to establish this without a more complete model of exchange-rate determination.

The effects of the increase in the U.S. trade deficit on other countries occur primarily through world prices and real exchange rates. The appreciation of the dollar in Table 1 corresponds to a depreciation of other currencies that in general expands other countries' exports and contracts their imports. These changes, too, correspond to the tightening of world markets in individual sectors that occurs when U.S. imports expand and exports contract as reported in Table 6.

The trade and employment results for Canada due to the increased trade deficit of the United States are shown in Tables 8 and 9. The largest percentage increases in Canada's exports are in leather products, footwear, wearing apparel, rubber products, and nonferrous metals. There are declines in imports, in the 1 percent range or less, except in the cases of agricultural products, iron and steel, and nonferrous metals where imports rise. The employment effects largely mirror the trade effects, including a shift away from nontradables. The results of the model suggest a depreciation of the Canadian dollar in the 2 to 3 percent range.

The results for Mexico in Tables 10 and 11 show unusually large percentage increases in exports and employment in petroleum and leather products, which may reflect the relatively high supply elasticities assigned to these sectors. Aside from these outliers, the export increases are in the 1 to 3 percent range and the import declines are somewhat larger. The percentage employment effects are highest in mining and quarrying, nonferrous metals, petroleum products, nonelectric machinery, and wood products. Finally, the model suggests a depreciation of the peso by 3 to 4 percent.

As we noted, the United States has experienced trade and current-account deficits ranging from 1 to 3.5 percent of GNP since 1980 coupled with a government deficit in excess of 5 percent of GNP in 1983 and 1986–87. The dollar appreciated substantially between 1980 and 1985 and has since depreciated to about its 1980 level. We have tried to provide some estimates of the sectoral impact of U.S. policy changes that are reflected in the macroeconomic data both for the United States and its two major North American trading partners, Canada and Mexico. While we have not attempted to take into account the full extent of the changes in exchange rates and associated changes in the U.S. trade and current

TABLE 8

Sectoral Percentage Trade Effects in Canada Due to an Increase in the U.S. Trade Deficit by 1 Percent of GDP Under Alternative Assumptions

	Exports				Imports			
	Capital inflow alone		Expenditure increase with capital inflow		Capital inflow alone		Expenditure increase with capital inflow	
	Flex. wage	Fixed wage	Flex. wage	Fixed wage	Flex. wage	Fixed wage	Flex. wage	Fixed wage
Traded goods								
Agr., for., & fishing (1)	0.04	0.13	0.06	0.06	0.29	0.61	0.23	0.09
Food, bev., & tobacco (310)	4.22	3.87	3.89	3.89	-0.72	-0.50	-0.69	-0.73
Textiles (321)	4.20	4.73	4.09	3.86	-0.36	-0.14	-0.36	-0.41
Wearing apparel (322)	7.14	6.94	6.44	5.88	-1.27	-1.06	-1.18	-1.15
Leather products (323)	16.99	17.80	15.98	15.46	-0.22	0.07	-0.24	-0.34
Footwear (324)	8.44	7.36	6.88	5.70	-0.96	-0.68	-0.86	-0.83
Wood products (331)	3.44	3.71	3.39	3.31	-0.33	-0.07	-0.32	-0.39
Furniture & fixtures (332)	3.48	3.89	3.19	2.86	-1.56	-1.28	-1.47	-1.47
Paper & paper products (341)	3.93	4.13	3.87	3.80	-0.12	0.15	-0.12	-0.18
Printing & publishing (342)	2.20	2.55	2.15	2.04	-1.41	-1.20	-1.37	-1.41
Chemicals (35A)	1.14	1.49	1.22	1.15	-0.04	0.17	-0.07	-0.13
Petrol. & rel. prod. (35B)	1.19	0.98	1.15	1.16	-0.20	0.03	-0.20	-0.25
Rubber products (355)	5.84	6.38	5.76	5.53	-1.40	-1.24	-1.39	-1.41
Nonmetallic min. prod. (36A)	0.57	0.76	0.55	0.49	-0.57	-0.28	-0.55	-0.61
Glass & glass products (362)	1.23	1.39	1.19	1.11	-0.24	0.01	-0.23	-0.29
Iron & steel (371)	-2.15	-1.69	-2.02	-2.12	1.58	1.96	1.56	1.51
Nonferrous metals (372)	5.04	6.00	4.98	4.99	1.66	2.08	1.64	1.59
Metal products (381)	2.06	2.29	2.01	1.88	-1.26	-0.98	-1.23	-1.26
Nonelectric machinery (382)	2.36	2.73	2.40	2.26	-0.44	-0.19	-0.43	-0.49
Electric machinery (383)	1.29	1.46	1.33	1.27	-0.71	-0.46	-0.72	-0.77
Transportation equip. (384)	1.65	1.74	1.65	1.62	-0.68	-0.49	-0.68	-0.72
Miscellaneous manufac. (38A)	2.48	2.66	2.36	2.18	-0.55	-0.26	-0.53	-0.58
Total traded	2.37	2.59	2.33	2.28	-0.43	-0.19	-0.43	-0.48

TABLE 9

Sectoral Percentage Employment Effects in Canada and Change in Effective Exchange Rate Due to an Increase in the U.S. Trade Deficit by 1 Percent of GDP Under Alternative Assumptions

		Capital inflow alone		Expenditure increase with capital inflow	
		Flex. wage	Fixed wage	Flex. wage	Fixed wage
Traded goods					
Agr., for., & fishing	(1)	0.41	1.01	0.41	0.29
Food, bev., & tobacco	(310)	−0.21	0.08	−0.23	−0.31
Textiles	(321)	0.41	0.82	0.40	0.28
Wearing apparel	(322)	−0.25	0.14	−0.28	−0.40
Leather products	(323)	17.78	18.69	16.71	16.15
Footwear	(324)	−0.15	0.16	−0.25	−0.42
Wood products	(331)	2.16	2.51	2.13	2.03
Furniture & fixtures	(332)	0.23	0.65	0.18	0.04
Paper & paper products	(341)	3.51	3.87	3.45	3.34
Printing & publishing	(342)	0.33	0.71	0.33	0.23
Chemicals	(35A)	0.98	1.46	1.02	0.90
Petrol. & rel. prod.	(35B)	2.08	1.83	2.01	2.01
Rubber products	(355)	2.04	2.45	2.02	1.88
Nonmetallic min. prod.	(36A)	0.28	0.66	0.27	0.16
Glass & glass products	(362)	0.50	0.83	0.48	0.38
Iron & steel	(371)	0.87	1.41	0.89	0.81
Nonferrous metals	(372)	6.56	7.83	6.49	6.50
Metal products	(381)	0.40	0.77	0.39	0.28
Nonelectric machinery	(382)	1.99	2.46	2.02	1.87
Electric machinery	(383)	0.38	0.78	0.39	0.29
Transportation equip.	(384)	1.26	1.49	1.25	1.20
Miscellaneous manufac.	(38A)	1.67	2.01	1.59	1.40
Total traded		1.01	1.44	0.99	0.88
Nontraded goods					
Mining & quarrying	(2)	2.63	3.05	2.57	2.44
Electric, gas & water	(4)	−0.08	0.66	−0.08	−0.25
Construction	(5)	−0.60	−0.17	−0.59	−0.68
Wholesale & ret. trade	(6)	−0.36	0.10	−0.35	−0.46
Transp., stor. & com.	(7)	−0.17	0.24	−0.17	−0.27
Fin., ins. & real est.	(8)	−0.49	0.16	−0.48	−0.64
Comm., soc. & pers. serv.	(9)	−0.46	−0.00	−0.45	−0.55
Total nontraded		−0.35	0.12	−0.34	−0.45
Total all industries		0.01	0.46	0.01	−0.10
Change in effective exchange rate		−3.20	−2.67	−2.04	−2.19

TABLE 10

Sectoral Percentage Trade Effects in Mexico Due to an Increase in the U.S. Trade Deficit by 1 Percent of GDP Under Alternative Assumptions

	Exports				Imports			
	Capital inflow alone		Expenditure increase with capital inflow		Capital inflow alone		Expenditure increase with capital inflow	
	Flex. wage	Fixed wage	Flex. wage	Fixed wage	Flex. wage	Fixed wage	Flex. wage	Fixed wage
Traded goods								
Agr., for., & fishing (1)	0.33	0.40	0.35	0.35	-2.15	-2.13	-2.25	-2.34
Food, bev., & tobacco (310)	3.47	3.59	3.49	3.45	-2.63	-2.53	-2.65	-2.69
Textiles (321)	2.02	2.16	2.05	2.00	-2.23	-2.11	-2.28	-2.31
Wearing apparel (322)	2.99	3.05	2.97	2.87	-9.11	-8.74	-9.07	-8.99
Leather products (323)	11.58	11.65	11.51	11.40	-4.35	-4.18	-4.34	-4.37
Footwear (324)	3.60	3.59	3.54	3.40	-6.17	-5.79	-6.10	-6.03
Wood products (331)	1.80	1.97	1.84	1.79	-2.19	-2.05	-2.23	-2.28
Furniture & fixtures (332)	5.65	5.70	5.67	5.54	-5.21	-5.02	-5.25	-5.24
Paper & paper products (341)	3.45	3.70	3.51	3.43	-2.51	-2.41	-2.56	-2.59
Printing & publishing (342)	1.64	1.81	1.67	1.61	-6.53	-6.43	-6.63	-6.66
Chemicals (35A)	0.70	0.79	0.73	0.70	-2.05	-1.92	-2.12	-2.18
Petrol. & rel. prod. (35B)	36.70	38.21	37.36	36.78	-0.87	-0.71	-0.88	-0.93
Rubber products (355)	1.44	1.55	1.47	1.43	-4.84	-4.60	-4.94	-5.01
Nonmetallic min. prod. (36A)	1.37	1.51	1.41	1.36	-4.17	-3.92	-4.26	-4.34
Glass & glass products (362)	1.65	1.79	1.69	1.63	-2.52	-2.37	-2.57	-2.60
Iron & steel (371)	1.75	1.88	1.81	1.76	-1.25	-1.08	-1.28	-1.34
Nonferrous metals (372)	1.98	2.16	2.02	1.98	0.16	0.26	0.16	0.12
Metal products (381)	1.76	1.89	1.79	1.74	-4.76	-4.58	-4.85	-4.88
Nonelectric machinery (382)	1.37	1.51	1.40	1.35	-2.08	-1.95	-2.13	-2.17
Electric machinery (383)	0.80	0.89	0.82	0.79	-1.95	-1.83	-2.00	-2.04
Transportation equip. (384)	0.63	0.68	0.64	0.63	-4.28	-4.11	-4.37	-4.42
Miscellaneous manufac. (38A)	1.59	1.70	1.61	1.55	-3.03	-2.82	-3.08	-3.11
Total traded	5.31	5.57	5.41	5.31	-2.56	-2.42	-2.62	-2.66

TABLE 11

*Sectoral Percentage Employment Effects in Mexico and Change
in Effective Exchange Rate Due to an Increase in the U.S. Trade Deficit
by 1 Percent of GDP Under Alternative Assumptions*

		Capital inflow alone		Expenditure increase with capital inflow	
		Flex. wage	Fixed wage	Flex. wage	Fixed wage
Traded goods					
Agr., for., & fishing	(1)	−0.11	0.25	−0.11	−0.22
Food, bev., & tobacco	(310)	−0.20	0.29	−0.21	−0.38
Textiles	(321)	2.48	2.87	2.52	2.37
Wearing apparel	(322)	0.11	0.50	0.08	−0.07
Leather products	(323)	0.77	1.15	0.73	0.58
Footwear	(324)	−0.49	−0.08	−0.53	−0.68
Wood products	(331)	3.10	3.54	3.15	3.02
Furniture & fixtures	(332)	−1.72	−1.44	−1.76	−1.85
Paper & paper products	(341)	0.95	1.46	0.96	0.79
Printing & publishing	(342)	−0.42	−0.05	−0.43	−0.55
Chemicals	(35A)	1.94	2.42	2.01	1.86
Petrol. & rel. prod.	(35B)	4.06	4.50	4.12	3.97
Rubber products	(355)	2.72	3.32	2.77	2.56
Nonmetallic min. prod.	(36A)	0.73	1.24	0.75	0.58
Glass & glass products	(362)	0.68	1.09	0.69	0.55
Iron & steel	(371)	1.18	1.75	1.22	1.04
Nonferrous metals	(372)	4.74	5.28	4.84	4.70
Metal products	(381)	1.21	1.58	1.23	1.09
Nonelectric machinery	(382)	3.27	3.63	3.36	3.23
Electric machinery	(383)	2.27	2.52	2.34	2.26
Transportation equip.	(384)	0.57	0.74	0.57	0.52
Miscellaneous manufac.	(38A)	0.86	1.31	0.86	0.69
Total traded		0.30	0.69	0.31	0.19
Nontraded goods					
Mining & quarrying	(2)	6.90	7.68	7.01	6.73
Electric, gas & water	(4)	−0.53	0.16	−0.54	−0.76
Construction	(5)	−1.05	−0.69	−1.07	−1.19
Wholesale & ret. trade	(6)	−0.75	−0.08	−0.77	−0.99
Transp., stor. & com.	(7)	−0.63	−0.18	−0.65	−0.79
Fin., ins. & real est.	(8)	−0.53	−0.04	−0.54	−0.70
Comm., soc. & pers. serv.	(9)	−0.77	−0.43	−0.79	−0.90
Total nontraded		−0.48	−0.03	−0.49	−0.64
Total all industries		0.01	0.42	0.01	−0.12
Change in effective exchange rate		−4.34	−4.00	−3.33	−3.46

accounts, the sectoral impacts that we have calculated are nonetheless substantial.

Because a very large proportion of the trade of both Canada and Mexico is carried on with the United States, it is reasonable to conclude that U.S. macroeconomic policies in the 1980s have had a major impact on the level and sectoral composition of bilateral trade flows in North America. It is also interesting to note how the nontradable sectors have been affected in each country.

While we have not attempted to calculate the effects of dollar depreciation, our analysis suggests that the sectoral impacts in the United States and in its major trading partners are bound to be substantial. The dollar depreciation has already brought about a significant expansion in the production of tradables in the United States, as exports have increased and expenditure has shifted from imports to domestic substitutes. At the same time, a shift away from nontradables has also been occurring in the United States. Opposite effects can be expected in Canada and Mexico, with a shift away from tradables toward nontradables. In view of the size and impact of the exchange-rate movements, it is possible that some dislocation may occur in particular sectors in the individual countries.

CONCLUSION

We have had occasion in this paper to use the Michigan Model of World Production and Trade to analyze changes in multilateral trade policies and U.S. macroeconomic policies, both of which have taken place in the 1980s and have had an important influence on North American economic relations.

Our analysis of the Tokyo Round tariff reductions, which were implemented in stages between 1980 and 1987, focused on the own-country and cross-country sectoral effects of the tariff reductions on Canada and the United States. It was shown that the effects were relatively small in view of the small size of the actual tariff reductions. Nonetheless, both negative and positive own-country effects were observed, which reflected the sectoral differences in the depth of the tariff reductions. When we decomposed the multilateral reductions, the own-country effects were dominant in relation to the overall effects. In addition, because of the similarities of the tariff reductions, the cross-country effects often tended to offset the own-country effects.

We found that changes in U.S. macroeconomic policies in the first half of the 1980s had much larger impacts on trade and employment in the North American setting than the Tokyo Round tariff changes. The computational results suggested relatively large increases in U.S. imports and declines in U.S. exports, with a shift away from U.S. tradable industries toward nontradables. The net percentage reductions in employment were fairly large in a number of the U.S. tradable sectors. Opposite effects were observed in Canada and Mexico, though with somewhat smaller relative sectoral changes in their trade and employment. When the full effects of the post-1985 dollar depreciation are realized, we can expect to witness significant sectoral impacts in a direction opposite to what occurred in the period of dollar appreciation.

It is interesting to view our Tokyo Round and macroeconomic experiments together. In the case of the Tokyo Round tariff reductions, the own-country effects brought about a shift toward tradables and away from nontradables in all major industrialized countries. But because of the similarities of the tariff reductions, the cross-country effects tended to dampen the own-country effects. U.S. macroeconomic policies in the first half of the 1980s had effects opposite to the Tokyo Round tariff reductions insofar as there was a shift away from tradables toward nontradables in the United States. In Canada, the own-country effects of its tariff reductions were reinforced by the changes in U.S. macroeconomic policies. The same is true for Mexico, except that our calculations suggest that the Tokyo Round tariff reductions had a negligible impact on Mexico.

One final note: our analysis of the own-country and cross-country effects of policy changes can be extended to other countries and regions covered in the Michigan model.

Trade Liberalization and Structural Adjustment in Canada: The Genesis of Intraindustry Trade

Richard E. Caves

A DJUSTING TO import competition is a conspicuous process because of the persistent policy debate over how much protection to grant producers afflicted by intensified overseas competition. For two decades, the debate has been highly audible in Canada, the United States, and other industrial countries as major exchange-rate changes, the rise of Japan and newly industrialized countries, and other disturbances turn the competitive heat on one sector after another. The Canada-U.S. Free Trade Agreement and the European Community's commitment to remove internal nontariff barriers in 1992 are exceptions to a trend toward managing international trade so as to slow import penetration to a politically acceptable rate.

Despite this generally restrictive policy climate, manufactured exports of the major industrial countries—Canada notably included—have quietly undergone a rapid expansion. Rising shares of output that is exported have more or less kept pace with the rising shares of domestic use, that is accounted for by imports. Furthermore, this parallel expansion of imports and exports has occurred not only for nations' entire manufacturing sectors but also for a surprising proportion of individual industries. The parallel growth of exports and imports gives rise to intraindustry trade, now a well-known phenomenon that has been intensively studied as a static ongoing feature of individual countries' trade patterns. However, little attention has been paid to how industries adjust to international disturbances so that increased intraindustry trade results.

Intraindustry trade was first noticed in the expansion of trade experienced by the European Community following the elimination of tariffs by the Treaty of Rome. Balassa and Grubel pointed out the phenomenon, which they associated with industries' adjustments to a general reduction of tariff protection—a reduction that both threatened producers with cheaper imports and offered them the opportunity for higher net revenue from exports.[1] Later, the growth of intraindustry trade was found to be widespread and not confined to countries taking vigorous part in multilateral trade liberalization.[2] Although that fact should have flagged the dynamics of trade expansion as a focus for research, academic interest in intraindustry trade chose to explain it with static equilibrium models of market structure. Research designs that explain the incidence of intraindustry trade in cross-sections of industries and countries have enjoyed considerable success.[3]

Those findings, however, tell us nothing about why intraindustry trade has grown so markedly. We know intraindustry trade is more prevalent in markets with certain structures; however, market structures have changed very little over time and thus do not account for intertemporal changes in two-way trade. This paper attempts to redirect attention to the process that has implemented the expansion of intraindustry trade. It grows out of a larger project on the adjustment of Canadian manufacturing industries to international disturbances, which permits analysis of adjustments to heightened import competition that can lead to increased exports and thus intraindustry trade. The first section reviews data that highlight the importance of intraindustry trade for Canadian manufacturing. The second reviews the market models that underlie our empirical study of adjustment in general and relates them to conditions that could enlarge intraindustry trade through supply-side adjustments. The third summarizes the structure and empirical results of the general model of adjustment to import competition. The fourth extends that model to ana-

---

[1] Bela Balassa, "Tariff Reductions and Trade in Manufactures among the Industrial Countries," *American Economic Review* 56 (June 1966), 466–73; Herbert G. Grubel, "Intra-Industry Specialization and the Pattern of Trade," *Canadian Journal of Economics and Political Science* vol. 33, no. 3 (Aug. 1967), 374–88.

[2] Helmut Hesse, "Hypotheses for the Explanation of Trade Between Industrial Countries, 1953–1970," in Herbert Giersch, ed., *The International Division of Labour: Problems and Perspectives* (Tubingen, 1974).

[3] For a literature survey, see David Greenaway and Chris Milner, *The Economics of Intra-Industry Trade* (Oxford, 1986). Significant recent contributions include Bela Balassa and Luc Bauwens, *Changing Trade Patterns in Manufactured Goods: An Econometric Investigation* (Amsterdam and New York, 1988), and Elhanan Helpman, "Imperfect Competition and International Trade: Evidence from Fourteen Industrial Countries," in A. Michael Spence and Heather A. Hazard, eds., *International Competitiveness* (Cambridge, Eng., 1988).

lyze industry-level interactions of changes in imports and exports, and the fifth reports the statistical results.

INCREASING INTRAINDUSTRY TRADE: THE CANADIAN CASE

Canada is an unlikely site for analyzing intraindustry trade because of its traditional structure of comparative advantage. Canada's factor endowment gave rise to exports of products intensive in natural resources, which paid for imports dominated by manufactured goods and consigned most of the manufacturing sector to competing with imports. However, a recent shift of Canadian exports away from the nation's traditional natural-resource base has been widely noted.[4] Much of this change can be explained by general equilibrium forces limiting expansion of the resource sectors and an important public policy, the Auto Pact. Nonetheless, many individual manufacturing industries have exhibited increases of both their imports' share of the market and their exports' share of industry shipments.

This pattern is illustrated by Matthews's calculations of trends in trade shares.[5] In a mixture of three- and four-digit industries, he observed imports, exports, total shipments, and apparent domestic disappearance (shipments minus exports plus imports) for various years between 1966 and 1980. He then determined whether an increase, decrease, or no change had occurred in each of three ratios: exports/shipments, imports/domestic disappearance, and shipments/domestic disappearance. His classifications are summarized in Table 1. The last of these three ratios indicates the change in an industry's net comparative-advantage position. As the bottom line shows, the typical industry experienced no change in its net position, and negative changes outnumbered positive ones. However, fully 42 percent of the industries exhibited increases in both imports and exports ratios. Another 20 percent experienced an increase in one ratio with no deterioration of the other. For only 6 of 132 industries did one ratio increase while the other decreased—the pattern predicted by traditional international trade theory.[6] And only twelve experienced a decline in either the exports or the imports ratio. Imports increased for 59 percent of the industries, but exports also increased for 49 percent.

As Matthews noted, despite this pattern dominated by expanding in-

[4] See Peter Morici, *Meeting the Competitive Challenge: Canada and the United States in the Global Economy* (Toronto and Washington, 1988).

[5] Roy A. Matthews, *Structural Change and Industrial Policy: The Redeployment of Canadian Manufacturing, 1960–1980* (Ottawa, 1985).

[6] The pattern was predicted by even some recent models of strategic trade policy. See Paul R. Krugman, "Import Competition as Export Promotion: International Competition in the Presence of Oligopoly and Economies of Scale," in H. Kierkowski, ed., *Monopolistic Competition and International Trade* (Oxford, 1984).

TABLE I

Changes in Exports/Shipments, Imports/Domestic Disappearance, and Shipments/Domestic Disappearance, Selected Manufacturing Industries, 1966–1980

Change in exports/ shipments	Change in imports/ domestic disappearance	Change in shipments/ domestic disappearance			Total number of industries
		+	0	−	
+	+	15	24	16	55
+	0	6	2	X	8
+	−	2	X	X	2
0	+	X	0	19	19
0	0	0	38	0	38
0	−	4	0	X	4
−	+	X	X	4	4
−	0	X	0	2	2
−	−	0	0	0	0
Total number of industries		27	64	41	132

SOURCE: Calculated from R. A. Matthews, *Structural Change and Industrial Policy: The Redeployment of Canadian Manufacturing, 1960–1980* (Ottawa, 1985) table A-6. Counts differ slightly from some reported in Matthews' text.

NOTE: Cells indicated by X should be empty if underlying trend estimates were consistent, and were in fact empty.

traindustry trade, a calculation of Canada's revealed comparative advantage (his Table 8–3) showed a strong advantage in wood products and paper, a weaker advantage in primary metals and transportation equipment, but a generally strong comparative disadvantage in everything else—exactly the traditional pattern. Thus, the changing participation of Canada's manufacturing industries in international trade seems part of a broad drift of industrial reorganization affecting all industrial countries. And it proceeds without greatly changing long-established patterns of net comparative advantage.

A corollary of this marked growth in intraindustry trade is that most classes of manufactured goods made and used in Canada should now show perceptible levels of intraindustry trade. These levels were confirmed by Hazledine, Guiton, and Wall, who analyzed data on 212 narrowly defined products in 1982.[7] Exposure to trade was defined as a share of imports or exports exceeding 5 percent of domestic shipments. Setting aside 9 products for which imports are prohibited, they counted 41 subject to import competition but without exports, 35 with exports but no import competition, 69 nontraded, and 58 (29 percent) with both

[7] Tim Hazledine, Steve Guiton, and Robert Wall, "Assessing the 'Canadian School' of Open Economy Industrial Organization. I: Theory," working paper (Vancouver, University of British Columbia, 1988).

imports and exports significant. Although 29 percent is a minority, it is striking for a manufacturing sector once confined to exporting processed raw materials (the poorest candidates for intraindustry trade).

These patterns clearly establish the prevalence of simultaneous expansions of imports and exports and justify an examination of how industries adjust to international disturbances by changing their exports. The next section therefore considers the theoretical background of imperfectly competitive market structures (the underpinning for this study of adjustment to international competition) and the theoretical bases for expecting an industry's exports to increase due to a disturbance that increases competing imports.

THEORETICAL BACKGROUND

The project from which this paper grows rests (as do static explanations of intraindustry trade) on market models of imperfectly competitive markets. Those models are identified and their implications for adjustments to increases in import competition are developed. The positive association between changes in imports and exports is treated as one consequence of an industry's adjustment of prices and activity levels to import disturbances.

Monopolistic Competition in the Open Economy

One theoretical cornerstone is the model of monopolistic competition in the open economy.[8] Its implications are shown by examining the effect of opening a closed economy with monopolistically competitive industries to international trade. Opening the economy to trade would affect a purely competitive industry's output (depending on whether it assumes exporting or import-competing status) but not the optimal scale of the individual, purely competitive firm in long-run equilibrium. When the market for a differentiated product is enlarged in the open-economy equilibrium, however, the size of the individual firm can increase (each firm is assumed to produce one "brand" or variety) as well as the total number of varieties available for consumption in each trading country. Whether the gains from trade are realized as more varieties consumed or lower costs (due to larger scale) per variety depends on particular assumptions about cost structures and consumers' tastes.

Consider how a tariff reduction or shift in cost conditions that favors foreign producers affects scales of activity and the incidence of fixed

[8] For example, Elhanan Helpman, "International Trade in the Presence of Product Differentiation, Economies of Scale, and Monopolistic Competition: A Chamberlin-Hecksher-Ohlin Approach," *Journal of International Economics* vol. 11, no. 3 (Aug. 1981), 305–40.

costs under monopolistic competition. According to the monopolistic-competition models, lower prices and/or an expanded array of importable varieties precludes some domestic producers from covering their costs. If it also raises the demand elasticity facing the surviving domestic producers, however, their scale of production is enlarged. That effect is independent of the increase in demand for any particular variety that stems from the concurrent arrival of export opportunities. A successful response by an industry to a change in its international competitive position includes rationalizing the scales and output configurations of producers who survive, regardless of whether the industry will contract or expand overall.

The Eastman-Stykolt Model

The Eastman-Stykolt model addresses the performance of an oligopoly when facing import competition characterized by a world price determined outside of the country.[9] The domestic industry's costs are assumed low enough (when minimized) to yield at least normal profits producing and selling in competition with tariff-afflicted imports, but not low enough to permit substantial export sales. Scale economies in production are assumed substantial, so that producers serving the domestic market are rather few and hence potentially able to collude. If collusion can be sustained, the natural price to agree on is the world price plus the domestic tariff and transfer costs applicable to imports. Indeed, the model suggests that this conspicuous focal point may make collusion easier to sustain than in the absence of such a clearly delineated international "limit price." Given these assumptions, excess profits are potentially available if domestic production facilities are organized to minimize the cost of the output supplied to the home market.

The model assumes that the structural conditions and information structures of domestic producer groups often make price collusion feasible. The success of price collusion, however, gives rise to two forms of rent seeking that supply much of the model's (negative) normative connotation. First, the assumptions about collusion and cost levels imply the attraction of entrants with suboptimally scaled facilities, able to earn normal profits because their presence does not crack the collusive price consensus. The market equilibrium then begins to resemble the Brander-Spencer model of free entry with collusion, a long-run equilibrium in

[9] H. C. Eastman and S. Stykolt, "A Model for the Study of Protected Oligopolies," *Economic Journal* 70 (June 1960), 336–47; H. C. Eastman and S. Stykolt, *The Tariff and Competition in Canada* (Toronto, 1967).

which all producers earn normal profits and the inefficiency (excess fixed costs) increases with the height of the collusive price.[10]

The second form of rent seeking materializes when we combine the original ES model (which did not address product differentiation) with the form of product differentiation assumed in the monopolistic-competition model. That combination allows additional forms of rent seeking and inefficiency. Assume—with the support of much empirical evidence validated by recent theoretical research—that collusion is harder to sustain on nonprice dimensions of rivalry than on price.[11] Producers may then undertake rent-seeking activities to increase sales made at collusively set prices that exceed marginal costs. Some of these activities take on particular importance in import-competing industries serving small markets. Producers may offer additional varieties of differentiated products, incurring extra fixed costs that manifest themselves in short production runs and in plants more diversified for their scales than those found in larger or more competitive markets. The possibility of entry at suboptimal scales is amplified, because product differentiation reduces cross-elasticities of demand among varieties and thus the likelihood that small-scale entry will crumble the price consensus. In the extreme case, a concentrated ES industry may fail to realize any excess profits if nonprice rivalry and new entries push average costs up to the level of the delivered tariff-ridden world price.

The interesting comparative-statics properties of this extended version of the ES model with product differentiation center on the effect of changes in the delivered price of imports, prototypically a tariff reduction. A compressed margin between the delivered world price and minimized domestic costs reduces the viable number of domestic producers and/or varieties. Although the number of producers falls, the scale of the individual producing unit or product variant increases; the domestic industry's total output can actually increase as long as the delivered world price stays sufficiently above minimized domestic costs. These predictions differ from those of the monopolistic-competition model in two respects: (1) the amount of rationalization of product lines and operating scales is potentially greater in the ES case, because the initial structure reflects rent-seeking activities induced by the collusive price, and (2) total output could expand in an ES industry rationalized due to tariff reduction, if the industry's minimized costs lie below the (reduced) delivered world price.

[10] James A. Brander and Barbara J. Spencer, "Tacit Collusion, Free Entry, and Welfare," *Journal of Industrial Economics* vol. 33, no. 3 (Mar. 1985), 277–94.
[11] Chaim Fershtman and Eitan Muller, "Capital Investments and Price Agreements in Semicollusive Markets," *Rand Journal of Economics* 17 (Summer 1986), 214–26.

This expanded ES model served as the framework for analyzing responses of Canadian manufacturing industries to the changes in import competition and the tariff reductions of the 1970s, and the consequences of these responses were pursued through reactive changes in domestic selling prices and the input choices (capital spending, employment) made by domestic producers. The question raised by intraindustry trade is the degree to which such responses to increased international competition can increase export sales. We first inquire whether the theoretical models just set forth yield that prediction.

Links Between Imports and Exports

Observers have conjectured that if producers were deprived of a profitable niche in the domestic market, they would expand their operating scales and sell more to both the domestic and export markets. Such an outcome, however, is tricky to model. Exporting must be shown to be profitable only because of pressure from competing imports. If the small-scale domestic firm producing in a protected market could enter profitably into the export market by enlarging its scale or simplifying the varieties it produces, one must explain why that strategy was elected only when competitive pressure from imports increased. This axiom rules out the simple hypothesis that sellers resort to exporting due to profit shrinkage in the domestic market.

The axiom seems to leave open only one means for predicting that an increase in import competition could by itself beget increased exports. Assume that the firm has some monopoly power in the domestic market but receives a parametric net price for any sales on export markets. Assume also that if it exports, the same price must be charged to domestic and foreign customers. The company would face this constraint if its exports can be arbitraged back to the domestic market without cost or if antidumping legislation is strictly enforced by governments in its export markets. As White showed, depending on the firm's cost function and the domestic demand that it faces, it might forego exporting even if its marginal costs are less than the net unit revenue it could obtain from exports, because the profits gained from exporting do not offset the profits lost on domestic sales when home and export prices are aligned.[12] By extension, a disturbance (such as increased import competition) that reduces the profitability of domestic sales could induce the producer to enter the export market. At some critical point, a little more import competition begets a lot of exports.

[12] Lawrence J. White, "Industrial Organization and International Trade: Some Theoretical Considerations," *American Economic Review* 64 (Dec. 1974), 1013–20.

The assumptions needed for this model are quite restrictive. An implicit assumption of the standard ES model, not challenged by any empirical test, is that a substantial margin exists between the delivered price of imports and the net (free on board) revenue obtainable on export sales. If that assumption is valid, then the potential exporter will not be deterred from price discrimination via arbitrage of reimports to undercut the high domestic price—although, of course, reductions in tariffs or international transport costs do tighten the arbitrage constraint on the difference between domestic and export prices. The constraint of foreign antidumping laws is real, but surely unimportant for the typical small Canadian manufacturer selling on world export markets. Also, abundant if casual evidence suggests that manufacturers typically price independently in their various national markets. Hence, antidumping constraints seem too weak to support White's model for empirical predictions, despite the charges of dumping lodged against a few Canadian industries.

If we assume that market participants are completely informed, then another explanation based on supply responses can link exports to import disturbances. Competing imports may be innovative, and the domestic producer's cost of imitation or innovative response may fall and/ or the benefit from innovative response may rise when competition is imminent.[13] Because information about external markets is costly, the Canadian firm may invest in learning about them and discover a new exporting opportunity only when beset by import competition.[14] This model of intraindustry trade based on learning or diffusion of innovation is consistent with the presence of product differentiation. Therefore, it naturally adds to the market-structure models and predictions already invoked for this project.

Other reasons exist to explain why imports and exports might exhibit parallel changes, but these reasons rely on mechanisms that do not in-

[13] Evidence for speedy imitation by local competitors of U.S. subsidiaries' innovations produced abroad is found in Edwin Mansfield and Anthony Romeo, "Technology Transfer to Overseas Subsidiaries of U.S.-Based Firms," *Quarterly Journal of Economics* vol. 95, no. 4 (Dec. 1980), 737–50.

[14] These hypotheses are supported by organizational and evolutionary approaches to the firm, which offer several ways of predicting that firms will make some major reallocation only in the face of a substantial change in threats or opportunities in the environment. The contract among the firm's participants embraces policy as well as pecuniary commitments, and is costly to renegotiate. Information is highly incomplete, and investment of search effort occurs only in the face of some unusual stimulus (opportunity or threat). Profit and other objectives are defined conventionally, and rule-of-thumb behavior persists as long as these objectives are reasonably attained. For analyses along these lines, see Richard M. Cyert and Kenneth D. George, "Competition, Growth, and Efficiency," *Economic Journal* vol. 79, no. 313 (Mar. 1969), 23–41; and Richard R. Nelson and Sidney G. Winter, *An Evolutionary Theory of Economic Change* (Cambridge, Mass., 1982), chap. 5.

volve supply responses by domestic producers. Consider the discovery of intraindustry trade in the context of European integration. When the members of the European Community simultaneously reduced their trade barriers, producers in their national industries found their potential unit revenues from exports increasing while more stringent competition arose from imports. In a differentiated-product industry, exports and imports plausibly expand at the same time if the net price realized from exports rises while the delivered price of competing imports falls; the process resembles the theoretical opening of monopolistically competitive markets to external trade, with the attendant increases in the production scales of individual brands and/or the number of brands produced worldwide and consumed in each country.

This scenario does not apply in partial equilibrium when the disturbance is assumed to come solely from the import side: if the disturbance comes from the lowering of a domestic tariff, an industry's net export revenue is unchanged. Nor does the scenario apply if the import disturbance comes from a deterioration of the industry's comparative advantage or an appreciation of the country's real exchange rate; those disturbances should cause the industry's potential net export revenue to fall. Therefore, the mechanism apparently responsible for expanding intraindustry trade during the European Community's formation should have promoted Canada's intraindustry trade in the 1920s only to the extent that tariffs (or natural transport and transaction costs restricting international trade) were being reduced both in Canada and abroad. Increased exports could be related statistically to increased imports, but the latter would merely proxy the reduction of trade barriers throughout the system.

Another explanation of expanding intraindustry trade poses the same interpretive hazard. Barker showed that intraindustry trade can expand simply due to the growth of per capita incomes.[15] When goods are differentiated, and each brand has different levels of various qualities, rising national incomes cause trade to expand faster than income (and intraindustry trade to increase) as consumers start buying imported brands with levels of qualities previously outside their budget constraints. The model's assumptions (which include the existence of international transportation costs) are restrictive but compatible with those used in this project. Like the EC-type model, which rests on multinational trade liberalization, this model implies that Canadian imports and exports could both increase without imports causing exports (or vice versa). In our analysis of the

[15] Terry Barker, "International Trade and Economic Growth: An Alternative to the Neoclassical Approach," *Cambridge Journal of Economics* vol. 1, no. 2 (June 1977), 153–72.

statistical dependence of exports on import disturbances, it will hence be important whether the link involves the allocative decisions of Canadian manufacturers.

INDUSTRIAL ADJUSTMENT TO INTERNATIONAL COMPETITION: THE GENERAL MODEL

Do imports beget exports? We have established that such a relation can be founded theoretically on market structures that involve differentiation (permitting learning and diffusion effects) and perhaps oligopoly (discrimination). Such structures are specialized but nonetheless seem a priori appropriate for undertaking a general investigation of industries' adjustments to international disturbances, and invite inclusion of induced exports as an industry adjustment in the model. In this section, other parts of the adjustment model are presented and their empirical results summarized as a background for incorporating exports as an endogenous variable.

Our strategy in designing our model has been to observe a maximum of 161 four-digit Canadian manufacturing industries from 1970 to 1979 and expose the industries' short-run process of adjustment to international competition.[16] Annual observations do not provide the evidence we need to test a rich model of the course of an industry's adjustment. However, the contrasting structures of industries permit tests of hypotheses about how adjustment processes differ with the domestic industry's structure. The study is thus an opportunity to use empirical procedures of industrial organization to understand short-run adjustment processes.[17]

Industry Selling Prices

We expect industry's selling prices to depend on its marginal costs and the delivered world price of competing imports. In a purely competitive model in long-run equilibrium, only the world price would matter and the behavior of marginal costs would determine only the equilibrium out-

---

[16] The analysis was executed on the database maintained by Statistics Canada. This organization makes available statistical analysis observations for some variables and industries that cannot be published (or revealed to the outsider researcher) because of disclosure restrictions. For a full report of the project, see Richard E. Caves, *Adjustment to International Competition: Short-Run Relations of Prices, Trade Flows, and Inputs in Canadian Manufacturing Industries* (Ottawa, 1990).

[17] Industrial organization theory has been preoccupied with testing hypotheses about market equilibria and not the processes by which they are reached. The main exceptions are the traditional hypotheses of sticky prices in oligopoly markets and the more recent interest in adjustments of prices and other variables in light of the theory of multiperiod games.

put of domestic producers. With differentiated products, imperfect competition in some sectors, and lags in the adjustment process, short-run movements of domestic prices should generally reflect both world price and variable cost. Using the selling-price indexes of counterpart U.S. industries (adjusted for the exchange rate and Canadian tariffs) to approximate delivered world prices, we found that both world prices and domestic variable costs significantly influence Canadian selling prices. World prices exert most of their effect on Canadian prices within a year, although a one-year lag is also statistically significant (about 56 percent of the induced change in Canadian prices occurs within one year, 70 percent in two years). The effect of variable-cost changes is quantitatively small.

Changes in both costs and world prices affect domestic prices according to the structure of the Canadian industry. Concentrated industries lag in adjusting prices to their own variable costs but respond quickly to world prices. That contrast supports the ES model, which identifies the delivered price of competing imports as the focal point for pricing by concentrated domestic sellers. Prices rose more relative to variable costs in capital-intensive industries during the 1970s—a puzzling pattern evident in U.S. as well as Canadian data.[18] Domestic prices were less sensitive to world prices in highly protected industries; apparently protection not only changes the intraindustry resource allocation but also desensitizes domestic sectors to international price changes. Domestic prices were also desensitized to world prices in industries that offered differentiated products. When these structural differences among industries were controlled, the prevalence of foreign subsidiaries exerted no systematic effect on price adjustment.

Quantity of Imports

The quantity of imports was assumed to vary with disturbances to domestic demand, disturbances to foreign supply, and imports' price relative to competing domestic goods. They indeed increase significantly with lagged shipments of the domestic industry to the Canadian market (indicating demand disturbances) and decrease with their relative price; changes in U.S. shipments did not significantly affect the supply of imports to Canada. Again, the magnitudes of these responses varied with the structural traits of the markets involved. Increases in the domestic

[18] I conjecture that this price increase results from two causes: first, the invasion of imports from newly industrializing countries was concentrated in the more labor-intensive sector; second, the energy crisis increased the long-run (real) marginal costs of capital-intensive industries disproportionately at the same time its macroeconomic consequences created excess capacity for them.

demands facing capital-intensive industries gave rise to smaller increases in imports apparently because those industries held significant excess capacity. Tariff protection desensitized the response of quantities imported to domestic demand disturbances, just as it desensitized domestic prices to changes in international prices. Relative-price changes had less effect on imports of structurally differentiated products. The price sensitivity of imports decreased with the prevalence of foreign subsidiaries in the Canadian industry—probably a reflection of intrafirm trade and the multinational firm's reliance on administrative links rather than market-price signals.

Capital Expenditures

The quantity of domestic output is not explicitly determined in the model, but the industry's key input decisions—capital expenditures and employment—are endogenized. Capital expenditures (normalized by the industry's capital stock at the start of the 1970s) were expected to increase with the two-year change in the industry's real output, decrease with its cost of capital, and decrease with the relative price of competing imports.

A striking finding emerged when we unbundled the relative price of imports and entered the change in tariffs protecting domestic producers as a separate component.[19] Reductions in protection caused capital spending to increase as producers adopted the different mixtures of product varieties and run lengths necessary to remain viable against intensified foreign competition. This finding is particularly arresting because a purely competitive industry would presumably contract its supply and reduce its capital expenditures. The result reaffirms the pervasive importance of differentiation (product and/or spatial) and perhaps of imperfections in competition. Furthermore, it sustains the hypothesis that increased exports result from adjustment to import disturbances.

We also found that stepped-up capital spending was strongly associated with the proportion of the industry's shipments made by foreign subsidiaries. Because data on capital spending are available separately for industries' domestic and foreign-controlled establishments, we could investigate whether the adjusting is done entirely by foreign subsidiaries, or rather is concentrated in industries with strong foreign presences but affects their domestic and foreign producers similarly. The results are mixed but lean toward the latter interpretation.

---

[19] This was expressed not as a year-to-year change but as the change over the whole period, because Canada's precommitment to these reductions presumably alerted producers about future protection levels.

Employment

Industries' annual average employment levels were analyzed using a model based on exploratory work by Siedule, which relates the logarithm of employment to the logarithm of shipments, the ratio of the wage to the cost of capital, and various structural variables that shift the employment-shipments relationship.[20] Employment of production workers and nonproduction staff proved sensitive to relative factor prices; along with the less-robust sensitivity of investment, this result indicates that appreciable factor substitution occurs during short-run adjustments.

The highly significant short-run relationship of employment to shipments varies according to a number of factors. It is reduced in the more concentrated industries due to these industries' greater capital-intensity and possibly their short-run output-setting behavior. Some evidence of labor hoarding appears: employment is slightly sensitive to short-run increases of shipments but insensitive to short-run decreases. Staff employment was insensitive to short-run increases, and indeed showed a downward trend in the 1970s that may have been related to the decline in market shares of foreign subsidiaries (which use higher ratios of staff to total employment).

The employment-shipments relation was not sensitive to changes in import penetration, but it did decrease in the face of long-run reductions in tariff protection. This finding is most important for the process of adjusting to international competition; the rationalization reduced staff employment almost proportionally to production-worker employment. Expansions of exports in the short run were associated with reductions in the employment-shipments relationship, a trend that is important for the role of exports in the model.

Links to Patterns of Exports

To conclude this section and provide background for an exports equation, we review some evidence that links the pattern of Canadian manufactured exports with structural elements central to the generalized ES model—product differentiation, scale economies, specialization, and run lengths. Particularly helpful is the survey by Balcome of 254 Canadian manufacturing firms that undertake some exports.[21] Balcome's evidence

[20] Tom Siedule, "International Trade Disturbances and Industry Adjustment," working paper (Ottawa, Economic Council of Canada, 1987).

[21] David L. Balcome, "Choosing Their Own Paths: Profiles of the Export Strategies of Canadian Manufacturers," report no. 06–86 (Ottawa, Conference Board of Canada, 1986).

is certainly consistent with the widespread prevalence of product differentiation. In designating factors most important to export sales performance, 50 percent of the respondents picked product characteristics and 42 percent named price, while marketing skills and production capabilities trailed behind. Furthermore, many firms reported they produce to order: 44 percent produce to order, 17 percent custom design, and only 39 percent produce to stock. These data strongly support an approach that assumes differentiation.

Balcome's findings downplay the importance of fixed costs, scale economies, and run lengths. When asked the main benefit of exporting, only 14 percent of the respondents cited reduced unit costs due to increased output, while 67 percent indicated simply the increased net revenue and 19 percent the diversification value of export sales. Furthermore, cost reduction was mentioned least frequently by small firms, the ones that should benefit most from increasing production for export. Cost reduction was least frequently cited by manufacturers of finished products, which suggests that scale economies are more important for the exporters of relatively homogeneous goods such as fabricated materials and food products. The ES model implies that increased orientation toward exports would accompany narrowing of a firm's product line, but Balcome found the opposite: a positive association between export orientation and the five-year change in product-line breadth. Finally, the survey offers no strong evidence that heavy fixed costs must be incurred to enter export markets. In short, Balcome's results suggest that a lot of Canadian manufactured exports might match the "bespoke tailoring" model, in that they are differentiated but not subject to important scale economies.

Certain conclusions of Baldwin and Gorecki also bear on the association of rationalization processes with export expansion.[22] For the period 1970–1979, they found that expansion of industries' exports was positively associated with acquisition of established plants by outside firms but not with the creation of new plants (although plant creation was strongly related to increased domestic-market shipments). The pattern can be interpreted two ways. As Baldwin and Gorecki noted, the pattern parallels corporate diversification, a process by which firms move resources from declining markets to those that are expanding due to changes in trade pattern. It is also consistent with export expansion caused by changed activity patterns of established plants, where changes result in

[22] John R. Baldwin and Paul K. Gorecki, "Plant Creation versus Plant Acquisition: The Entry Process in Canadian Manufacturing," *International Journal of Industrial Organization* 5 (Mar. 1987), 27–41.

part from the infusion of cash and other resources by firms based in other industries.[23]

A final empirical finding bears on dumping and the exporter's ability to vary its pricing policies among markets. Balcome found no strong evidence of dumping: 44 percent of respondents reported unit profits on export sales about the same as those on domestic sales, and the proportion of respondents reporting lower profits (35 percent) did not greatly exceed the proportion reporting higher profits (21 percent). These data do not proclaim the ubiquity of dumping. However, they indicate that export pricing varies too much among markets to warrant relying on the theoretical assumption that dumping is infeasible—an assumption necessary for White's model.

MODELING EXPORT SHIPMENTS

In our export model, we assume that Canadian exporters are small sellers on the world market but that their goods may be differentiated, so that exports depend on more than the world price and the domestic supply schedule. The dependent variable is the logarithm of the value of exports for each industry and year (EXP_{it}). No export-price indexes exist for finely disaggregated industries, so the variable must be used undeflated.

Demand Variations

The first explanatory variable is an index of demand for Canadian exports, taken from the CANDIDE model and based on national incomes of customer countries weighted by the proportion of Canadian exports they receive. This index is calculated at the two-digit level of industry classification, and we assume that a given two-digit index can serve for each four-digit industry that is included within it. This variable is expressed in logarithmic form as $DEMAND_{it}$. Exports should increase with *DEMAND*, even with price held constant, if they are differentiated products that enter as normal goods into buyers' consumption.

Prices and Variable Costs

Exports should be sensitive to variations in exchange-rate-adjusted world prices relative to Canadian prices or costs. These variations should

[23] Tim Hazeldine, in his "The Anatomy of Productivity Growth Slowdown and Recovery in Canadian Manufacturing Industries," *International Journal of Industrial Organization* 3 (Sept. 1985), 307–25, found that nearly all productivity growth within Canadian industries in the 1970s was associated with cost reduction in ongoing plants and not with the exit of (old) inefficient and entry of (new) efficient facilities. The renewal of ongoing plants is evidenced by the constantly changing efficiency rankings of these continuing operations.

indicate shifts of domestic marginal-cost curves in relation to marginal revenues from export sales. The selling-price index of the U.S. counterpart industry serves as a proxy for external prices in Canada's export markets, as it was for world prices of competing imports. With the majority of Canada's manufactured exports going to the United States during the period under analysis, the assumption is more appropriate here than in the imports equation, where the U.S. selling price nonetheless behaved well. If we assume that exports are homogeneous and Canadian exportables sell at the same price at home and abroad, the quantity of exports should depend on the external price of exportables relative to domestic marginal costs. With exports differentiated, the external price may be more appropriately compared to the price obtained from domestic sales, which reflects influences of both costs and domestic market conditions. Although the market-structure evidence developed in this study favors the latter hypothesis, we employ both:

$PRICE\ 1_{(i,t-1)}$ U.S. industry selling price-index multiplied by effective exchange rate (price of foreign exchange), divided by Canadian industry selling-price index, industry i in year $t - 1$.

$PRICE\ 2_{(i,t-1)}$ U.S. industry selling-price index multiplied by effective exchange rate, divided by average of indexes of unit-labor and unit-materials costs (weighted by their importance in the industry's total costs), industry i in year $t - 1$.

Exports should increase with the relative prices of competing goods abroad. It should be recalled when interpreting the coefficient that the dependent variable is not deflated.

Capacity

The expansion of an industry's exports may be constrained in the short run by its available capacity. The unit variable costs controlled by *PRICE 2* are short-run-average rather than marginal costs, and hence will not represent this constraint accurately (we can think of additions to an industry's capacity decreasing the unobserved short-run marginal cost relative to this average). The following variable approximates the extra output producible as a result of the preceding year's capital expenditures:

$SUPPLY_{(i,t-1)}$ Logarithm of previous year's current-dollar value of industry shipments, multiplied by the ratio of previous year's capital expenditures to the value of the industry's capital stock in 1970; this figure is inflated to the current year's prices by the ratio of industry i's selling price in year t to its value in year $t - 1$.

The variable is inflated to current prices because the dependent variable is undeflated; capital-stock data are available only for 1970, not for each year of our analysis.[24] *EXP* should increase with *SUPPLY*.

The presence of lagged output in the variable SUPPLY converts the model into an explanation of the industry's ratio of exports to shipments and indicates the need for exogenous variables to show comparative-advantage factors. Previous research designed to test this type of relationship has not been very successful, and Leamer's work made us acutely aware of the misspecification that occurs when explaining international trade structures in this manner.[25] Thus, although hypotheses about comparative-advantage are not optimally tested on national exports/shipments ratios, omission of these factors could affect other coefficients of the model.

The following standard indicators of comparative-advantage are included without specific justification:

> RND_i Research and development outlays of industry i divided by value of shipments, 1975.

> ADS_i Advertising outlays of industry i divided by value of shipments, 1970.

> K/L_i Value of gross capital stock per employee, industry i, 1970.

Finally, industries affected by the Canada-U.S. Auto Pact have exceptionally large export sales because of that agreement's structure; the pact's effects are controlled by the dummy variable:

> $AUTO_i$ Dummy variable set equal to 1 for sectors affected by the Auto Pact.

Links to Import Disturbances

The simplest approach to the question of whether import competition promotes exports is to include the following as a regressor:

> $IMP_{(i,t-1)}$ Logarithm of the value of imports classified to industry i in year $t-1$.

This reduced-form approach bypasses the question of the mechanism by which import induced responses could affect exports. However, it in-

---

[24] A more refined specification would capture the *net* addition to the capital stock available at the beginning of the preceding year. The unavailability of annual capital-stock and depreciation data and the importance of productivity improvements in new plants and equipment justify the specified variable.

[25] Edward E. Leamer, *Sources of International Comparative Advantage: Theory and Evidence* (Cambridge, Mass., 1984).

cludes the possibility (noted previously) that import expansion could reflect conditions such as reduced protection, transport costs, or rising per-capita incomes for a product line. No prediction is made whether the coefficient $IMP_{(i,t-1)}$ is positive or negative; after all, traditional international trade theory implies that an increase in competing imports is associated with a deterioration of an industry's comparative advantage and a reduction of its export sales.

Interactions

Other hypotheses are tested by allowing the coefficients of previously defined time-series variables to vary with the industry's structure. A number of hypotheses about slope shifts can be formulated.

One of these hypotheses provides a strategic test of the ES model. The ES model rests on the assumption that import competition causes an industry to suffer a comparative disadvantage substantial enough to put export markets well out of its reach. If industries marked with the ES characteristics—high concentration and tariff protection—increase their exports smoothly when protection is reduced, the hypothesis of protected oligopoly would be undermined and a generalized monopolistic-competition model (assuming Nash behavior) would appear more appropriate. Conversely, if import disturbances should beget less exports in highly concentrated and protected industries, the ES model could claim strong support. The crucial interaction term then is $IMP_{(i,t-1)} * C4C_i * NT_{i0}$, where $C4C_i$ is the four-firm seller concentration ratio for the Canadian industry and NT_{i0} is the average nominal tariff in 1970.

Foreign subsidiaries have been assigned conflicting roles in Canada's trade adjustment. Some survey evidence indicates that foreign subsidiaries have been less active than domestic companies in developing export sales.[26] That conclusion is not surprising, because Canadian subsidiaries may remain less-cost-effective producers than their overseas siblings; even when a domestic firm operating the same facilities might anticipate positive profits from exporting, a multinational would source more profitably from abroad. On the other hand, capital expenditures prompted by tariff reductions are found chiefly in industries populated by foreign subsidiaries, although expenditures on rationalizing activities are not confined to foreigners.

Differences in the behavior of subsidiaries, or in industries they populate, can be tested in other ways. With FSH_{it} defined as the share of shipments by foreign-controlled establishments divided by industry shipments, the term $SUPPLY_{(i,t-1)} * FSH_{it}$ tests whether capacity additions have

[26] Donald J. Daly and Donald C. MacCharles, *Canadian Manufactured Exports: Constraints and Opportunities* (Montreal, 1986).

been more or less oriented toward foreign markets in industries marked by foreign control. No sign is predicted a priori. In the same spirit, we can make the coefficient *IMP* conditional on multinationals' participation in an industry by means of the interaction $IMP_{(i,t-1)} * FSH_{it}$. Its coefficient is predicted to be negative on the basis of the Daly-MacCharles results. It is also appropriate to determine whether *FSH*, used as an interactive variable, has an additive influence on *EXP*. Foreign investment in Canada (apart from extractive sectors and the automotive industries) originally tended to substitute local production for imports. That pattern implies a negative (but nonbehavioral) relation between *FSH* and *EXP*, if *FSH* proxies elements of Canada's comparative (dis)advantage not represented by the variables *RND, ADS,* and *K/L.*

The effects of import changes (*IMP*) and increments to industry capacity (*SUPPLY*) may also depend on the comparative-advantage variables just mentioned. Our attention was drawn to *K/L* in particular, because capital-intensive Canadian industries behaved in the 1970s as if they were raising prices in response to increases in their variable costs and as a result carried substantial excess capacity. If this behavior was unique to Canada—probably not the case—their exports should have been low relative to their supply capability, and the access they gained to export markets through rationalization should have been attenuated (predicting a negative coefficient of *SUPPLY* K/L*).

The ability of imports to beget exports should be influenced by the character of product differentiation, bound up as it is with the process of rationalization. The interactions *IMP* RND* and *IMP* ADS* test this conjecture. The former interaction should certainly take a positive coefficient if research-intensive markets offer more possibilities for learning or successful experimentation following import-based disturbances. The sign for the interaction with advertising is less clear. While in general advertising indicates product differentiation, Canada appears to have an overall comparative disadvantage in consumer nondurables, the most heavily advertised goods.

STATISTICAL RESULTS

It is useful to report the results in two steps. *EXP* has a group of fundamental determinants based on shifts in foreign demands and domestic capacity, relative prices, and the Auto Pact. We report that core of the model first, then set forth the results for other variables and modified specifications. Initial empirical results prompted one change from the basic specifications proposed above when we determined that the variables *PRICE 1* and *PRICE 2* were best disaggregated into their components: the selling price of the U.S. counterpart industry $USP_{(i,t-1)}$ and the Canadian industry selling price $CSP_{(i,t-1)}$, or the variable-cost index. The foreign and domestic components of *PRICE* take coefficients with rather different absolute values. Furthermore, *PRICE 1*, which incorporates the Canadian industry selling price, is considerably more significant than *PRICE 2*, which includes an index of variable cost.

Basic Results

Our core model is reported in Equation 2.1 of Table 2. Except as noted below, the equations were estimated by ordinary least squares. We did employ the corrections for autoregression and heteroskedasticity that were recommended by Kmenta, but we encountered both budget constraints and problems with the performance of corrections in models with extensive interactions between variables.[27] In Equation 2.1, all signs are correct and all coefficients significant. Because of marginal-supplier effects (documented in empirical research on short-run trade changes), we expect a high elasticity of exports with respect to external demand. The elasticity should be overestimated, because export shipments could not be deflated.[28] A comparison of the equations in Table 2 shows that the estimated value of this elasticity is sensitive to specification, reaching 2.13 in Equation 2.4 (which includes the structural comparative-advantage variables), but insignificant and below unity in other models. The elasticity of exports' value with respect to external prices is similarly overestimated, while the negative effect of Canadian price increases on exports (very sensitive to specification) correspondingly understates the elasticity of quantity with respect to supply price.

Because the variable *SUPPLY* combines the effects of industry capacity changes and interindustry scale differences, we added the term Q_{10}, real shipments of industry i in 1970 (Eqs. 2.3 and 2.5). Its coefficient is highly significant, but the coefficient of *SUPPLY*, which should now be picking up strictly a capacity-expansion effect, also remains highly significant.

Equation 2.2 introduces the fulcrum of this analysis, $IMP_{(i,t-1)}$. Its coefficient, positive and highly significant, indicates a responsiveness elasticity of the value of exports to the preceding change in imports of 0.44.[29] Our series were too short to allow a sensitive investigation of this relation's time structure, but we did partition *IMP* into its interindustry and

---

[27] Jan Kmenta, *Elements of Econometrics*, 2d ed. (New York, 1986), 618–25.

[28] If we assume that export prices adjust fully to changes in prices (including the exchange rate) outside of Canada, we can of course convert the regression coefficient into an income-elasticity of demand for export quantities. Evidence from diverse sources on export pricing suggests, however, that export prices underadjust in the short run, so the assumption would lead to an overstated correction.

[29] The absence of deflation again means that this elasticity overestimates one based on real quantities.

TABLE 2

Determinants of Industries' Export Shipments

Equation 2.1 $EXP_{it} = -12.115 + 1.305 \; DEMAND_{it} + 0.775 \; SUPPLY_{it} + 3.090 \; AUTO_i$
$\qquad\qquad\quad$ (2.30)$\quad$ (1.91)$\qquad\qquad\qquad$ (29.69)$\qquad\qquad$ (8.61)
$\qquad\qquad\quad$ $0.859 \; USP_{(i,t-1)} - 1.354 \; CSP_{(i,t-1)}$
$\qquad\qquad\quad$ (1.84)$\qquad\qquad$ (3.01)
$\qquad\qquad\qquad\qquad\qquad\qquad\qquad\qquad\qquad$ $\bar{R}^2 = 0.491; F = 251$

Equation 2.2 $EXP_{it} = -10.534 + 0.735 \; DEMAND_{it} + 0.543 \; SUPPLY_{it} + 1.750 \; AUTO_i$
$\qquad\qquad\quad$ (2.16)$\quad$ (1.03)$\qquad\qquad\qquad$ (18.52)$\qquad\qquad$ (5.00)
$\qquad\qquad\quad$ $+0.609 \; USP_{(i,t-1)} - 0.865 \; CSP_{(i,t-1)} + 0.445 \; IMP_{(i,t-1)}$
$\qquad\qquad\quad$ (1.40)$\qquad\qquad$ (2.08)$\qquad\qquad$ (16.51)
$\qquad\qquad\qquad\qquad\qquad\qquad\qquad\qquad\qquad$ $\bar{R}^2 = 0.595; F = 280$

Equation 2.3 $EXP_{it} = -12.476 + 0.987 \; DEMAND_{it} + 0.256 \; SUPPLY_{it} + 1.547 \; AUTO_i$
$\qquad\qquad\quad$ (2.60)$\quad$ (1.37)$\qquad\qquad\qquad$ (5.27)$\qquad\qquad$ (4.56)
$\qquad\qquad\quad$ $+0.642 \; USP_{(i,t-1)} - 0.196 \; CSP_{(i,t-1)} - 0.483 \; Q_{i0}$
$\qquad\qquad\quad$ (1.51)$\qquad\qquad$ (0.46)$\qquad\qquad$ (7.66)
$\qquad\qquad\quad$ $+0.368 \; IMP_{i0} + 0.037 \; DIMP_{it}$
$\qquad\qquad\quad$ (6.94)$\qquad\qquad$ (0.71)
$\qquad\qquad\qquad\qquad\qquad\qquad\qquad\qquad\qquad$ $\bar{R}^2 = 0.622; F = 233$

Equation 2.4 $EXP_{it} = -3.740 + 2.128 \; DEMAND_{it} + 0.729 \; SUPPLY_{it} + 3.048 \; AUTO_i$
$\qquad\qquad\quad$ (0.76)$\quad$ (3.38)$\qquad\qquad\qquad$ (30.27)$\qquad\qquad$ (9.03)
$\qquad\qquad\quad$ $-0.171 \; USP_{(i,t-1)} - 0.555 \; CSP_{(i,t-1)} + 0.417 \; FSH_{i0}$
$\qquad\qquad\quad$ (0.39)$\qquad\qquad$ (1.32)$\qquad\qquad$ (2.72)
$\qquad\qquad\quad$ $+1.257 \; RND_i - 1.739 \; ADS_i + 0.007 \; K/L_i$
$\qquad\qquad\quad$ (11.53)$\qquad\quad$ (8.80)$\qquad$ (6.51)
$\qquad\qquad\qquad\qquad\qquad\qquad\qquad\qquad\qquad$ $\bar{R}^2 = 0.581; F = 200$

Equation 2.5 $EXP_i = -14.31 + 1.051 \; DEMAND_{it} + 0.227 \; SUPPLY_{it} + 1.392 \; AUTO_i$
$\qquad\qquad\quad$ (3.03)$\quad$ (1.52)$\qquad\qquad\qquad$ (4.81)$\qquad\qquad$ (4.10)
$\qquad\qquad\quad$ $+0.519 \; Q_{i0} + 0.792 \; USP_{(i,t-1)} - 0.469 \; CSP_{(i,t-1)} + 0.400 \; IMP_{(i,t-1)}$
$\qquad\qquad\quad$ (8.48)$\qquad$ (1.88)$\qquad\qquad$ (1.14)$\qquad\qquad$ (15.09)
$\qquad\qquad\quad$ $-0.066 \; IMP_{(i,t-1)}*NT_{i0}$
$\qquad\qquad\quad$ (3.98)
$\qquad\qquad\qquad\qquad\qquad\qquad\qquad\qquad\qquad$ $\bar{R}^2 = 0.624; F = 238$

Equation 2.6 $EXP_{it} = -14.04 + 2.387 \; DEMAND_{it} + 0.382 \; SUPPLY_{it} + 1.104 \; USP_{(i,t-1)}$
$\qquad\qquad\quad$ (6.06)$\quad$ (5.68)$\qquad\qquad\qquad$ (13.66)$\qquad\qquad$ (6.84)
$\qquad\qquad\quad$ $-1.078 \; CSP_{(i,t-1)}$
$\qquad\qquad\quad$ (9.73)

intertemporal components, the level of imports at the beginning of the period (1971, IMP_{i0}), and the logarithm of the change in imports between 1971 and the year of observation ($DIMP_{it}$).[30] In Equation 2.3, the coefficient of *DIMP* is only 10 percent as large as that of IMP_{i0} and not

---

[30] When the change was negative, $DIMP_{it}$ was set equal to zero, because the logic of the mechanism of intraindustry trade changes pertains only to positive changes (apart from the nonexistence of logarithms of negative numbers).

statistically significant. This finding suggests that the following considerations operate in some combination: (1) the export-inducing effect of
import changes operates with substantial lag, and (2) the expansion of
Canada's manufactured exports depends partly on differences in the potential for intraindustry trade proxied by initial imports. Both channels
of influence are probably at work, but it seems infeasible to establish their
relative importance with the data at hand.

Equation 2.4 includes several additive variables that may affect the extent of industries' export orientation, and three of these prove highly significant in two-tail tests. Exports increase with the industry's research
intensity, confirming that Canada's stock of intellectual and research
capital has come to exert an appreciable effect on its exports. Foreign
investment also has a positive effect. This outcome suggests that multinational enterprises operating in Canada have shifted away from predominantly import-replacing production, a claim supported by evidence
of their increasing roles in international trade among the industrial countries generally.[31] The advertising intensity of an industry exerts a significant negative influence and probably filters out what would otherwise
appear as a negative component in the influence of multinational enterprises. Finally, the coefficient of the capital-intensity variable is positive
and significant, a finding consistent with evidence on the capital-intensive
processing of natural resources for export.

A comparison of the models in Table 2 shows that the coefficients of
the core variables and their significance levels unfortunately tend to be
rather sensitive to specification changes. This sensitivity is especially evident for *DEMAND* and the price terms *USP* and *CSP*, which become
insignificant in some specifications. It appears imprudent to give much
emphasis to predictions based on the quantified coefficients.

Corrections for autoregression and heteroskedasticity were applied to
Equation 2.1 with the dummy variable for industries affected by the Auto
Pact omitted. The result is Equation 2.6. The significance of all variables
but *SUPPLY* increase substantially, as do the magnitudes of the coefficients of *DEMAND* and *ISP*. None of the qualitative conclusions drawn
from Table 2 change, although magnitudes shift enough to discourage
emphasis of conclusions based on the sizes of OLS coefficients.

Interaction Terms

Following the specifications discussed above, interactions were inves-
tigated between industry-structure variables and *IMP* or *SUPPLY*. Spe-

---

[31] This expansion includes, but is not confined to, intrafirm trade and international specialization within these enterprises.

cifically, the interaction and the variable that interacted with *IMP* or *SUPPLY* were both added to Equation 2. A positive and highly significant interaction (t = 4.11) appears between *IMP* and FSH_{i0}, the share of shipments initially accounted for by foreign subsidiaries. *IMP* also interacts positively with *RND* (t = 3.03), and these influences are collinear.[32] The coefficient of *IMP*FSH* at face value implies that imports' export-increasing effect is enlarged 38 percent in an industry where foreign subsidiaries hold a 50 percent share over an industry occupied solely by domestic enterprises. In evaluating the degree of inconsistency between this result and that of Daly-MacCharles,[33] we should recognize two distinct interpretations of this statistical relation: (1) in the short run, rationalization by foreign subsidiaries facing import competition generates more exports than responses by similarly situated domestic enterprises, and (2) Canada's exports are expanding more rapidly in those industries that in the long run have been both import-competing and conducive to multinationals' operations. In light of Equation 2.3, the latter interpretation certainly carries force.

We checked whether other structural variables affect the export-generating effect of import disturbances. One such variable is used to discriminate industries that most closely fit the ES model—highly concentrated and protected initially by high tariffs. When *IMP* interacts with the product of the four-firm concentration ratio and the initial nominal tariff, the interaction's positive coefficient is not statistically significant.[34] Thus, we obtain no clear conclusion about the existence of "pure" ES industries in oligopolistic equilibria that have no access to export markets: neither a significant negative coefficient confirming their presence nor a significant positive coefficient implied by a generalized monopolistic-competition model are present.

Variables related to bases for comparative advantage in Canada's manufacturing industries were also interacted with *IMP*. A significant positive interaction between *IMP* and *RND* was mentioned above. No remotely significant interaction exists with advertising (*ADS*). However, the interaction $IMP_{(i,t-1)}^* K/L_i$ takes a significant negative coefficient (t = -3.80), and the coefficient of the additive term K/L_i is positive and significant (t = 4.72). Examination of the coefficients' magnitudes shows that

[32] Neither *FSH* nor *RND* shows a positive interaction with *SUPPLY*, indicating that the positive roles of these two factors in the expansion of exports were specifically associated with international factors and not just with the general growth of domestic supply capability.

[33] See Daly and MacCharles, *Canadian Manufactured Exports*.

[34] The model also includes the product of concentration and initial protection as an additive regressor. Its coefficient is negative but also not significant.

although capital intensity slows the reorientation of domestic production facilities toward exports, it does not actually eliminate the positive net influence of import disturbances within the observed range of values. In addition, a significant negative interaction exists between K/L and *SUPPLY*. This is consistent with both the pricing behavior we noted in capital-intensive industries during the 1970s and the fact that capital- and resource-intensive activities have traditionally dominated Canadian manufactured exports but do not contribute much to export growth at the margin.[35]

In Equation 2.5, interaction between the lagged level of imports and the initial level of nominal tariff protection is tested. Tariff protection not only distorts resource allocation in the long run but also desensitizes it to international disturbances in the short run. That finding applies as well to the influence of import increases on exports: the higher the initial level of protection, the smaller the export-inducing effect of any disturbance that increases imports. A significant negative interaction was also observed between the effect on exports of the decade-long tariff change and the incidence of foreign investment ($t = -3.13$). This implies that tariff reductions tended to expand exports from industries heavily populated by "tariff factories." These findings about interactive effects of Canada's tariff policies are important for confirming some role for domestic supply-side adjustments in expanding intraindustry trade.

We conclude that the export-inducing effect of imports is modified by certain structural features (initial protection, prevalence of foreign subsidiaries, or research intensity). This result can be related to the problem of whether the positive influence of imports on exports operates in cross-section, time series, or both. Evidence has clearly favored cross-section, with time-series supported only by a nonsignificant though substantial coefficient. The likelihood that a substantial short-run influence exists (though not well represented in this model) increases if these comparative-advantage variables display the same interactions with $SUPPLY_{it}$, the measure of lagged capacity expansion, as with $IMP_{(i,t-1)}$. In fact, none of the interactions with $SUPPLY_{(i,t-1)}$ proved statistically significant except for a negative interaction with ADS_i, which can be interpreted simply as the marginal counterpart of the finding that Canadian manufacturers suffer a comparative disadvantage in promotion-intensive consumer goods (Eq. 2.4). The lack of abundant interactive effects on *SUPPLY* tends to confirm that the positive association of exports with imports picks up mainly the effect of market-structure elements and changes in the market worldwide, not just changes in the Canadian market. Although the responses of domestic industries to import competition

[35] Recall the significant positive coefficient of K/L in Equation 2.4.

have certainly not reduced exports, no positive response has been shown that is focused within Canada. One can attribute this largely negative finding either to the relatively small intertemporal variance of imports or the weak theoretical foundations of a country-specific effect, noted previously.

CONCLUSIONS

Two questions can be asked about intraindustry trade: Why does it occur where it does among sectors and countries? Why has it grown as it has? While most empirical and theoretical research on the subject focuses on the former question, this paper investigates the development of intraindustry trade as part of an extensive study of the adjustment of Canada's manufacturing industries to international competition. Exogenously increased imports or lowered tariff protection can generate increased exports by inducing adjustments of domestic producers in industries subject to product differentiation and/or protected collusive oligopoly, although the theoretical bases are weak. Export and import expansion could also be correlated because of common external changes independent of induced adjustments by domestic producers.

The statistical results are strongly consistent with a positive long-run relationship of some sort between imports and exports, contrary to the traditional neoclassical model of comparative advantage. It also is clear that short-run changes in industries' exports and competing imports are positively correlated. Furthermore, Canadian industries' short-run adjustments to import competition through rationalizing capital expenditures and productivity gains are certainly consistent with an ultimate positive effect of import increases on exports. Nonetheless, we did not find a statistically significant direct short-run effect of imports on exports.

Other interesting results concern structural factors affecting Canadian manufactured exports. Capital intensity and research intensity have a positive effect, but advertising intensity deters exports. Foreign subsidiaries apparently play a trade-expanding role in these adjustments and are strongly involved in the rationalization of production facilities induced by trade liberalization.

This study's conclusions are limited (for example, in isolating the factors that explain the growth of intraindustry trade) by their reliance on Canadian data and changes occurring within Canada. Also limiting, in the wisdom of hindsight, is the focus of the underlying study on domestic adjustments induced by import disturbances. Can export-increasing disturbances have positive effects on imports as well? Future research in this area might well consider a more symmetrical form with respect to exports and imports.

PART II
Multilateral Trade Negotiations

Global Implications of the Canada-U.S. Free Trade Agreement

Jeffrey J. Schott

T HE NEGOTIATION of the Canada-U.S. Free Trade Agreement (FTA) creates both a challenge to the multilateral trading system and an opportunity to reinvigorate the General Agreement on Tariffs and Trade (GATT), which provides the cornerstone for that system. Will the FTA reinforce interest in bilateral negotiations to the detriment of multilateral talks now underway in GATT? Or will the agreement further multilateral trade liberalization and be a building block for broader GATT agreements?

The negotiations themselves were born amid these conflicting objectives. Both countries hoped the FTA would complement efforts to launch a new GATT round of multilateral trade negotiations, but they also considered the bilateral agreement to be a fallback against the possible breakdown of the GATT process.[1]

The GATT has always had an inherent tension between bilateral and multilateral negotiations. Besides being a body of multilateral trading rules and a forum for multilateral negotiations, the GATT is a repository for each member's schedule of trade concessions. These concessions are negotiated bilaterally but generally applied to all signatories under the GATT's most-favored-nation principle. Bilateral negotiations are thus an integral part of the GATT negotiating process.

This paper examines the broad implications of the Canada-U.S. Free Trade Agreement for the GATT trading system. The first section summarizes the objectives and achievements of the U.S. and Canadian nego-

[1] James A. Baker III, "The Geopolitical Implications of the U.S.-Canada Trade Pact," *The International Economy* (Jan.-Feb., 1988).

tiators.[2] The next section discusses the relationship of free trade areas to GATT. The final sections analyze whether the free trade agreement could weaken the commitment of both countries to the GATT system, promote multilateral agreements during the current Uruguay Round of GATT negotiations, or be a model for additional bilateral free trade agreements.

THE FTA: OBJECTIVES AND ACHIEVEMENTS

At the start of the FTA negotiations, each country had specific objectives they considered essential to secure political acceptance of the overall pact. The main Canadian concern related to access to the U.S. market and conditions for participating in that market. In particular, Canada sought (1) greater certainty about how U.S. trade-remedy laws would be administered, and (2) liberalized market access, obtained through U.S. tariff cuts and increased U.S. direct investment in Canada, to stimulate production and employment. The two are clearly related. Market access is of limited value unless it is sustainable, hence the Canadian interest in more disciplined U.S. import-control policies.

In contrast, U.S. objectives focused primarily on improved rule making. The aggregate growth stimulus from the FTA was of lesser priority, although it was important for some industries. In particular, the United States sought (1) a "standstill" on new trade barriers, (2) agreements on services, investment, and intellectual property rights that could be used as building blocks for GATT accords and to facilitate cross-border trade and investment, and (3) resolution of long-standing disputes in particular sectors (for example, the elimination of auto subsidies).

These goals were reshaped during the negotiations. In the end, both countries focused on the broad goal of integrating the North American market to facilitate cross-border trade and investment in goods and services. It was hoped that the FTA would encourage inter- and intraindustry specialization so that industries in both countries could reap the benefits of the expanding North American market. But there was a broader purpose to be served by this underlying trend: both countries needed to promote increased competitiveness of their firms to sustain the export-led growth required to redress each country's large trade imbalance with the rest of the world.

The results of the Canada-U.S. Free Trade Agreement can be classified in three categories: trade liberalization, rule making, and standstill.

[2] For a more extensive evaluation of the agreement, see Jeffrey Schott and Murray Smith, eds., *The Canada-United States Free Trade Agreement: The Global Impact* (Washington, 1988) and Economic Council of Canada, *Venturing Forth: An Assessment of the Canada-U.S. Trade Agreement* (Ottawa, 1988).

Trade Liberalization

The FTA eliminates all tariffs on bilateral trade within ten years. In addition, it will open up more government contracts to competitive bidding and bar most border restraints and minimum price requirements on bilateral energy trade. Less progress was made on other nontariff barriers, most of which were grandfathered, though there are some notable exceptions (for example, duty-remission schemes for autos, discriminatory pricing regulations for wines and spirits, and import restraints on enriched uranium).

Trade liberalization achieved by the FTA should have notable income, employment, and trade effects. The gains will be small in absolute terms, but governments seldom can take actions that will have such permanently beneficial impacts on their economies. As a smaller country obtaining enhanced access to markets in a much larger country, Canada will gain relatively more—with the agreement boosting real income by 2.5 percent of GNP and adding 251,000 jobs over ten years—but will also face greater adjustment needs to adapt to freer trade.[3] By comparison, the United States will gain considerably less than 1 percent of GNP, and employment effects will be barely noticeable from normal labor-market fluctuations in almost all sectors.[4]

The trade liberalization should also spur increased exports by both countries, even though the average duty on total bilateral trade in 1985 was only 0.9 percent and 2.4 percent for the United States and Canada respectively. However, average duties on dutiable goods in 1985 were 3.3 percent for the United States and 9.9 percent for Canada, and high tariffs remain on certain products.

In the short run, there should be a modest improvement in the U.S. trade balance with Canada. Some U.S. gains will result from total elimination of tariffs that, on average, are three times higher on dutiable imports in Canada than in the United States. This factor alone may boost by 18 percent U.S. exports to Canada currently subject to duties.[5] Some gains will also occur as U.S. exports displace goods from Europe and Japan in the Canadian market as a result of removing bilateral trade bar-

[3] Economic Council of Canada, *Venturing Forth.*
[4] For the effects of the FTA on the U.S. labor market, see Brian F. Shea, "The Canada-United States Free Trade Agreement: A Summary of Empirical Studies and an Industrial Profile of the Tariff Reductions," Economic Discussion Paper 28 (Washington, U.S. Department of Labor, March 1988).
[5] Estimates of the impact of the tariff cuts are in Table 4 of Jeffrey J. Schott, "United States-Canada Free Trade: An Evaluation of the Agreement," *Policy Analyses in International Economics* 24 (Washington, Institute for International Economics, April 1988).

riers. Over the medium-to-long term, Canadian exports should increase as a result of efficiency gained from FTA reforms.

Rule Making

The FTA establishes a legal framework under which businesses can operate in both markets and under which governments can resolve disputes. There are two notable results. First, the FTA establishes innovative approaches to dispute settlement and binational surveillance of trade policies. It provides for two separate dispute mechanisms: one for disputes on bilateral countervailing duty (CVD) cases and one for all other issues. The former provides for binding arbitration after issuance of final CVD rulings to determine whether the decision was consistent with national law and administrative practices. This mechanism is a compromise between initial Canadian demands for total exemption from U.S. unfair trade laws and the status quo (which had provoked bilateral tensions most recently in the softwood lumber case).

Second, the FTA establishes contractual obligations regarding public policies toward investment and service-industry regulation. The FTA provisions do not necessarily seek to promote identical policies or regulations, only those compatible with the agreed guidelines or principles. Importantly, the FTA commitments apply to state and provincial government policies. In most instances, most-favored-nation treatment is to be accorded goods and services from the other country, effectively placing U.S. and Canadian firms on the same footing in activities regulated at the subnational level.

For investment, the FTA reinforces the recent trend toward liberalization of Canadian investment policies and makes the investment restrictions that remain on both sides more transparent. The agreement's obligations are wide-ranging, covering areas such as national treatment, performance requirements, remittance restrictions, expropriation, and domestic-equity requirements. Although most existing discriminatory policies and restrictions affecting foreign investment are grandfathered, notably in the energy sector, changes in policies and regulations must be consistent with FTA principles.

The national treatment obligation with respect to future investment policies applies to the establishment, operation, and acquisition or sale of a business. However, Canada retains the right to screen certain direct acquisitions above a specific threshold, affecting roughly the top six hundred companies and sectors where investment restrictions are grandfathered. The FTA also prohibits all new trade-related performance requirements, although the sharp reduction in investments subject to screening by Investment Canada will make it more difficult to impose and enforce performance requirements in any event.

The FTA establishes rights and obligations to guide future government policy regarding the provision of services and the rollback or liberalization of existing trade barriers in certain service sectors. The agreement establishes obligations regarding (1) national treatment to prohibit new discrimination against foreign service providers in specified sectors, (2) right of establishment or right of commercial presence to provide appropriate market-access guarantees to ensure that the national treatment obligation is meaningful, (3) licensing and certification procedures to ensure that, with limited exceptions, government regulators judge service providers solely on their competence, and (4) procedures facilitating cross-border travel by businesspersons. While most trade barriers in services are grandfathered, the separate FTA financial services obligations provide for substantial liberalization of Canadian restrictions on market share, asset growth, and capital expansion.

Standstill

In essence, the "standstill" sets an inventory date or baseline for border restrictions and regulatory barriers from which changes are to be no more restrictive or distortive of trade than before and should evolve toward liberalization and nondiscrimination. In other words, the standstill precludes a return to the interventionist policies of past decades—especially the Canadian energy and investment programs that led to many bilateral disputes. The purpose of the standstill is preemptive: to forestall future attempts to impose protection. The standstill does not require changes in existing policies, laws, and regulations even if they have discriminatory effects. At the same time, the standstill obligation does not prevent either government from implementing changes in domestic policies and regulations, but it does require that any change not mask protectionist intent nor discriminate against goods and services provided by U.S. and Canadian interests in either country. As a result, businesses should be able to better plan their trade and investment strategies.

Over time, one could expect the standstill commitment to reinforce the existing trend toward similar regulatory policies in both countries. The standstill will constrain changes in future policies and trade measures and therefore promote convergence of U.S. and Canadian policies from the current baseline. Such convergence has prompted Canadian concern about loss of sovereignty over their domestic policies, although in an important respect this already occurs in the macroeconomic arena because of Canadian participation in exchange-rate management with the Group of Seven.

FREE TRADE AREAS AND GATT

The explicit bilateral preferences in free trade areas might at first seem to run counter to the nondiscrimination and most-favored-nation principles of GATT. However, GATT signatories recognized that the benefits of trade liberalization by free trade agreement partners may confer benefits to third countries beyond the costs inherent in discriminatory free trade agreement preferences. Thus, GATT allows free trade agreements if they meet a three-part test: detailed notification to GATT signatories; coverage of substantially all the trade between the partner countries; and avoidance of new barriers to third-country trade.[6] These criteria are spelled out in GATT Article 24.

GATT reviews of agreements under Article 24 have been held quite frequently, but they have been conducted without great rigor. More than fifty-three free-trade-area and preferential-trade arrangements have been notified to the GATT. While numerous pacts have been criticized by some members of the GATT Working Party as being inconsistent with GATT rules, the GATT Council has never formally censured any agreement brought before it. The lax enforcement of Article 24 obligations was sharply criticized in the GATT Wisemen's report to the director-general of GATT: "The exceptions and ambiguities which have thus been permitted have seriously weakened the trade rules, and make it very difficult to resolve disputes to which Article 24 is relevant. They have set a dangerous precedent for further special deals, fragmentation of the trading system, and damage to the trade interests of non-participants."[7]

The Wisemen were concerned about the increase in preferential trading arrangements and the threat that such agreements pose to the multilateral trading system. The clear implication of their report was that many of those agreements do not meet the three-part test of Article 24 but have been accepted by GATT members nonetheless. A review of reports by the GATT Working Party on the various complaints of preferential trading arrangements bears this out. Only four agreements were deemed to be fully compatible with Article 24; in most cases, there were disagreements among Working Party members about the agreements'

[6] While there is no obligation that the agreement be on balance trade creating, GATT reviews have established the presumption that a free trade agreement should have a net trade-creation effect to qualify for the Article 24 exception.

[7] Fritz Lekutwiler et al., *Trade Policies for a Better Future: Proposals for Action* (Geneva, 1985).

conformity with GATT rules on third-country effects, trade coverage, and timing and implementation. In those cases, no decision was made, although countries reserved their retaliatory rights under GATT Article 23 (regarding nullification and impairment of trade concessions).

Since the publication of the Wisemen's report, the U.S.-Israel and Canada-U.S. Free Trade Agreements have been submitted to GATT for scrutiny under Article 24. These agreements have been deemed by most countries to have generally met the GATT test, though some members noted concerns about the agricultural trade provisions.

WILL THE FTA WEAKEN THE COMMITMENT OF THE UNITED STATES AND CANADA TO THE GATT?

Any bilateral agreement covering more than $160 billion in trade (1988) is bound to raise questions about its impact on the multilateral trading system. This section examines whether the Canada-U.S. Free Trade Agreement is a retreat toward bilateralism or is supportive of efforts to strengthen the GATT trading system.

Some analysts argue that the agreement represents a strengthening of bilateralism and therefore is antithetical to the GATT system.[8] For Canada, the need for further GATT talks is questioned because most of Canada's trade is with the United States and covered by the FTA. For the United States, the lengthy duration of GATT talks and their diluted influence contrast sharply with the relative speed and success of the FTA. The prospects of more bilateral free trade agreements thus have some appeal.[9]

Both countries, however, have broader trade interests that can be best served by the multilateral system. First, the free trade agreement comes at a crucial juncture for the U.S. and Canadian economies. Both the United States and Canada need to bolster their external positions and promote a stronger world trading system. Both need to substantially improve their market shares at home and abroad to correct large trade deficits. Both will benefit from the expanded home base that the FTA provides, and the corresponding opportunity to improve their firms' competitiveness at home and abroad. The FTA contributes to these goals by promoting increased efficiency and productivity of industries in both countries, and by reinforcing a strong and effective multilateral trading system that helps open foreign markets.

[8] John Whalley, "Comments," in Schott and Smith, *Global Impact.*
[9] The question of the feasibility and desirability of prospective FTAs, as well as their implications for third countries and the GATT system, is examined in Jeffrey J. Schott, "More Free Trade Areas?" *Policy Analyses in International Economics* 27 (Washington, Institute for International Economics, May 1989).

Second, key aspects of the bilateral trade relationship—subsidies and agriculture—depend on the development of multilateral discipline in GATT. The FTA failed to increase discipline on subsidies, although the issue is the subject of continuing bilateral negotiations over the next five to seven years. This is not altogether surprising, because discipline on subsidies can often be effective only if applied to the trade of other major trading countries—as is clearly the case with regard to agricultural subsidies.[10] Moreover, concessions on subsidies involve some of the most substantial and politically difficult concessions that a country can offer in a trade negotiation; the stakes were clearly not high enough in the bilateral FTA to prompt such concessions. Only a multilateral negotiation can generate a package of benefits large enough to induce countries to surmount domestic political opposition and offer reciprocal concessions on subsidies.

The same rationale holds true for agricultural trade restrictions in general. Agriculture accounts for only 4.5 percent of total bilateral trade. While the FTA will eliminate tariffs on bilateral trade, nontariff barriers remain largely unscathed. Both countries maintain substantial farm-support programs and compete furiously for export markets. Both want stringent discipline on these subsidies. Yet if they act bilaterally or unilaterally to disarm their farm-support programs, an influx of subsidized imports from third countries would likely result. As with subsidies, farm reform is untenable unless reciprocal liberalization is achieved in other markets.

In several respects, the Canada-United States Free Trade Agreement provides a big boost for GATT in general and for the current Uruguay Round of multilateral trade negotiations in particular. First, the FTA counters the worldwide protectionist trend. It demonstrates that countries can negotiate the elimination or reduction of trade barriers despite the presence of strong protectionist pressures. As such, the FTA is true to the "bicycle theory" of trade policy that postulates that trade liberalization must maintain forward momentum or fall off into protectionism. Thus, it should reinforce GATT efforts to reduce trade barriers and to reform the trading system; indeed, the FTA reaffirms the open-trade principles that underpin GATT.

Second, the Canada-U.S. agreement is fully consistent with GATT requirements for bilateral free-trade areas. FTA provisions cover all merchandise trade and many traded services, except some trade and invest-

[10]For a detailed examination of this issue, see Dale E. Hathaway, "Agriculture and the GATT: Rewriting the Rules," *Policy Analyses in International Economics* 20 (Washington, Institute for International Economics, Sept. 1987) and *Reforming World Agricultural Trade* (Washington, and Ottawa, 1988).

ment in Canadian cultural industries. Tariffs are eliminated for all products, including agriculture. No new restrictions will be applied to trade with third countries, though some trade diversion may occur. However, the FTA should have a net trade-creating effect due to income growth in both countries, which should enable third countries to maintain or even expand sales in absolute terms even if they lose some market share.[11] In sum, the Canada-U.S. Free Trade Agreement meets the requirements of GATT Article 24 regarding trade coverage, trade creation, and the absence of new trade restrictions.

Third, the FTA contains provisions that could serve as models for prospective GATT accords under negotiation in the Uruguay Round. In particular, the FTA pioneers new agreements on dispute settlement, services, and investment on which GATT negotiators can build to develop better multilateral accords. The main implications for the Uruguay Round are addressed below.

WILL THE FTA PROMOTE MULTILATERAL AGREEMENTS IN THE URUGUAY ROUND?

The Canada-U.S. Free Trade Agreement contains many important implications for the Uruguay Round of GATT negotiations. Its innovative approach to dispute settlement could prove particularly important, while its provisions on services and investment could provide useful precedents for areas not currently subject to extensive GATT discipline. In each of these areas, experience gained by U.S. and Canadian negotiators should contribute to development of better GATT agreements.[12]

Dispute Settlement

Reform of GATT dispute-settlement procedures is of utmost importance to the future of the GATT system; countries will be loath to agree to new rules and obligations if they believe existing provisions are inadequately enforced. For this reason, the FTA procedures, which set up mechanisms to preempt disputes and expeditiously resolve those that emerge, may be particularly instructive for GATT negotiators.

What is wrong with current GATT dispute-settlement procedures? The problem is twofold. First, GATT provisions are vague in certain areas such as agriculture. Second, many countries refuse to give panels the au-

---

[11] Schott, "United States-Canada Free Trade," 5–6.

[12] This section draws heavily on Jeffrey J. Schott, "Implications for the Uruguay Round," in Schott and Smith, *Global Impact.* That chapter also points out that GATT negotiators can learn a great deal from U.S. and Canadian efforts in areas where the FTA results left much to be desired. This is particularly true regarding subsidies and intellectual property rights, where both countries committed to pursue multilateral accords in the GATT.

thority to interpret and elaborate GATT rules and issue binding recommendations. Moreover, countries do not always abide by panel rulings and GATT does not have sufficient power or leverage to force them to do so. The task of the Uruguay Round is to better define certain GATT provisions. The dispute-settlement provisions of the FTA establish procedures that could help remedy the enforcement problem.

In particular, surveillance of national trade policies and resorting to binding arbitration in certain disputes would be useful precedents for GATT reforms. The introduction of such procedures in GATT would make the dispute-settlement process more equitable and objective. Monitoring trade policies would help ensure greater conformity with GATT obligations and preempt some problems. The resulting information would also facilitate preparation of more authoritative panel reports. Moreover, with binding arbitration, countries would no longer be able to block with impunity the adoption of panel reports.

In addition, introduction of national trade-policy surveillance—when combined with a more structured consultation and dispute settlement mechanism—could prove instructive for negotiators seeking to reinforce the GATT safeguards system. The trade-policy reviews would be indispensable for monitoring compliance with prospective safeguards obligations, especially if a new safeguards code requires adjustment by the industry benefitting from temporary protection.[13]

Services

The FTA provides a model of the type of "umbrella code" or framework agreement on services that the United States has been advocating for several years in Geneva. The agreement's provisions establish firm contractual obligations regarding national treatment, establishment, and licensing and certification procedures for trade in services. Provisions in these areas are carefully crafted and could serve as a model for a GATT code.

In other respects, however, the agreement is less useful as a model for a GATT accord. First, the agreement does little to liberalize existing restrictions on services trade. A successful GATT negotiation will require liberalization of specific trade barriers.

Second, a comprehensive standstill on new trade barriers for services was arrived at relatively easily by the United States and Canada, given the level of development and openness of their service sectors, but it will

[13] See Gary Clyde Hufbauer and Jeffrey J. Schott, "Trading for Growth: The Next Round of Trade Negotiations," *Policy Analyses in International Economics* 11 (Washington, Institute for International Economics, 1985).

be much more difficult to reach in GATT. The principles contained in the services code may not be universally applied, and countries may not want to subject certain service sectors to code obligations. Therefore, flexibility may be needed in the range of concessions countries are able to offer.

Third, the application of the most-favored-nation principle, which was not as relevant in the bilateral context, will have to be addressed. To preempt the free-rider problem, a GATT agreement needs to be applied on a conditional most-favored-nation basis as between signatories and nonsignatories.[14] However, a question remains whether the most-favored-nation principle should apply among signatories if some countries assume more detailed obligations in particular sectors than do other countries.

Fourth, the U.S.-Canada services agreement casts doubt on the efficacy of negotiating self-contained sectoral agreements. The failure to agree on even minimal liberalization in the maritime sector is instructive. The rollback of barriers on a multilateral basis requires the additional leverage gained from being able to trade off concessions between sectors covered by a common GATT framework agreement.

In addition, the FTA coverage of labor services sets an interesting precedent for GATT talks. There has been some concern, especially among developing countries, that such services would be excluded from the GATT agenda and considered solely as an immigration issue. Although coverage of labor services is incomplete—the FTA primarily covers the temporary entry of businesspersons and traders and excludes blue-collar labor services—the distinction drawn between professional and blue-collar labor services sets useful parameters for a GATT negotiation.

Investment

As in services, several provisions of the FTA set out useful models for a GATT accord on trade-related investment measures, especially those dealing with the national treatment, performance requirements, remittance restrictions, expropriation, and domestic-equity requirements. Obligations in the agreement for trade-related performance requirements are particularly important, since they go further than existing GATT practice, which pursuant to the 1983 panel report on the Canadian Foreign Investment Review Agency only censures domestic sourcing rules.

The FTA also sets an interesting precedent for a GATT accord in its coverage of practices by state and provincial authorities. Both countries undertake to ensure that subnational authorities comply with FTA obligations and, in particular, grant most-favored-nation treatment to goods

---

[14]Hufbauer and Schott, "Trading for Growth."

and services from the other country. Extending this obligation to GATT would have important implications for GATT discipline on subsidies, government procurement practices, services, and investment.

The main omission of the FTA is the thorny area of investment incentives. This is not surprising, because many investment incentives are granted by states and provinces. A GATT agreement on investment will have to deal with the subsidies issue, either head-on or by referring to changes in the GATT Subsidies Code, to avoid proliferation in the use of subsidies as a substitute for newly liberalized trade and investment barriers.

In sum, the FTA provides many useful lessons for the Uruguay Round. It demonstrates that countries still recognize the value of trade liberalization and are willing to reduce trade barriers. It also demonstrates that rules can be crafted to subject new areas such as services and investment heretofore not covered by GATT to multilateral discipline, and that different regulatory regimes can coexist under an international agreement. As such, lack of homogeneity between regulations imposed by different countries should not bar a GATT agreement on services. Although more work needs to be done in Geneva to bridge various national positions in these areas, the FTA will help clarify the issues for the GATT negotiators.

IS THE FTA A MODEL FOR FUTURE BILATERAL AGREEMENTS?

Could the FTA be replicated with other countries? The successful negotiation of the Canada-U.S. pact has reinforced interest in bilateral free trade agreements to liberalize trade and resolve longstanding trade disputes. Several countries have already expressed an interest in exploring just such an arrangement with the United States. Studies are underway in Japan, Korea, and the Association of Southeast Asian Nations in response to initial U.S. overtures for a possible free trade agreement. Only Australia rejected the notion of such an agreement, after considering a detailed report issued in June 1986.[15]

As a practical matter, however, it would be very difficult for any other country to negotiate a free trade agreement with the United States as comprehensive as the Canada-U.S. agreement. In many respects, the FTA is unique.

First, the U.S. and Canadian economies are already substantially interdependent. The two countries are the world's largest bilateral trading partners, with more than $162 billion in total trade of goods and services

[15] Richard H. Snape, "Should Australia Seek a Trade Agreement with the United States?" discussion paper 86–01 (Canberra, Australia, Economic Planning Advisory Council and the Department of Trade, 1986).

in 1987. The stock of U.S. foreign direct investment (FDI) in Canada and Canadian FDI in the United States totaled $50 billion and $18 billion respectively in 1987. There is substantial cross ownership in key sectors such as autos and petroleum. Even the labor market is somewhat integrated, with affiliated unions in sectors such as autos, steel, and textiles and apparel. Such interdependence made it easier to negotiate a standstill obligation, a key aspect of the FTA.

Second, domestic support for the FTA is facilitated by the absence (in most respects) of significant adjustment pressures from politically powerful industries such as textiles, apparel, and steel[16]—partly reflecting the absence of a large disparity in wage rates in these sectors. Thus, the habitual complaint about unfair competition from low wage suppliers does not arise. In addition, these industries for the most part face competitive pressures from foreign producers, not other North American firms. Moreover, these industries have been shielded from much of the postwar multilateral trade reforms as a result of both domestic subsidies and extra-GATT quotas negotiated under the Multi-Fiber Arrangement.[17] The FTA does not diminish this protection against third-country competition; if anything, it strengthens the competitiveness of North American firms.

Third, there already is substantial convergence of key trade-related regulatory policies in both countries, and common standards for exchange-rate management are being developed in consultations among the industrial countries in the Group of Seven. Both countries have been deregulating financial markets and reforming agricultural support programs. Moreover, Canada and the United States administer their statutes on countervailing and antidumping duties in much the same way.[18] As a result, the two countries encountered fewer problems in reconciling their trade-policy regime to the shared discipline of the FTA.

No other free trade agreement would have these advantages or could realistically meet the GATT tests. U.S. labor unions would complain about wage disparities, and import-sensitive industries such as steel and textiles would balk at having to liberalize their quotas to secure an agree-

[16] With the notable exception of the U.S. uranium industry, the FTA has raised few U.S. concerns about potential dislocations and industrial restructuring that may arise from the implementation of the trade reforms. In Canada, the adjustment concerns have been more widespread, but the prospect of a significant increment to real income as a result of the FTA means that adjustment will take place in the context of economic growth and job creation (See Economic Council of Canada, *Venturing Forth*).

[17] William R. Cline, *The Future of World Trade in Textiles and Apparel* (Washington, 1987).

[18] Gary N. Horlick, Geoffrey D. Oliver, and Debra P. Steger, "Dispute Resolution Mechanisms," in Schott and Smith, *Global Impact*.

ment. As a result, prospective accords would likely evolve into sectoral free trade agreements or preference schemes in which the balance between trade creation and trade diversion would be less distinct.

The benefits of such agreements for the United States could well be transitory. When past U.S. efforts to open foreign markets have succeeded, they have resulted in special preferences for U.S. suppliers to the detriment of other exporters. Indeed, at times U.S. pressure has only resulted in a redistribution of import shares and not overall liberalization. Such a result is applauded by those who seek to use free trade agreements in ill-conceived attempts to improve the U.S. bilateral trade balance.[19] However, such efforts are inevitably imitated by other countries seeking their own special deals. Soon U.S. trade gains are offset by foreign reactions. More importantly, such actions often lead to market-sharing arrangements instead of market liberalization—an outcome clearly inferior, for U.S. trading interests, to the maintenance of GATT. As such, the Canada-U.S. Free Trade Agreement seems to be the exception that proves the rule that bilateral agreements between the United States and other countries do not further a strong multilateral trading system.

A U.S.-MEXICO FREE TRADE AGREEMENT?

Another exception to the multilateral approach could be the negotiation of a bilateral trade agreement with Mexico.[20] The political, economic, and social benefits of such an accord arguably could justify extending discriminatory preferences to Mexico. Given that Mexico already conducts the predominant share of its trade with the United States, a prospective trade pact with Mexico would be less likely to result in trade diversion and thus undercut the broader effort to secure multilateral trade liberalization.

What form could a prospective U.S.-Mexico trade agreement take? Three options are available: a comprehensive agreement like the Canada-U.S. agreement; a sectoral free trade agreement; or bilateral preferences like the Caribbean Basin Initiative.

A quick examination of the main objectives of the FTA exposes several serious problems for Mexico should it want to enter a comprehensive agreement with the United States.

[19] Pat Choate and Juyne Linger, "Tailored Trade: Dealing with the World as It Is," *Harvard Business Review* (Jan.-Feb., 1988).

[20] Since this paper was written in 1988, the dramatic rush of events in Mexico has accelerated progress toward the initiation of negotiations for a bilateral U.S.-Mexico free trade area. See my "The Mexican Free Trade Illusion," *International Economy*, June/July 1990, pp. 32–34.

Trade Liberalization

The breadth and scope of the trade liberalization achieved in the Canada-U.S. agreement would be hard to duplicate. Tariff elimination is possible, given the substantial reductions in Mexican levies since 1985, which have lowered Mexico's average weighted tariff to 6.2 percent and harmonized its tariff schedule. Removing quotas on industrial products, however, would cause problems for both the United States (in steel, textiles, and apparel) and Mexico (in autos). Agricultural reforms also would remain problematic.

Although some flexibility may be possible regarding liberalization of nontariff barriers given the precedent of grandfathering many existing nontariff barriers in the FTA, reforms of discriminatory public procurement policies would be more difficult since Mexico is not a signatory of the GATT Government Procurement Code (and thus has not committed specific public entities to the GATT's transparency and nondiscrimination requirements). Eliminating tariffs and nontariff barriers on bilateral trade would sharply increase the competitive pressure on Mexican industry, which is still adjusting to reforms implemented pursuant to GATT accession and programs for domestic economic stabilization. The adjustment problem, however, could be mitigated somewhat by staggering the implementation of trade concessions so that Mexico gets more time to phase in its reforms.

Investment

Mexican policies toward foreign direct investment historically have been quite restrictive. In May 1989, however, Mexico instituted significant reforms in its Foreign Investment Law that facilitate foreign participation in substantial sectors of the Mexican economy, and align Mexican policy much closer to the requirements set out in the Canada-U.S. pact. Recent reforms have not been as extensive as Canada's revamping of the Foreign Investment Review Agency. This is due in part to the development objectives of Mexican government planners and in part to sovereignty concerns (which have been similarly raised in the debate about Canadian energy industries). As such, Mexico would be hard-pressed to commit to the prohibitions on performance requirements, the extensive reduction in screening of foreign direct investment, and the national treatment provisions included in the Canada-U.S. agreement. Similarly, the FTA commitments on energy pricing and supply access—key U.S. concerns—would be hard to duplicate.

Subsidies/Countervailing Duties

Mexico and Canada share many of the same concerns about the U.S. countervailing duty (CVD) law. In addition, U.S. concerns about domestic subsidies in Mexico—especially in the energy and natural resource sectors—mirror those raised about Canadian policies. The United States and Mexico have had an understanding concerning subsidies and CVDs since 1985. The pact provided the foundation for the application of an injury test in U.S. CVD cases involving Mexican goods, and for Mexico's subsequent participation in the GATT Subsidies Code.

Mexico undoubtedly would benefit from the type of commitments the United States gave Canada regarding prospective changes in U.S. CVD law and binding arbitration in bilateral subsidy/CVD disputes. Given the harsh reaction by the U.S. Congress to those provisions when complementary discipline on subsidies was not achieved, however, it will be difficult for the United States to extend similar assurances to Mexico. Moreover, as in the U.S.-Canada talks, most of the subsidy issues that confront U.S.-Mexico trade are unlikely to be resolvable in bilateral negotiations. Many of the needed reforms require significantly higher concessions than could be offered in a bilateral deal, and, in any event, new discipline on many key subsidy programs could be effective only if applied to other major trading countries as well. Thus, the key to success in this area lies in the Uruguay Round—where the United States, Canada, and Mexico (among others) need to play an active role in developing new multilateral discipline over domestic subsidies.

Services

For the most part, the FTA provides little immediate liberalization in services, except for the separate chapter on financial services. Most existing restrictions have been grandfathered. Liberalization is designed to be an evolutionary process, sector by sector, starting from the baseline established by the standstill commitment. As such, there would be substantial flexibility in negotiating a bilateral agreement on services between the United States and Mexico, especially since such talks would not yet be constrained by GATT obligations. The main question is whether Mexico could accept the principles of a framework agreement on services—including national treatment—that are included in the Canada-U.S. pact. The United States hopes to have a framework agreement included in the prospective GATT code on services, even though the application of those principles may be limited from the beginning to a few service industries.

Institutional Issues

Mexico clearly would benefit from a binational commission and formal consultation and dispute-settlement procedures similar to those negotiated in the FTA. Indeed, the framework agreement negotiated in 1987 between the United States and Mexico seeks to provide a foundation for just such arrangements.

Joint administration may prove difficult, however, in the absence of both equivalent obligations and similar legal procedures. First, the different levels of U.S. and Mexican economic development means that even a reciprocal bargain will result in a different degree of commitment to trade liberalization by each country. If Mexico does not put up a full share of concessions, support for joint administration will be more difficult to generate. This issue did not arise in the Canada-U.S. context and thus posed no obstacle to the acceptance of the binational commission.

Second, binational review of subsidy/CVD cases and the general dispute-settlement procedures of the FTA were relatively easy to negotiate because of the similar legal procedures and unfair-trade regulations of Canada and the United States. This has not been the case with Mexico, although the issue has been moot until recently because of the comprehensive nature of Mexican import controls. However, import liberalization pursuant to GATT accession and IMF programs has opened up new trade opportunities requiring new administrative responses by the Mexican government. Innovative institutional procedures in a bilateral U.S.-Mexico pact could help shape dispute-settlement procedures and build a stronger foundation for the bilateral trade relationship.

In sum, numerous obstacles confront efforts to negotiate a U.S.-Mexico free trade agreement, so that free trade is unlikely to be a near-term prospect. However, freer trade is possible. Only the degree of liberalization and the context in which such reforms would be implemented—multilaterally in the GATT round, and/or bilaterally through sectoral pacts or preference agreements—has yet to be determined.

As one of GATT's newest members, Mexico has a particularly strong interest in strengthening multilateral trading rules. For both political and economic reasons, a bilateral free trade agreement with the United States would need to promote both bilateral and multilateral objectives. As noted above, in some respects a prospective agreement could be a building block for broader GATT accords in services and dispute settlement; significant problems arise, however, over investment and general trade-liberalization issues.

A principal attraction of a sectoral pact is its pragmatic and defined approach to resolving trade problems. By limiting coverage, it also limits the scope of spillover effects to other sectors and the political opposition that might entail. However, such an approach complicates the negotiation of trade reforms because it is difficult to balance concessions within a specific product sector or between a few sectors.[21] Indeed, the failure to achieve such a balance led the United States and Canada to expand their sectoral talks in 1985 to include negotiation of a more comprehensive free trade agreement.

Mexico followed Canada's lead in the late 1980s by proposing talks on liberalization in both industrial and service sectors. Much of the interest was in expanding existing quotas affecting Mexican exports of textiles, apparel, and steel to the United States. In that sense, bilateral preferences would also achieve Mexico's goals. But neither a sectoral agreement nor special preferences are consistent with GATT, and either approach would require a GATT waiver under Article 25. Ample precedents exist for waivers under both situations (for example, the Auto Pact for sectoral agreements and the Caribbean Basin Initiative for trade preferences). However, proliferation of such waivers could do extensive damage to the multilateral fabric of the GATT system. Mexico and the United States would need to examine closely the relative costs and benefits of such agreements to determine whether they are superior to potential GATT results.

CONCLUSION

The Canada-U.S. Free Trade Agreement is an example of a bilateral agreement that promotes both U.S. economic interests and the multilateral trading system. The agreement counters the worldwide protectionist trend and thus strongly boosts GATT efforts to liberalize trade. It demonstrates that two countries can negotiate tariff elimination and the liberalization of many other trade barriers despite the presence of strong protectionist pressure. Furthermore, the FTA contains provisions, especially in areas such as services, investment, and dispute settlement, that could serve as models for prospective GATT accords under negotiation in the Uruguay Round.

The FTA is a complement to, not a substitute for, the GATT. Both countries still need to work for multilateral trade liberalization to ensure market access for their growing volume of exports. Thus one can conclude that the perceived threat to the GATT system of new regional blocs is not worrisome—unless efforts to reinvigorate the GATT in the Uruguay Round falter. If this should happen, the United States and others would undoubtedly pursue preferential trade agreements, admittedly a second-best alternative to a multilateral trading system.

[21] The U.S.-Canada Auto Pact of 1965 is the notable exception, in large part due to the integration of the auto industry in both countries.

Canada, the United States, and Mexico: North American Economies in a Global Context

Murray G. Smith

A T FIRST GLANCE, it would appear that in the 1980s Mexico and Canada are pursuing opposite tacks in conducting their economic relations with the United States. After decades of pursuing a bilateral approach, Mexico has joined the GATT and become an active participant in the Uruguay Round of GATT negotiations. Canada, a founding member of the GATT, has negotiated a bilateral free trade agreement with the United States. Mexicans, however, have an interest in the potential implications for their economy of the Canada-U.S. Free Trade Agreement, and in assessing this impact, it is important to consider how all three countries (in particular, Canada) deal with the Uruguay Round of GATT negotiations and to examine the subsequent implications for economic relations among these three economies.

This paper considers the interactions or tensions between bilateralism and multilateralism, both in general and in particular with respect to the trade and international economic policies of Canada, the United States, and Mexico.[1] All three countries face common challenges and have common interests in the multilateral trading system. The main focus will be trade and investment policies, but it is useful to take account of macroeconomic factors, which can have significant implications for trade and investment flows.

THE MACROECONOMIC DIMENSION

One remarkable similarity about these three North American economies, which otherwise are different in many ways, has recently emerged.

---

[1] An overview of these issues is available in William Diebold, ed., *Bilateralism, Multilateralism, and Canada in U.S. Trade Policy* (Cambridge, Mass., 1988).

As a result of the large U.S. trade and current-account deficits of the 1980s, the United States, like Mexico and Canada, has become a substantial international debtor. In fact, the United States is, at least according to official data, considered to be the largest external debtor, although of course there are questions about exactly how one should value the U.S. external position. Clearly, international indebtedness will have important implications over the medium and the longer terms for the real exchange rates of these three economies, and for trade flows both within North America and between North America and the rest of the world.[2]

The sharp appreciation of the U.S. dollar in the mid-1980s and the substantial U.S. trade deficit that resulted has diverted Canadian trade flows and inhibited the private sector from expanding trade and investment links with Pacific economies. During the 1990s, however, continuing pressures in financial markets resulting from the changes in national balance sheets will act to reverse the massive global trade imbalances of the 1980s. The realignment of exchange rates (which has sharply reduced the value of the U.S. dollar in terms of the yen and West German mark since 1985) has started reversing global trade imbalances. However, the prospect for further short-term improvement in the U.S. trade balance is limited in light of the continuing U.S. budget deficit and the resilience of the U.S. dollar in 1989. The rapid buildup of U.S. international liabilities and the expanding U.S. deficit on investment income will put downward pressures on the real exchange rate of the U.S. dollar through the 1990s.

Similarly, the pattern of Canadian trade is affected by the exchange-rate alignment among the major industrial countries. During the 1970s when the U.S. dollar was low, Canada earned all of the trade surplus required to service its substantial international liabilities from offshore trade. During the 1980s with the strong U.S. dollar, Canada obtained all of the necessary trade surplus from trade with the United States and ran a trade deficit with the rest of the world. Other macroeconomic factors, of course, were also operating.

There are some parallels between Mexico and Canada in the economic impact of shifts in exchange rates, interest rates, and commodity prices over the last two decades. Both countries enjoyed improvements in their terms of trade during the 1970s because of rising energy prices. And owing to low real interest rates in global capital markets, the costs of large domestic budget and external current account deficits appeared low. The collapse of commodity prices and high real interest rates in the early

[2] See Richard G. Lipsey and Murray G. Smith, *Global Imbalances and U.S. Policy Responses* (Washington and Toronto, Canadian American Committee, 1987).

1980s resulted in a severe contraction in both economies. In Canada's case, economic growth was restored starting in 1983, while Mexico has had a much more painful adjustment process.

Although the process could be irregular—depending on the budgetary policies that emerge from the continuing struggle between the U.S. administration and the U.S. Congress—during the 1990s, the United States will be obliged by mounting foreign debt service requirements to continue to reduce its trade deficit. Thus collectively Canada, the United States, and Mexico will need to look to offshore markets for growing export opportunities.

The slow and irregular process of macroeconomic adjustment could make it difficult to make progress in the Uruguay Round. Protectionism may be waning in the United States, albeit slowly, but the legacy of protectionist attitudes will likely linger. At the same time, Japan and Europe (both with strong currencies) could become less willing to open their markets to competition from foreign agricultural producers and manufacturers in developing countries if they anticipate that their currencies will likely appreciate against North American currencies in the 1990s.

EVOLUTION OF COMMERCIAL POLICIES

Through most of the post-war period, the United States was outward-looking in its trade policies, while Canada was only leaning toward this perspective. Certainly Canada participated in the GATT along with the United States, but the enthusiasm of Canadian participation in the individual rounds of tariff negotiations was variable; it was not always as intense as is now so fondly remembered. It is interesting to observe that from 1945 to 1947, U.S. tariffs were higher than Canadian tariffs but at the end of the Tokyo Round the reverse was true. Mexico was inward-looking for most of the postwar period, and previously as well.

During the 1980s, each country switched places to some extent. Canada became more outward-looking in its trade policies, Mexico started drifting outward, more in accord with the earlier Canadian model, and the United States became more inward-looking in the conduct of its trade policy and trade relations.

The apparent contrast between Canada, which pursued a bilateral option negotiating a free trade agreement with the United States, and Mexico, which shifted to a multilateral approach by joining the GATT, should not be overstated. In fact, Mexico had a bilateral most-favored-nation treaty with the United States and received many of the benefits of the GATT system. For its part, Canada often negotiated on a bilateral basis with the United States in a GATT context and did negotiate an explicit bilateral agreement, the Canada-U.S. Automotive Agreement (Auto Pact) in the 1960s.

THE ARCHITECTURE OF THE CANADA-U.S.
FREE TRADE AGREEMENT

Although the Canada-U.S. Free Trade Agreement is shaped by the many pressures and interests impinging on the world's largest bilateral commercial linkage, it is compatible with the multilateral system. Not only are the two nations proposing a classic free trade area, consistent with Article 24 of the GATT, but the agreement is interwoven with their respective multilateral trade obligations in the GATT and interlinked with the Uruguay Round negotiations.

The Canada-U.S. Free Trade Agreement will eliminate over ten years all tariffs, not only in the industrial sector but also in food and agricultural products. Thus the agreement goes further in liberalizing agricultural trade and in avoiding sectoral exclusions than do many other free trade agreements that have been reviewed under Article 24 of the GATT. True, the United States and Canada retain quotas that serve to buttress supply-management regimes and price-support mechanisms for agricultural products. However, such selective exceptions are permitted under Article 24 if the measures conform with GATT Article 11 or Article 20. Similarly, only limited progress was made in resolving agricultural subsidy issues—both sides will cease export subsidies on bilateral trade—because the real problems in world agricultural trade result from the interaction of European and Japanese with U.S. and Canadian policies and can be only addressed in the Uruguay Round.

The obligations in the Canada-U.S. Free Trade Agreement regarding technical barriers to trade and government procurement build on the GATT codes negotiated in the Tokyo Round. The procurement and technical-barriers provisions of the agreement are not sweeping and revolutionary, but they further liberalize trade and make more transparent the impediments that remain. The limited scope of the procurement provisions is one area where the negotiations fell short.

Drafting general rules of competition to deal with subsidies, dumping, and other allegations of unfair trade practices, and creating rules to liberalize trade in services and investment were the major challenges in the Canada-U.S. talks. The two models that provide the most relevant basis for comparison are the rules of competition that are contained in the Stockholm Convention, which created the European Free Trade Association (EFTA), and the Treaty of Rome, which created the European Community (EC). Neither model provides a perfectly appropriate analogy for Canada and the United States. Instead, the bilateral talks have produced a hybrid, which shares elements of the EFTA system, the EC system, and includes some unique and distinctive elements not found in any other free trade area.

Other bilateral free trade areas, such as between Switzerland, Austria, or Sweden and the European Community, or the U.S.-Israel Agreement, do not have such formal dispute-settlement processes. The principal mechanism for resolving disputes in these other bilateral agreements is a joint committee of the two governments. The Canada-U.S. Trade Commission is a similar type of joint committee, but there are some important and unique innovations in the dispute settlement process in the Canada-U.S. agreement.

The agreement will institute an expeditious binding process of binational appeal for antidumping and countervailing-duty cases and a binational review process governing changes in the trade laws. Furthermore, the potential recourse to judicial review should have a sobering effect on the administrative processes. Thus, the agreement seeks to stop the protectionist drift in each country's trade laws and to buffer the administration of those laws from political influences.

In the services and investment areas as well, the Canada-U.S. agreement goes further than the EFTA-EC bilateral agreements, but falls well short of the full commitment to national treatment that applies within the European Community. (One might take note that one goal of the European Community is to narrow this gap by 1992.) Many existing laws and measures that derogate from national treatment are grandfathered on both sides of the Canada-U.S. border.

The cultural and transportation sectors were exempted from the service and investment provisions of the agreement, because of Canadian concerns about the vulnerability of the cultural industries in light of heavy penetration by U.S. media, and because of lobbying pressures from U.S. maritime interests to permit new cargo-preference legislation in addition to existing Jones Act restrictions. For Canada, the most sensitive national concerns involve issues of cultural sovereignty and identity, while in the United States, national security goals demand special consideration.

It must be stressed that the agreement creates a free trade area, not a customs union. Thus, each country retains separate commercial policies for trade and economic relations with third countries. Maintaining this commercial policy independence while preventing undesired pass-through trade or deflections of trade and production requires negotiating clear and predictable rules of origin. On a technical level, the rules of origin in this agreement are much clearer and will involve much less paper burden and uncertainty than do the rules used by European Free Trade Association-European Community bilateral agreements. Of course, some of the most difficult issues in balancing conflicting sectoral interests required special rules of origin for textiles, apparel, and automotive trade.

BILATERALISM VERSUS MULTILATERALISM

The tension between bilateralism and multilateralism in terms of the evolution of the trade policy can be characterized in terms of two criteria. The first criterion is whether those various trade agreements or negotiations deal with trade disputes and trade conflicts in a way that can be characterized as rule-based or power-based.[3] The second question, apart from this issue of management of economic relations, is whether genuine liberalization exists or whether the arrangements reinforce a drift toward managed trade in the world trading system.

The FTA contains some significant institutional innovations and provides a useful basis for managing economic relations between Canada and the United States.[4] In general, the FTA is much closer to the rule-based system of resolving trade issues and trade disputes than the power-based system. Indeed it is closer in that regard than the GATT at the present time, although hopefully the GATT dispute-settlement procedures and institutions will be strengthened in the Uruguay Round.[5] I also think that the Canada-U.S. introduces more competition in the North American market between the two countries, and in that sense is likely to reinforce the multilateral system.

There are two basic questions we have to ask about regional trade arrangements such as the FTA: Will the agreement lead to trade creation or trade diversion? And what would be the longer term impact on the trading system in terms of both the management of trade relations and subsequent conduct of those countries in trade negotiations? I would argue that in each of those respects, Canadian commercial policy after the FTA will likely continue to be outward-looking.

[3] See John H. Jackson, "Governmental Disputes in International Trade Relations: A Proposal in the Context of GATT," *Journal of World Trade Law* 13 (1979), 1–29.

[4] A fuller discussion is available in Jeffrey Schott, "The Free Trade Agreement: A U.S. Assessment," and Murray Smith, "The Free Trade Agreement in Context: A Canadian Perspective," in Jeffrey Schott and Murray Smith, eds., *The Canada-United States Free Trade Agreement: The Global Impact* (Washington and Halifax, N.S., Institute for International Economics and Institute for Research on Public Policy, 1988).

[5] See papers by Leonard Legault, Robert Hudec, Julius Katz, and Debra Steger, in D. Macrae and D. Steger, *Understanding the Free Trade Agreement* (Halifax, N.S., Institute for Research on Public Policy, 1988).

There is a dearth of empirical estimates measuring the trade-creation or trade-diversion effects of the agreement on Mexico, but I presume that if one were to analyze the effects on Mexico with a general equilibrium model—such as the Harris-Cox model, which embodies significant economies of scale—that the trade-creation effects will dominate the trade-diversion effects for Mexico. It is worth noting that third-country barriers are not being increased in the FTA and either country is free to lower its barriers on third-country commerce. Of course, to the extent that there are trade-diversion effects adversely affecting Canadian economic welfare, they are largely the result of Canada's own import policy.

The much more important question in my view is the dynamic of subsequent trade liberalization. For the purposes of this discussion, I will focus on tariffs. Some Canadian industries may feel that digesting the reductions in tariffs that are resulting from the Canada-U.S. Free Trade Agreement is really a sufficient challenge, both in terms of the competitive opportunities and competitive threats. Those industries might prefer to coast through the Uruguay Round without placing a high priority on improved access to offshore markets. Other industries, however, are likely to be concerned about their input costs and will be concerned that they are paying higher Canadian tariffs on their inputs when they are now competing with U.S. firms; these firms will probably lobby for reduced Canadian tariffs in the context of the Uruguay Round. A third set of industries may feel that the rationalization of the North American marketplace improves their competitiveness and as a result may attach higher priority to access to offshore markets.

One qualitative example of how these cross-pressures affecting trade policy come into play is illustrated by the textiles and apparel sector. There was considerable pressure in the United States to exclude the textiles and apparel industry from the FTA. In the end the industry was included with some restrictive rules of origin that limit untrammelled access to apparel made from either Canadian or U.S. fabrics. This part of the agreement was disappointing to segments of the Canadian apparel industry that use fabrics made offshore, but duty-free quotas for Canadian apparel utilizing third-country fabrics exist that permit exports to the United States. There was a lot of concern among the Canadian apparel industry about how they could compete in a free trade context with the U.S. apparel industry without access to low-cost offshore imports of textiles. Canada has accordingly indicated its intention to lower most-favored-nation tariffs on textiles in the years ahead. Telling your partners that you are planning to reduce these tariffs may not be the best negotiating strategy in the context of the Uruguay Round, but it is interesting to note that the FTA had dislodged some very entrenched protectionist interests in the Canadian textile industry. This example, with both its positive and negative aspects, illustrates the very different dynamic of a free trade area as compared to a customs union or a common market such as the European Community. At least on the Canadian side, there will be continued interest in liberalizing trade in the Uruguay Round and negotiating significant improvements in market access, including tariff reductions.

Two points are appropriate to summarize the potential interaction between the FTA and the Uruguay Round. First of all, whatever the merits of the outcome of the FTA, the FTA deals with many of the issues and problems that the Uruguay Round is attempting to resolve. Consider the example of services, in which the Canada-U.S. experience shows some of the problems that multilateral services negotiations are likely to encounter, but also suggests some ways in which the issues may be dealt with in a GATT-like context. Certainly, the structure of the FTA is interwoven with the GATT and interlinked with the Uruguay Round negotiations. The Uruguay Round can be expected to have a different dynamic and will likely solve some of these issues in slightly different ways than did the Canada-U.S. Free Trade Agreement, but the FTA negotiating experience will have been useful in this larger context.[6]

Second, Mexico has had some experience with U.S. antidumping and countervailing-duty laws in the 1980s. As a result, Mexico may support Canada if efforts are made to revise GATT rules for antidumping and countervailing duties in the Uruguay Round. This interest is likely to be shared by some of the Asia-Pacific economies who have experienced particular difficulties with EC antidumping procedures.

In terms of concerns that the FTA will create bilateral trade preferences and reduce each partner's interest in subsequent trade liberalization, I would suggest that it is much better to move ahead in the Uruguay Round than to defer some of those issues, since the attitude of Canada and the United States in some subsequent round of multilateral negotiations may become more complacent.

I will attempt to characterize three possible outcomes to the Uruguay Round. One outcome would be relatively modest: the Uruguay Round would basically paper over the cracks in the multilateral trading and financial system with some very modest institutional developments, which would tend to reinforce the regionalism and sectoralism that is undermining the multilateral system. The second possible outcome of the Uruguay Round is that not much would be achieved in the way of trade

---

[6] See Jeffrey Schott, "Implications for the Uruguay Round," and Jules Katz, "Comments," in Schott and Smith, *The Global Impact*.

liberalization but important progress would be made in rule making, which could strengthen the system, develop new institutions, and forge better links among the Bretton Woods Institutions (which have not really been revitalized since the early post-war days). The third possible outcome would be that both significant liberalization of trade in the Uruguay Round and a rule-making round that strengthens the system would occur. I suggest that the interests of Canada and the United States would be served best by such an outcome even with the implementation of the FTA.

There is another very important regional development in the world trading system: the efforts of the European Community to complete its internal market by 1992. It remains to be seen how that process will interact with the Uruguay Round. Much of the EC internal mechanisms and liberalization proposals may be genuinely trade-creating, but given the past behavior of the European Community, one has some grounds for concern that they will not structure those arrangements in such a way as to link them closely with what happens in the multilateral system, or to make the internal EC market more open to the rest of the world. Again, this is a case for urgency, since early progress in the Uruguay Round before the EC completes its internal process would be highly desirable. Stronger multilateral rules increase the likelihood that it will be possible to structure the EC internal arrangements so that they are more open to the rest of the world.

INHERENT DIFFICULTIES OF THE MULTILATERAL TRADING SYSTEM

It must be acknowledged that we face some deep existential problems in the multilateral trading system. On the one hand, developing countries have been deeply attached to their rights to special and differential treatment and they want credit for some of their "unilateral" trade liberalization steps implemented under the IMF/World Bank programs. Granting advance credit for these liberalization measures is problematic, but perhaps it could be negotiated if such countries were prepared not only to bind their specific tariff policies but in a sense to give up their rights under Article 18 of the GATT, where they are permitted to impose quotas and other restrictive arrangements for balance-of-payments or development purposes.[7] Unfortunately, it is going to be very difficult to engage the developing countries in a constructive dialogue in the system, in terms of taking a slightly different stance on these traditional issues of special and

[7] See Robert Hudec, *Developing Countries in the GATT Legal System* (London, Gower for the Trade Policy Research Centre, 1987).

differential treatment. However, significant steps in that regard by a few of the major developing countries such as Mexico, Korea, Thailand, and one or two others would have a major impact on the whole dynamic of the Uruguay Round and the development of the trading system.

The other problem is that on the other side of the equation, major players, particularly the United States and the European Community, are interested only in high-technology and services issues—issues that do not appeal to the developing countries. In addition, the major industrial countries are not predisposed to significant liberalization in sectors such as textiles and apparel.

The asymmetries of interest between industrial and developing economies put us in a difficult situation. Perhaps the best parallel that is sometimes used in the context of the Canada-U.S. negotiations is that the only deal that is feasible is a big deal. In short, you either have a big deal that incorporates a lot of the issues permitting cross-issue and cross-sectoral trade-offs, or you unravel down to a very small deal. Michael Aho has termed this "package paradox," and it may well be the most credible basis for achieving a broad-based liberalization of trade and a strengthening of the system in the Uruguay Round.[8]

Smaller countries are playing a much more vigorous and effective role in the Uruguay Round. Canada is playing its traditional role as a middle power in the GATT, and now that Mexico has become an effective GATT participant, there is greater scope for common strategies to overcome some of the obstacles that confront us in the Uruguay Round. For that matter, all three North American countries have a significant interest in liberalizing trade and strengthening the GATT system in the Uruguay Round. The trading system right now is very fluid and fragile, but this presents some creative opportunities. Certainly, there is more ferment about the institutions and the interrelationship among the Bretton Woods institutions than there has been for some time.

There is some risk that the United States will attach the wrong priority to import relief as compared to getting better market access through the Uruguay Round. My positive hypothesis is that sometime in the 1990s the United States will experience the full consequences of its accumulation of international liabilities during the 1980s and become obliged, as Canada and Mexico are, to sustain a trade surplus of 2 to 3 percent of GNP in order to service its international liabilities. At that point, the

[8] See C. Michael Aho and Jonathan Aronson, *Trade Talks: America Better Listen* (New York, Council on Foreign Relations, 1985), 133–64; Gary Hufbauer and Jeffrey Schott, *Trading for Growth: The Next Round of Trade Negotiations* (Washington, Institute for International Economics, 1985), 82–85.

United States will become a born-again evangelist for the multilateral trading system. I hope that the sleeping giant wakes up before the opportunities have been lost. I must say I am always impressed by the ability of the U.S. Congress and the international economic policymaking apparatus in Washington to drift to the brink of disaster and then suddenly steer back on a remarkably clever and astute course.

CONCLUSION

As debtor economies, Canada, the United States, and Mexico face common challenges in expanding their exports of goods and services to offshore markets in the 1990s. The liberalization of trade and investment that has occurred on a bilateral basis under the Canada-U.S. Free Trade Agreement and through Mexico's liberalization will stimulate the expansion of trade and investment links among the three North American economies. All three economies have a strong interest in promoting a broad-based liberalization of trade in the Uruguay Round that will deepen the liberalization of commerce among the North American economies and provide enhanced and more stable access to offshore markets.

PART III
Investment Strategies and Fiscal Harmonization

Resource Mobilization
and Investment Promotion:
Current Growth Perspectives for Mexico

Alain Ize

AFTER THREE DECADES of fast growth, Mexico's economy seems to have come to a halt. The average growth rate of output in the period 1982–1987 was slightly negative, in sharp contrast with an average of 6.4 percent yearly growth from 1965 to 1981 (see Fig. 1). After remaining in the single-digit range for two decades, inflation also started to creep upward in the mid-1970s, and in 1987 reached a record 159 percent (Fig. 2). At the same time, after rising by 38 percent from 1965 to 1981, real wages fell by 34 percent from 1982 to 1987 (Fig. 3). Finally, total external debt rose, as a proportion of GDP, from 12 percent in 1965 to 77 percent in 1987 (Fig. 4).

The poor performance of the Mexican economy occurred in the context of a 52 percent drop in the terms of trade from 1982 to 1987 due to a combination of falling oil prices and severe real exchange rate depreciation, and a sharp reversal of net foreign capital flows, from an average 2 percent of GDP inflow in the period 1977–1981 to an average 5 percent of GDP outflow during 1982–1987 (Figs. 5 and 6). The magnitude of these negative external shocks will tax the economy's ability to recover a satisfactory growth rate of output and employment in the near future; it implies both a sharp compression of domestic consumption and an unprecedented effort to reorient the structure of production toward exports and away from imports. Yet, with a population growing at 2.7 percent per year and a labor force growing at close to 4 percent, Mexico's need for growth is clearly pressing.

Three recommendations are generally made to countries attempting to

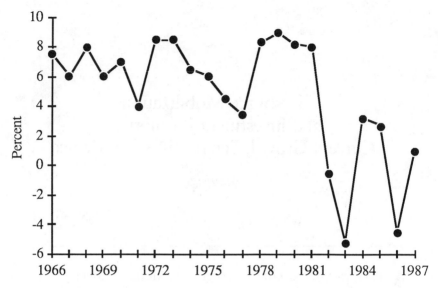

Fig. 1. Mexico's GDP growth rates, 1966–1987. SOURCE: *Indicadores Económicos*, Banco de México.

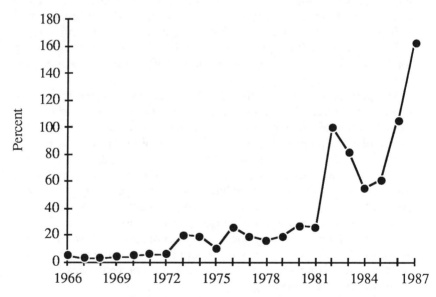

Fig. 2. Mexico's rate of inflation, 1966–1987. SOURCE: Same as Fig. 1.

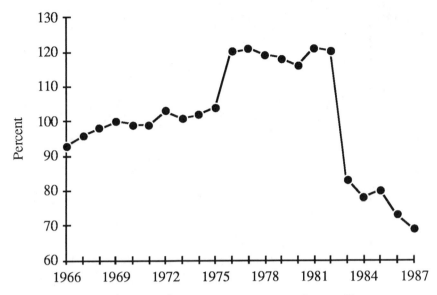

Fig. 3. Mexico's real wages index, 1966–1987. SOURCE: Same as Fig. 1.

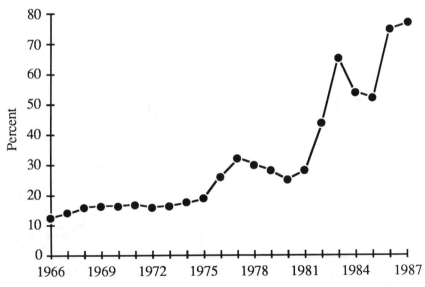

Fig. 4. Mexico's foreign debt as percent of GDP. SOURCE: Díaz and Tercero 1987.

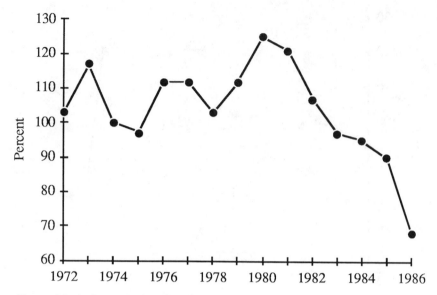

Fig. 5. Mexico's terms-of-trade index, 1966–1986. SOURCE: Same as Fig. 1.

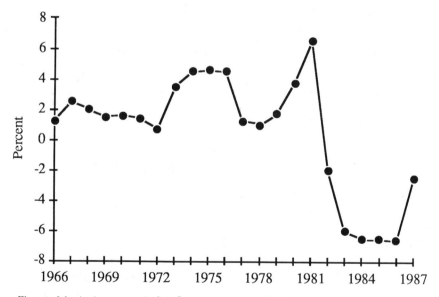

Fig. 6. Mexico's net capital inflow as percent of GDP, 1966–1987. SOURCE: Same as Fig. 1.

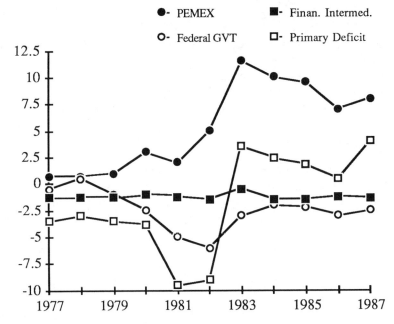

Fig. 7. Mexico's primary deficit, 1977–1987.

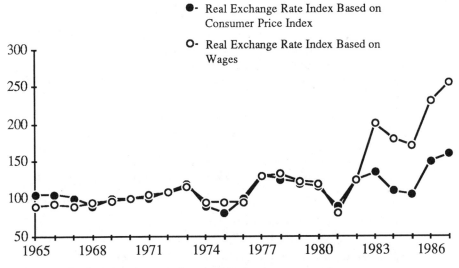

Fig. 8. Real exchange rate indices for Mexico (1970 = 100).

raise their growth rate: (1) set key macroeconomic prices correctly—in particular, adjust the real exchange rate to accommodate available foreign resources, (2) raise domestic resource mobilization for investment, particularly through increasing public savings, and (3) increase the overall efficiency of investment; structural policies to achieve this goal include trade liberalization and privatization. Mexico has made remarkable progress in all these areas. The primary fiscal deficit has fallen by more than 12 percentage points of GDP between 1982 and 1987 (Fig. 7), the real exchange rate in 1987 had depreciated by at least 50 percent with respect to its 1981 level (Fig. 8), and an extremely ambitious economic restructuring program has been under way since 1985 that has taken the form of accelerated trade liberalization and wide-ranging privatization.

In order to reach and sustain a satisfactory rate of growth over the next few years, Mexico needs to complete two additional requirements. The quality and depth of fiscal adjustment should be further improved to reach significantly higher domestic savings rates. At the same time, however, increased public savings should effectively lead to higher investment, rather than be offset by lower private or foreign savings resulting from recession, capital flight, or reserve accumulation. To that end, a reduction in the overall level of systemic uncertainty that has surrounded business conditions in Mexico since 1982 would be needed to boost the private sector's willingness to invest. In addition to stabilizing prices and finding lasting solutions to the debt issue, Mexican policies should simultaneously give priority to promoting trade. A strategy that would focus exclusively on the debt without furthering trade could stop short Mexico's structural adjustment, lessen Mexico's economic integration with the rest of the world, and ultimately exacerbate rather than solve Mexico's domestic resource gap.

I will first mention the evolution of the macroeconomic balance over the last four administrations (*sexenios*), then use some simple growth simulations to comment on the need for further fiscal adjustments. The third part of my paper will focus on measures needed to encourage investment, with particular emphasis on the issues of stabilization, trade, and debt.

THE MACROECONOMIC BALANCE
OVER THE LAST FOUR *SEXENIOS*

Table 1 shows the evolution of Mexico's savings-investment identity over the last four *sexenios*, starting with Díaz-Ordaz's (GDO) last *sexenio* of the "stabilizing development" era (1965–1971), and proceeding

TABLE I

Savings-Investment Identity

(*Ratios to GDP—average of yearly observations*)

	GDO	LEA	JLP	MDM
Total savings	21.3	21.8	25.1	19.7
External savings	2.9	3.7	3.1	−1.4
Foreign capital inflows	2.9	4.8	5.4	1.9
Domestic capital outflows	—	−1.1	−2.3	−3.3
Banking system	−0.2	−0.1	0.1	−1.7
Private sector	0.1	−1.0	−2.4	−1.6
Domestic savings	18.4	18.1	22.1	21.1
Public	3.7	3.0	5.0	7.7
Pemex[a]	0.8	1.1	4.5	9.6
Other	2.9	1.9	0.5	−1.9
Private	14.8	15.2	17.0	13.4
Total investment	21.3	21.8	25.1	19.7
Public	5.2	7.0	9.7	6.1
Private	15.7	14.9	15.4	13.6

SOURCES: *Indicadores Económicos*, Banco de México; and *Estadísticas Hacendarias del Sector Público, 1965–1982*, Secretaría de Hacienda y Crédito Público.

NOTE: The acronyms stand for the *sexenios* of the different presidents of Mexico. GDO is for Díaz-Ordaz; LEA is Echeverría; JLP is López Portillo; and MDM is De la Madrid.

[a]Includes the domestic tax on gasoline.

with Echeverría's (LEA) "shared development" period (1972–1976), López Portillo's (JLP) "oil boom" (1977–1982), and finally, De la Madrid's (MDM) *sexenio* of "crisis and adjustment" (1983–1987). Figures are averaged over each *sexenio* and adjusted for the inflation tax on peso-denominated financial instruments.

The first striking feature of Table 1 is the abrupt downfall of foreign savings after 1982, from an average 3 percent of GDP during the three administrations preceding the crisis to about −1.5 percent during the last administration. Although public savings increased after the crisis because of a large rise in the petroleum-sector surplus, this increase was offset by a reduction in other domestic savings, particularly private savings. Total savings and investment fell by more than 5 percentage points of GDP. It would thus appear that investment was forced down by the reduced availability of savings. This "savings gap" interpretation calls for higher savings as the only required condition for stronger investment and growth.

An alternative interpretation, however, can be offered. The very depressed investment levels since the crisis have led to an underutilization of total potentially available savings. This underutilization resulted in domestic capital outflows, which rose from an already high 2.3 percent of GDP each year of the López-Portillo administration to 3.3 percent after the crisis (in the form of reserve accumulation and capital flight). Low investment has also tended to depress output, hence contributing to re- duce private savings. A resumption of growth would then require a sus- tained recovery of investment (particularly of the private sector's willing- ness to invest) and an effort to mobilize additional savings.

There are many reasons why private investment should have fallen more than available savings. In the nontradable sector, some key factors were the higher price of imported equipment, large excess capacity, and the increase in the burden of external debt following the 1982 devalua- tion. In the tradable sector, and particularly in the exportable sector, most investors have adopted a wait-and-see attitude because of doubts about the feasibility and sustainability of an abrupt shift toward export- led growth. That uncertainty concerns, among other things, the path of future relative prices—in particular the real exchange rate and the ever- pervasive threat of protectionist measures by industrial countries such as the United States, Mexico's main trading partner.

FISCAL ADJUSTMENT

Figures 7 and 9 provide a more detailed view of the extent of fiscal adjustment after the crisis. As shown in Figure 7, the primary deficit made an abrupt recovery after 1982. Most of this recovery was due to the petroleum sector, whose large rent is directly appropriated by the state. The primary deficit of the federal government and other public entities also show improvements, however.

Figure 9 indicates the composition of the adjustment by types of expen- diture. It gives the breakdown of the primary deficit reduction between 1982 and each year after the crisis. The first point to emphasize is, of course, the sheer magnitude of adjustment, 11.5 percentage points of GDP on average. However, after isolating the exchange losses suffered in 1982, which were a one-time event linked to the nationalization of the banking system, the average adjustment shrinks to 8 points of GDP, of which about half was obtained through cuts in capital expenditure. The continuous fall in real wages is responsible for an additional 1.5 to 2 percentage points of deficit reduction. The rest of the adjustment during 1983–1985 was obtained through higher petroleum revenues, gener- ated largely from domestic price adjustment. The steep fall in interna- tional prices and some lag in domestic price adjustments resulting from accelerating inflation, however, have practically eliminated this source of

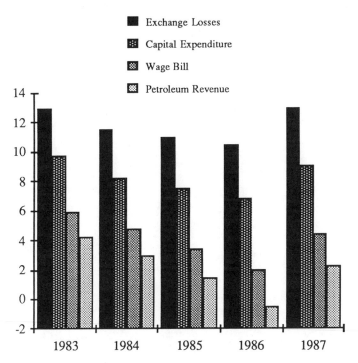

Fig. 9. Fiscal adjustment, 1983–1987.

adjustment in 1986–87. Notice that other budgetary items, including nonpetroleum-based public-sector revenue and other current expenditures such as current transfers, have not contributed to the adjustment (with the exception of 1987, when an adjustment of 2 percentage points of GDP was achieved mostly through cuts in current transfers and other current expenditure). Except for 1987, when a substantial effort was made to cut nonwage current expenditure, it appears that the quality of the adjustment has not been fully adequate.

Most of the adjustment outside exchange losses has so far been supported by excessive compression of capital expenditure, deep cuts in real wages that may not be sustainable, and a strong reliance on a petroleum sector that remains vulnerable to international price fluctuations and to lags in domestic price adjustments. Deeper fiscal measures to boost tax revenue, stabilize domestic petroleum receipts, reduce public-sector employment, and achieve further cuts in noninterest current expenditure

TABLE 2
Growth Simulations

	Historical averages		Base Scenarios			Fiscal adjustment	
	MDM[a] (a)	1986–87 (b)	World inflation (c)	Higher inflation (d)	Lower oil price (e)	Strong current account (f)	Weaker current account (g)
Macro balance							
Current account	1.4	-0.6	1.4	1.4	1.4	1.4	-2.5
Public sector balance[b]	1.6	1.6	-3.3	-1.5	-4.9	0.7	0.7
Savings	7.7	7.2	4.2	6.0	2.6	8.2	8.2
Investment	6.1	5.6	7.5	7.5	7.5	7.5	7.5
Private sector balance[b]	-0.2	-1.0	4.7	3.0	6.3	0.7	-4.2
Savings	13.4	11.4	14.9	14.6	15.3	14.3	14.3
Investment	13.6	12.4	10.2	11.6	9.0	13.6	17.5
Parameters							
Growth	-0.4	-1.6	2.6	3.3	2.0	4.4	6.3
Inflation	83.5	105.0	3.0	20.0	3.0	3.0	3.0
Solvency constraints							
Public	-8.4	-9.5	0.0	2.6	-1.6	6.1	7.5
External	-11.4	-11.1	3.6	4.1	3.3	5.2	4.0

[a]The De la Madrid *sexenio*.
[b]Deficits are shown with minus signs.

still mostly lie ahead, although recent measures taken in 1987 and 1988 take significant steps in that direction.

The potential impact on growth of further fiscal adjustment can best be appreciated by observing the results obtained from a simple simulation model, shown in Table 2. The model is based on a constant incremental capital output ratio (ICOR) and a constant private propensity to save private disposable income, defined as total income minus taxes (including the inflation tax) plus net real interest earnings on private assets, minus public enterprises' net operating surplus.[1] The base scenarios have the same current-account surplus as the average one obtained during the De la Madrid administration. Public savings are taken at their average value during 1986–87—corrected, however, for a reduction of inflation either to 3 percent, assuming a complete success of the current stabilization program (scenario (c)), or to 20 percent (scenario (d)) under a probably more realistic hypothesis. In scenario (c), the government loses nearly all the proceeds from the inflation tax, which represent about 3 points of GDP. In scenario (d), however, it recovers more than half of these proceeds. The third basic scenario, (e), supposes that the world price for Mexican oil falls from $15 to $10 per barrel. Assuming no impact on domestic prices of petroleum products, this reduction in the world price of oil implies a fall of nearly 2 percentage points of GDP in public-sector revenue.

Suppose in all cases that public capital spending returns to a level of 7.5 percent of GDP, closer to its historic pre-crisis average, but still substantially below the probably excessive levels reached during the oil boom. The operational balance would then switch from a surplus of 1.6 percent of GDP reached during 1986–87 to a deficit ranging from 1.5 percent to 4.9 percent of GDP. Compared to their 1986–87 average, private savings would increase by 3 to 4 percentage points of GDP, essentially as a result of a lower inflation tax and faster growth. This assumes that the private propensity to save would rise from the extremely low level reached in 1986–87, while remaining significantly below the level attained during the mini-boom years of 1984–85. Assume finally that the ICOR, while remaining higher than its pre-crisis average, falls somewhat from the abnormally high average level observed after the crisis. The higher saving propensity and lower ICOR should then allow for a growth rate of 2.6 percent in scenario (c), while in scenario (d) growth would be somewhat higher as a result of forced savings induced by the higher inflation tax. In scenario (e), however, growth would fall to 2 percent as a result of a substantial worsening of the public-sector balance.

---

[1] Details on the structure of the model and the choice of relevant parameters are given in the appendix.

Table 2 also indicates the rates at which the ratios of public and external debt over GDP would evolve over time. Notice in particular that although external debt would fall over time in all basic scenarios (thus ensuring the external "solvency" of the economy), the public debt over GDP would not fall in scenario (c) and would actually keep rising in (e). The "internal transfer" problem appears therefore to be the dominant solvency constraint, which pinpoints the critical need for further fiscal adjustment. Given the rate of growth of the labor force and the need for a minimum steady increase in per capita income, though, it is clear that a 2 percent to 3 percent growth rate is not satisfactory. Thus, further fiscal adjustment is also a requirement for faster growth.

On the revenue side, assume that tax revenue outside the petroleum sector can be raised to 12 percent of GDP, up from 10.3 percent. As Table 3 suggests on the basis of 1983 data, this increase seems reasonable when comparing Mexico's total tax revenue with the averages of developing and industrial countries, and considering also that Mexico has a comparatively very large petroleum tax base, which provides about 40 percent of total tax revenue. Notice in particular that direct taxes and nonpetroleum indirect taxes are rather low despite sizable tax rates for income and value-added taxes—a sign that seems to indicate much tax evasion. Suppose, on the other hand, (1) a 0.3 percent increase in revenue from nonpetroleum parastatals, which would require some moderate price adjustment, and (2) a 2 percent reduction in noninterest spending, which would amount to a 1 percent further reduction with respect to the 1987 level. Under the 3 percent inflation hypothesis, this adjustment would thus increase public savings by 4 percentage points of GDP, from 4.2 percent to 8.2 percent, and result in a small operational surplus. Growth would then increase by nearly 2 percent to 4.4 percent, while public debt would fall steadily.

A further boost of the growth rate could then be obtained by relaxing the current-account constraint from a surplus 1.4 percent of GDP to a 2.5 percent deficit, either by stopping capital flight or through greater foreign borrowing. Under the same fiscal effort as the previous scenario and assuming additional foreign resources are invested, growth would then increase to 6.3 percent (Mexico's average performance before the crisis), while still allowing for a safe decline over time of the ratio of external debt over GDP, even in the case where all additional foreign resources are borrowed. Provided private investment could pick up the resources left available by fiscal adjustment and foreign lending (rising from around 10 percent of GDP in the basic scenarios to over 17 percent in the last scenario), Mexico could return to its historic growth perfor-

TABLE 3

Composition of General Government Tax Revenue, 1983

(*as a proportion of GDP*)

	Mexico	Chile	Brazil	Developing countries	Industrial countries
Total tax revenue[a]	17.6%	20.3%	17.8%	18.2%	23.3%
Direct taxes	4.2	3.9	3.8	5.4	13.1
Indirect taxes	11.9	11.8	11.4	8.8	7.4
Petroleum	7.2	—	1.9	—	—
Other	4.7	—	9.5	—	—
Trade taxes	1.3	1.9	1.1	3.0	0.3
Property taxes and other	0.2	2.7	1.5	1.0	2.5

SOURCE: IMF, *Government Finance Statistics Yearbook.*
[a]Does not include social security contributions.

mance while safely reducing over time its public and external debts. The main issue is therefore the extent to which the private sector is willing to pick up and invest the slack.

UNCERTAINTY, BUSINESS CONFIDENCE, AND INVESTMENT

In spite of a quite impressive response of nontraditional exports (Fig. 10), investment in the tradable sector has not yet picked up satisfactorily because many domestic investors have adopted a wait-and-see attitude. Given the depressed current real wage and the large real depreciation of the exchange rate since 1981, current profitability does not seem to justify using additional investment incentives. Although that situation could change according to how key relative prices evolve, what seems most needed under current conditions is a sharp reduction in systemic uncertainty about overall business conditions. This, in turn, requires at least four basic economic conditions: large foreign reserves, a stabilization or indexation of key macroeconomic prices, a lasting resolution to the debt crisis, and definition of an ambitious agenda for trade with the United States.

Reserves

The desirability of large buffer stocks in a climate of uncertainty is a well-admitted principle. In Mexico's situation, large foreign reserves are particularly desirable because (1) the Mexican economy remains very dependent on widely fluctuating oil prices (in 1987, petroleum products still represented about 40 percent of both total exports or goods and public sector revenue), and (2) the high degree of financial openness im-

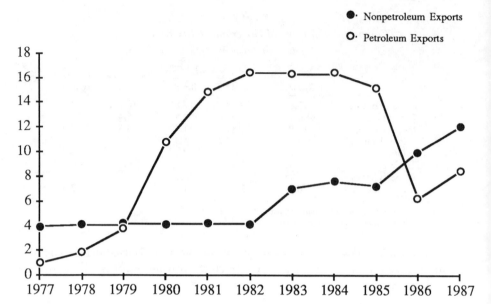

Fig. 10. Petroleum and nonpetroleum exports in Mexico, 1977–1987.

plied by Mexico's large border with the United States facilitates shifts in
asset demands and frequent bouts of self-fulfilling speculation, as movements out of peso assets induced by rumors of devaluation can force the
authorities to devalue. Although large foreign reserves cannot completely
protect against real or financial shocks, they should greatly facilitate the
task of the Central Bank by reducing swings in interest rates (which may
otherwise be necessary to defend the currency). Mexico currently has
foreign reserves of almost 50 percent of the liabilities of the financial
system to the private sector. Although it had costly stagflationary implications, this reserve accumulation—which took place mostly in 1987 as
a result of exchange-rate depreciation and restrictive demand management—should help accommodate temporary external shocks and stabilize expectations.

Stabilization and Indexation

The structure of relative prices has oscillated since the crisis. The real
exchange rate index, which depreciated sharply in 1982 and 1983,
appreciated again quite strongly in 1984–85 before shooting up in

1986–87 as a result of the oil crisis (Fig. 8). These fluctuations have not prevented real returns in domestic financial assets from oscillating widely as well (Fig. 11). Coming in the wake of the large losses suffered in 1982 by investors with peso-denominated assets (who according to Figure 11 would have earned three times as much in comparable investments in the United States) this volatility helps explain why confidence in local assets has not yet fully recovered and their demand remains depressed in spite of substantial premiums paid since the crisis.

On the other hand, the variance of sectoral prices, which should increase with inflation, has been particularly high in Mexico as a result of the lack of a general anchor and the discreteness and unpredictability of the government's adjustments to administered prices. Inflation has thus tended to be more chaotic in Mexico than in countries with well-defined indexation mechanisms.

A reduction in the volatility of relative prices is thus desirable as long as it remains compatible with macroeconomic equilibrium. That reduction can be obtained through stabilization or indexation. Given the need for large relative price adjustments, in particular of real wages; the wide uncertainty about the "right" equilibrium price structure; and the low level of reserves that existed at the end of 1982, it is unlikely that prices

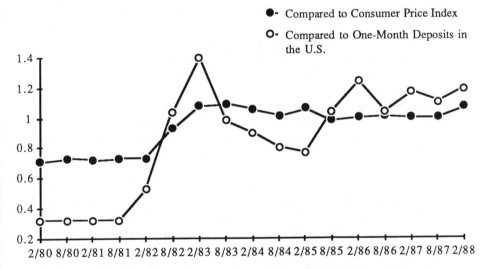

Fig. 11. Compounded returns on one-month deposits in Mexico, Feb. 1980–Mar. 1988.

could have been frozen at that time. It was politically impractical to index the real exchange rate and real interest rates without indexing wages. At the end of 1987, however, given the size of the relative price adjustments that had already occurred and the more adequate level of reserves, it became more feasible to shoot for a rapid stabilization or indexation. Although the authorities may have briefly considered indexation, the stock market crash of September 1987 and the resulting capital flight and exchange-rate depreciation that sent inflation rapidly past the 15 percent per month mark signaled the need for more radical actions and led to the Solidarity Pact of 1988.

In retrospect, stabilization, in spite of the risks involved and possible short-run costs, appears to have been a good alternative to general indexation for at least four reasons. First, underlying conditions and fundamentals were generally appropriate for a shock program to succeed. The fiscal position, although improvable, was not grossly out of equilibrium; foreign reserves were high; and the real exchange rate was sufficiently undervalued to provide a reasonable margin of safety. In addition, the government had managed so far to avoid explicit wage indexation, exploiting instead its ability to negotiate centralized wage settlements discretely. Thus it made even more sense to attempt to retain wage flexibility. Also, as already discussed, the very substantial—and largely unavoidable—degree of financial openness present in Mexico implies that confidence-induced shifts in asset demands can have a direct and very large impact on inflation through largely self-fulfilling movements in the exchange rate. In this context, indexation could give rise to very sharp upward swings in inflation, which may be difficult to revert, especially if wage indexation is backward-looking. Finally, as it will be argued below, Mexico would greatly benefit from strengthening its trade relations with the United States, its main economic partner, particularly if a North American free-trade zone can come to life. A steadier currency, that would perhaps be able to join at some point a North American equivalent of the European Monetary System, would then greatly facilitate that objective.

It is too soon to tell whether the current Solidarity Pact will be successful, although results attained so far are encouraging; inflation has fallen from 15 percent a month to less than 2 percent in just five months without a general freeze on prices. One significant problem encountered by authorities has been the high level of real interest rates. Indexation could have been an appropriate way to deal with this problem, because an indexed instrument would have reduced substantially the costs of funds if the program succeeded, and yet provided adequate coverage if it failed. The political difficulties involved in shielding asset holders from risk while avoiding any type of formal wage indexation may have blocked this alternative.

Debt

Links between the foreign debt burden and willingness to invest can be formalized in various ways. A high debt burden can depress investment through at least two channels: it can reduce investment returns directly by raising the taxes needed to service public debt, or it can force a reduction in per capita consumption to a level that may be politically difficult to sustain. In either case, multiple expectational equilibria can exist and large jumps in investment can be derived from small changes in debt, if it forces a switch from a "pessimistic" to an "optimistic" equilibrium. In cases where a country appears to be stuck in a low investment equilibrium, a strong argument can be made for reducing its debt burden.

Market-based mechanisms that would reduce the face value of outstanding debt on the basis of such a rationale would thus be a welcome development. Chances that these mechanisms will reduce the debt burden significantly appear dubious, however, because of uncertainty about relevant parameters, coordination problems between creditors, moral hazard, and other issues. Yet we should remember that value-preserving debt arrangements that would secure a steady flow of financing could also have a positive impact on private confidence and investment if those resources were used to induce higher sustainable growth. As shown earlier, a substantial permanent increase in external borrowing could in fact be consistent with a falling debt-to-GDP ratio over time. Finally, furthering and steadying trade relations between Mexico and its trading partners could do much to permanently settle the debt issue. It is thus essential that debt arrangements do not hinder trade agreements.

Trade

The De la Madrid administration did not make much progress in reshaping its foreign trade policies before mid-1985. It has made remarkable progress, however, since that time. Import-licensing requirements have been reduced drastically; controlled items, which represented only about 25 percent of import value at the end of 1987, equalled 85 percent in 1984, and the production-weighted average tariff has fallen from 29 percent in mid-1985 to about 14 percent at the end of 1987. The GATT, which Mexico joined in August 1986, has also provided a valuable framework for defining Mexico's trade policies and for negotiating trade agreements.

So far, however, most of the trade reforms have been a unilateral affair (other than two important bilateral agreements on trade with the United States, one signed in 1985 that restricts the ability of U.S. firms to apply for countervailing duties, and one in 1987 that establishes a framework for discussing bilateral trade issues between the two countries). The ever-pervasive threat of protectionism from industrial countries, particularly the United States, is still nevertheless a troubling issue for potential Mexican investors in export-oriented activities. That uncertainty has slowed large investments in the exportable sector, particularly those by Mexican firms. Hence, much of the recent growth in nontraditional exports depends on existing capacity, a situation that may revert itself as growth recovers. U.S. firms, in particular the in-bond industries and automobile companies, have felt less vulnerable and therefore benefited most from favorable exchange rates and Mexico's changing trade policies.

There is great potential for further trade development between Mexico and the United States, in spite of the fact that the United States already takes the lion's share of Mexican trade. Mexico's comparatively cheap labor, both skilled and unskilled; abundant natural resources; and geographical location complement the U.S. economy—creating an opportunity that until recently has been barely exploited.

Furthermore, an increase in trade with other countries could parallel a rapid development of U.S.-Mexico trade based on bilateral agreements. Recent changes in Mexican attitudes toward trade and the signing of the Canada-U.S. Free Trade Agreement provide an opportunity to launch an ambitious agenda toward creating a North American free-trade zone. Setting such an agenda would limit uncertainties on both sides of the border about future trade and exchange-rate policies, helping in this way to promote investment. Also, by promoting trade and reinforcing economic ties between Mexico and its main creditors, a North American free-trade zone could have a beneficial impact on the debt issue, as both the ability to repay the debt and the penalty associated with default would sharply increase. A sustained effort is also needed on the Mexican side to increase foreign investment, particularly by U.S. firms. A further liberalization of foreign investment regulations and large investments in infrastructure, particularly transportation, telecommunications, and education, are required. In contrast, a policy on the Mexican side that emphasizes the debt issue without promoting trade could slow Mexico's structural adjustment and lessen instead of reinforce Mexico's economic integration with the rest of the world, thereby undermining its potential for lasting growth.

TABLE 4

Notation for the Growth Model

Y = GDP	B_G^F = Public foreign debt
C_p = Private consumption	B_p^F = Private foreign debt (net of private
C_G = Public consumption	assets held abroad)
I_p = Private investment	ρ = Rate of nominal depreciation
I_G = Public investment	π = Rate of domestic inflation
Z = Trade deficit	g = Rate of real GDP growth
r^H = Nominal domestic interest rate	d_G = Current fiscal deficit
r^F = Nominal foreign interest rate	d^F = Current account deficit
E = Nominal exchange rate	α = Propensity to save
T = Tax revenue	β = Incremental capital output ratio
T^F = Net transfers from abroad to the	y_d = Private disposable income
private sector	s_G = Seignorage on public debt
B_G^{II} = Public domestic debt (including money)	s^F – Seignorage on external debt

APPENDIX: GROWTH SIMULATIONS

The Underlying Growth Model

The underlying model is as follows. Consider the following macro-identities, defined in domestic currency at current prices:

$$Y = C_P + C_G + I_P + I_G - Z \tag{1}$$

$$C_G + r^H B_G^H + r^F E B_G^B + I_G - T = \dot{B}_G^H + E\dot{B}_G^F \tag{2}$$

$$Z + r^F E(B_G^F + B_P^F) - T^F = E(\dot{B}_G^F + \dot{B}_P^F). \tag{3}$$

The notation is explained in Table 4. Deflating equations (2) and (3) by Y, and using lowercase letters to define the deflated variables, those equations become

$$c_G + i_G - t + (r^H - \pi - g)b_G^H$$
$$+ (r^F + \rho - \pi - g)Eb_G^F = \dot{b}_G \tag{4}$$

$$z - t^F + (r^F + \rho - \pi - g)b^F = \dot{b}^F \tag{5}$$

where ρ is the rate of nominal depreciation, π the rate of inflation, g the real rate of GDP growth, and where

$$b_G = b_G^H + b_G^F \tag{6}$$

$$b^F = E(b_P^F + b_G^F). \tag{7}$$

Define d_G and d^F as the current fiscal and external deficits, inclusive of the inflation tax on domestic debt:

$$d_G = c_G - t + (r^H - \pi)b_G^H + r^F E b_G^F \tag{8}$$

$$d^F = z - t^F + r^F E(b_G^F + b_P^F). \tag{9}$$

Define s_G and s^F as the seignorage obtained on public and external debt:

$$s_G = gB_G + (\pi - \rho)E b_G^F \tag{10}$$

$$s^F = (g + \pi - \rho)b^F. \tag{11}$$

Define finally private disposable income as

$$y_d = 1 - t + t^F + (r^H - \pi)b_G^H - r^F E b_P^F \tag{12}$$

and assume

$$c_p = (1 - \alpha)y_d \tag{13}$$

$$g = \frac{1}{\beta}(i_p + i_G) \tag{14}$$

where α is the propensity to save and β the incremental capital = output ratios (ICOR).[2]

Solving the model gives growth as a function of the current fiscal and external deficits, private disposable income, the propensity to save, and the ICOR:

$$g = \frac{1}{\beta}(d^F - d_G + \alpha y_d). \tag{15}$$

The following sets of solvency constraints for the public sector and the economy as a whole is also obtained:

$$\dot{b}_G = d_G + i_G - s_G \leq 0 \tag{16}$$

$$\dot{b}^F = d^F - s^F \leq 0. \tag{17}$$

The Choice of an ICOR and a Savings Propensity

Table 5 gives a range of values for the ICOR obtained on the basis of an assumed 5 percent average yearly depreciation of the capital stock.[3] The use of gross nominal investment, given by National Accounts data (excluding changes in inventories), leads to values around 1.8 for the years 1965 to 1981. The average ICOR then jumps to 2.3 after the crisis,

[2] The model assumes away the possibility of Ricardian equivalence, even in partial form. This assumption seems to be backed by the data; alternative consumption functions that include government spending instead of taxes seem to lead to more variable average saving propensities.

[3] The ICOR value is: $\beta = i/(\delta + g)$, where δ is the rate of depreciation.

TABLE 5

Incremental Capital-Output Ratios

	1965–72	1973–76	1977–81	1980–81	1984/85–87
Gross aggregate investment (National Accounts)	1.7	1.9	1.8	–	2.3
Investment volume index	–	–	1.9	–	2.0
Machinery index	–	–	–	2.0	1.7

even after excluding 1983 and 1986, the years of falling output. Although this could reflect the higher price of imported machinery, the use of real investment instead of nominal investment does not significantly alter the results.[4] The investment volume index published by Banco de México, however, shows a much smaller increase after the crisis. Finally, leaving aside investment in construction, which has been substantial after the earthquake and which includes a large share of residential construction, and focusing instead only on machinery, the data show a decline of the ICOR from 1980–1981 to the period after the crisis, which is what one would expect in a situation where a large initial excess capacity is eroded over time.

The ICOR in forthcoming years could thus be slightly higher than before the crisis because of the higher price of imported equipment, although reductions in capital intensity should offset at least part of this increase. On the other hand, it is likely that the average productivity of investment should rise during faster and more stable growth than that experienced so far after the crisis, as the relative share of residential and other relatively unproductive investment diminishes. An average ICOR of 2, which is slightly higher than the pre-crisis average but somewhat lower than the observed post-crisis average, can therefore be assumed for the forthcoming sexenio.[5]

Table 6 indicates, on the other hand, that the average private saving propensity rose from 17 percent during the GDO sexenio to 21 percent during the oil boom, and fell back to slightly above 17 percent after the crisis. The average during 1984–1985, the years of the aborted recovery, was much higher, however, at 19.7 percent. A saving propensity of 18 percent is therefore a reasonable estimate for the near future.

[4] The higher price of imported machinery seems to be offset by the lower price of construction, owing to the fall in real wages.

[5] A value of 2 would also correspond to an interpolation of the average oil-boom ICOR of 1.8, based on a 30 percent real devaluation on a 33 percent share of imported machinery (assuming no reduction of capital intensity).

TABLE 6

Average Propensity to Save

(*percent*)

	1965–72	1973–76	1977–81	1983–87	1984–85
Propensity to save	16.9%	17.7%	21.1%	17.3%	19.7%

Other Basic Parameters

Other basic parameters for the base simulations were taken from averages observed in 1986–1987: a petroleum price of $15 (U.S.) per barrel, yielding 11.2 percent of GDP in petroleum revenue; an 8 percent foreign interest rate; a tax pressure (excluding petroleum products) of 10.3 percent of GDP; an income for parastatals, excluding Pemex, of 8.7 percent of GDP; and noninterest current expenditure for the entire public sector of 21.5 percent of GDP.[6]

The net inflation tax (including interest payments on domestic interest-bearing debt) was computed on the basis of a real domestic interest rate of 3 percent. Changes in the inflation tax induced by changes in inflation were derived from the following demand equation for M1, estimated over the period 1965–1987:

$$\text{Log } m_t = 0.44 \text{ Log } m_{t-1} + 0.53 \text{ Log } y_t - 0.31\pi_t - 0.78 \quad (18)$$
$$\phantom{\text{Log } m_t = } (3.60) \qquad\qquad (4.33) \qquad (5.71) \quad (1.34)$$

where m is real money holdings deflated by the CPI, y is real GDP, π is CPI inflation, and figures in parenthesis are t statistics.

The impact of world oil price changes is computed on the basis of export revenues only. It is therefore assumed that the domestic price of petroleum products remains constant when the world price changes (a rather conservative assumption). Basic public investment, excluding on-lending, is assumed to be 7.5 percent, nearly 2 percentage points higher than the level reached during 1986–1987 so as to provide the country with sufficient infrastructure and to maintain a minimum parastatal capacity. This figure was obtained as follows: 3.3 percent for the federal government, which corresponds to the average reached during the oil boom; 1.2 percent for Pemex which is the average for the last three years; and 3 percent for other parastatals including social security, a figure

---

[6] Notice, however, that these figures may be altered to a significant extent depending on the final outcome of the current stabilization scheme. Petroleum revenue and income from other parastatals could turn out to be substantially lower if the government is forced to accept some appreciation of the peso and lags in public-sector prices during the inflation-stabilization process. However, tax revenue may increase as a result of the Tanzi effect.

somewhat higher than the levels reached during the stabilizing development and post-crisis periods, but short of the probably excessive levels reached during the Echeverría and López-Portillo years.

The base simulations also consider a current account surplus of 1.4 percent of GDP, the average observed after the crisis. Assuming a continuation of capital flight at the rate observed after 1982 (1.6 percent of GDP) and a steady reserve accumulation of 0.2 percent of GDP (the amount necessary to maintain the ratio of reserves to GDP at its average 1986–1987 level) a net positive foreign financing of only about 0.4 percent of GDP is implied, which is well below the 2 percent of GDP observed during 1983–1987. Finally, an inventories increase of 2.5 percent of GDP is assumed, which corresponds to the average during the oil boom, a more normal period than the highly unstable and speculative post-crisis years.

Saving, Investment, and Fiscal Harmonization

Charles E. McLure, Jr.

S EVERAL DEVELOPMENTS in recent years make it important to examine both the relationship between taxes, saving, and investment and the need for harmonizing the taxation of capital within the three nations of North America. The most obvious development is the increased internationalization of capital markets; it has become increasingly unrealistic to formulate tax policy using a model that assumes, if only implicitly, that economies are closed to international capital flows. This is especially true of the capital markets of Canada, Mexico, and the United States.[1]

The second development is the growing interest in direct taxation based on consumption rather than income. The possibility of switching to a consumption-based direct tax has intrigued academics in all three North American countries, and all three governments have toyed with moving toward such a tax.[2] For the most part, discussion has thus far

[1] For arguments along these lines, see Donald J. S. Brean, "International Portfolio Capital: The Wedge of the Withholding Tax," *National Tax Journal* vol. 37, no. 2 (June 1984), 239–47.

[2] Among academic analyses, see William D. Andrews, "A Consumption-Type or Cash Flow Personal Income Tax," *Harvard Law Review* 87 (April 1974), 1113–88; Institute for Fiscal Studies, *The Structure and Reform of Direct Taxation* (London, 1978); Peter Mieszkowski, "The Feasibility and Advisability of an Expenditure Tax System," in *The Economics of Taxation* (Washington, 1980), 179–201; Joseph A. Pechman, *What Should Be Taxed: Income or Consumption?* (Washington, 1980); Robin W. Boadway, Neil Bruce, and Jack M. Mintz, "Corporate Taxation in Canada: Toward an Efficient System," in *Tax Policy Options in the 1980s* (Toronto, 1982), 171–213; Robert E. Hall and Alvin Rabuska, *Low Tax, Simple Tax, Flat Tax* (New York, 1983); Robert E. Hall and Alvin Rabuska, *The Flat Tax* (Stanford, Calif., 1985); David F. Bradford, *Untangling the Income Tax* (Cambridge, Mass., 1986); David F. Bradford, "What Are Consumption Taxes and Who Pays Them?" *Tax Notes* vol. 39, no. 3 (18 Apr. 1988), 383–91; George R. Zodrow and Charles E. McLure, Jr., "Implementing Direct Consumption Taxes in Developing

focused on domestic aspects of consumption-based direct taxation—the economic and equity arguments and, more important, administrative advantages of consumption-based taxes. The treatment of international flows of income under a consumption-based tax is extremely important, however, because world capital markets are becoming so closely linked. Unfortunately, relatively little attention has been paid to the taxation of income from international investment under the direct consumption tax.

This paper briefly describes the differences between direct tax systems based on income and those based on consumption. It suggests that even in an economy closed to international capital flows, the greater simplicity of the consumption-based variant makes it an attractive alternative to the income tax.

The advantages of a consumption-based direct tax are perhaps even greater in the more realistic context of an open economy. In this chapter, I examine the principles that ostensibly govern the taxation of income flowing between countries, noting that practice often differs greatly from the conceptual ideal embodied in such principles, especially where portfolio investment is concerned. I then describe some of the distortions of international capital flows that have developed under the traditional income tax, particularly as it has been implemented by the United States. Finally, I ask whether the consumption-based alternative could rationalize the system. This discussion examines both the possible gains for all countries if consumption-based taxation were to become the world norm and the gains that might be available to a single country trying to adopt such a system in a world that continues to rely primarily on income taxation. My intent is not so much to propose particular solutions as it is to evoke discussion and research.

This paper reflects both the enormous role the United States plays in world capital markets and my familiarity with U.S. institutions. Although I focus on how U.S. practice causes problems for other countries, including Canada and Mexico, my discussion of potential solutions goes beyond the realm of U.S. relations with Canada and Mexico and is particularly germane to developing countries. These countries face problems both in administering an income tax and in obtaining capital from devel-

Countries," working paper WPS131 (World Bank, December 1988); and Charles E. Mc-Lure, Jr., "The 1986 Act: Tax Reform's Finest Hour or Death Throes of the Income Tax?" *National Tax Journal* vol. 41, no. 3 (Sept. 1988), 303–16. Among government studies are U.S. Department of the Treasury, *Blueprints for Basic Tax Reform* (Washington, 1977), and U.S. Department of the Treasury, *Tax Reform for Fairness, Simplicity, and Economic Growth* (Washington, 1984). A detailed analysis in a developing country context is Charles E. McLure, Jr., et al., *The Taxation of Income from Business and Capital in Colombia* (Durham, N.C., 1989).

oped countries because of tax-induced difficulties. Developed countries need to employ responsible fiscal policies that avoid worsening the plight of these capital-poor countries.

The paper begins in section 2 with a thumbnail sketch of taxation of business income and capital under the two alternative approaches, income and consumption. The first part of the discussion notes the greater simplicity of the consumption-based alternative, the second concentrates on the different economic effects of the two taxes (as indicated by the marginal effective tax rate), and the third assesses relative advantages and disadvantages of the two alternatives.

Section 3 describes traditional conventions for dealing with income generated from international investment under the income tax. It notes that as actually implemented, these rules create important incentives for capital flows that make no sense. This is particularly true of the tax treatment of income from portfolio investment, the primary focus of this paper.

Section 4 examines whether adoption of a consumption-based tax could eliminate—or at least alleviate—international problems with the income tax.

THE TWO ALTERNATIVES[3]

The most important distinction between income- and consumption-based taxes is their treatment of timing, debt, and interest. Some income taxes also allow for inflation when measuring income—or are harmed by failing to do so; under a consumption-based tax, inflation adjustment is not necessary.

Administrative Differences

The present tax liability may be significantly affected by when income is recognized for tax purposes and when deductions can be taken for expenses. Depreciation allowances are the best-known timing issue.[4] If an income tax is truly to measure economic income, depreciation allowances must be based on accurate estimates of economic depreciation—the loss of assets' income-producing capacity. By comparison, if the tax

---

[3] This discussion draws heavily on my joint work with George Zodrow. See especially McLure et al., *Taxation of Income from Business and Capital in Colombia*; and Zodrow and McLure, "Implementing Direct Consumption Taxes in Developing Countries." These are hereafter cited by shortened forms of the titles only.

[4] Issues similar to those involving the tax treatment of depreciable assets arise for many other types of long-lived assets, such as depletable assets and assets subject to amortization. These are not examined in detail; rather they are subsumed under the broad term "depreciable assets."

base is consumption, expensing—immediate write-off for the entire cost of the asset in the first year—must be allowed.

Under the income tax, borrowing and lending (and repayment of debt) have no tax consequences. Interest income is included in the tax base, and a deduction is allowed for interest expense. Because of the tax treatment of debt and interest, there are inevitably complicated questions of when income is deemed earned and when deductions can be taken.[5] It is also difficult to differentiate between interest and dividends, which are taxable to the recipient but not deductible by the payer; this problem is less important in countries such as Mexico that have a corporate deduction for dividends paid or in countries such as Canada where corporation income tax is treated (at least in part) as a withholding tax.

There are two ways to deal with debt and interest under a consumption-based tax.[6] Under the cash-flow version, the proceeds of borrowing (and debt repayments received) are included with interest income in the tax base; similarly, lending (and repayment of debt) is deductible along with interest expense. The tax base is clearly consumption, because it includes the amount borrowed but not reinvested (through either investment in depreciable assets or relending).

Although this approach defines the base of a consumption-based tax in the most conceptually appealing way, it would be more difficult to administer than an alternative that has received less attention.[7] For this reason, the rest of the discussion will focus on the alternative called the "tax prepayment approach," the Simplified Alternative Tax, or simply Plan X.[8]

---

[5] One of the most straightforward of these issues is deciding when to recognize income and allow deductions for interest of original-issue "discount" bonds. Allowing the lender to recognize income only when the debt is repaid improperly postpones recognition of income. Allowing the borrower to deduct the interest implicit in the discount on a straight-line basis is also too generous. In both cases, the same compound interest assumption should be used to determine accrual for tax purposes.

[6] For a more complete discussion, see *Taxation of Income in Colombia* or "Implementing Direct Consumption Taxes in Developing Countries"; for earlier discussions, see U.S. Department of the Treasury, *Blueprints for Basic Tax Reform* and Institute for Fiscal Studies, *Structure and Reform of Direct Taxation*.

[7] See *Taxation of Income in Colombia* or "Implementing Direct Consumption Taxes in Developing Countries," for both the rationale for the terms used to describe these two approaches and the reason the tax prepayment approach is administratively superior to the cash-flow approach. Boadway, Bruce, and Mintz, in their "Corporate Taxation in Canada," reject the cash-flow approach because it fails to reach inframarginal returns to financial transactions.

[8] See, for example, *Taxation of Income in Colombia*; "Implementing Direct Consumption Taxes in Developing Countries"; and Bradford, *Untangling the Income Tax*; and Bradford, "What Are Consumption Taxes and Who Pays Them?"

Under the Simplified Alternative Tax, there would be separate taxes for businesses and individuals. The individual tax would apply only to labor income and to gifts and bequests received.[9] For both businesses and individuals, borrowing and lending would have no tax consequences. But interest income (and dividends) would be tax-exempt, and interest expense (and dividends paid) would be nondeductible. Capital assets (with the possible exception of owner-occupied housing) would be held in business form.

Under special circumstances, the present value of the tax base under the Simplified Alternative Tax is equivalent to that under the cash-flow approach.[10] Thus the Simplified Alternative Tax is commonly classified as a consumption-based tax, although it is more obviously a tax on labor income.[11]

Inflation poses special problems for an income tax, which has traditionally been based on recorded historical values. Since inflation erodes the value of principle, it causes both real interest income and deductions for real interest expense to be overstated. It also causes tax to be paid on capital gains that are not real and even when losses occur. Finally, capital cannot be recovered tax-free when inflation erodes the real value of depreciation allowances and costs of goods sold from investors. It is clear that under such a system, taxable income will equal real economic income under inflationary conditions only by accident; more often income will be mismeasured, and inequities and distortions will result. Introducing partial and/or ad hoc adjustments for inflation may relieve some of these problems, but may accentuate others and open opportunities for arbitrage.[12]

Inflation poses no such problems for consumption-based taxes such as the Simplified Alternative Tax. Since neither debt nor interest flows have

[9] No deduction would be allowed donors. This treatment of gifts and bequests is not inherent in the tax-prepayment approach. Many tax experts, including myself, consider this treatment indispensible on equity grounds. See "Implementing Direct Consumption Taxes in Developing Countries." For a discussion of the analogous treatment under the cash-flow approach, see Henry J. Aaron and Harvy Galper, *Assessing Tax Reform* (Washington, 1985).

[10] See, for example, *Taxation of Income in Colombia* or "Implementing Direct Consumption Taxes in Developing Countries."

[11] This statement would be modified if gifts and bequests were included in the tax base of transferees, as suggested, but so would the characterization of the individual cash-flow tax, as a tax on consumption, be altered if the tax applied to gifts and bequests were made; for ease of exposition this qualification is ignored in what follows.

[12] See *Taxation of Income in Colombia* for further discussion of the problems caused by an unindexed income tax and means of dealing with the problem. See Francisco Gil Diaz, "Some Lessons from Mexico's Tax Reform," in *The Theory of Taxation for Developing Countries* (Oxford, 1987), for a description of Mexican attempts to deal with inflation in capital-gains taxes and corporate income taxes.

any tax consequences and all expenditures (including those on depreciable assets, other capital assets, and additions to inventories) are immediately expensed, there is no need for inflation adjustment under the Simplified Alternative Tax.

Economic Differences

It is difficult to compare tax systems that have different structural features such as the treatment of capital assets and inflation in measuring income from business and capital. Economists have recently developed the marginal effective tax rate (METR) to compare how alternative regimes tax an investment's income over its lifetime.[13] The METR is the percentage by which taxation reduces the before-tax real rate of return to a marginal investment. For example, if the before-tax return on a marginal investment is 10 percent and the after-tax return is 6.5 percent, the METR would be 35 percent.

An income tax based on an accurate measure of real economic income reduces the return to a marginal investment by a fraction equal to the statutory tax rate; thus the METR equals the statutory rate. By comparison, under a consumption-based tax the METR is zero. Take an equity-financed investment, for example. Suppose that a business investor subject to a 35 percent marginal tax rate contemplates a marginal investment of $1,000 that yields 10 percent before taxes. With expensing, the $1,000 investment produces a $350 tax saving, and thus really costs the private investor only $650. When the investment yields $100 before taxes, the government takes $35 and the investor keeps $65. Since the investor earns the same 10 percent rate of return on the $650 investment as in absence of taxation, the METR is zero. In essence, the government is a 35 percent partner in the venture, and the $35 in "tax revenues" it receives are best understood as the return on its $350 investment of forgone tax revenues. The individual portion of the Simplified Alternative Tax achieves the same result (a zero METR) simply by exempting income from capital.[14]

If investment incentives (accelerated depreciation allowances, investment tax credits, and so on) are provided under an income tax, the METR will be lower than the statutory rate, at least in a world without inflation. If equally generous allowances are not available for all investments, METRs will not be uniform across industries and assets, and capi-

[13] For the development of this concept, see Mervyn A. King and Don Fullerton, eds., *The Taxation of Income from Capital* (Chicago, 1984).
[14] For a more detailed exposition of this proposition, see Charles E. McLure, Jr., "Expensing," in *The Jamaican Tax Reform* (Boston, forthcoming); or "Implementing Direct Consumption Taxes in Developing Countries."

tal will be misallocated. During inflationary times, mismeasurement of real income and misallocation of resources occur even under a system that would measure income accurately and be neutral in the context of price stability. This explains much of the impetus for attempting to unify METRs across investments by conforming taxable income to real economic income.[15]

Of special interest here is the fact that if METRs applied to a particular industry differ greatly between countries, a distortion of the international allocation of resources may result.[16] Moreover, proposals that would produce differentials of this type are likely to be politically vulnerable because they would work to the disadvantage of domestic producers. In discussions leading to the U.S. Tax Reform Act of 1986, those who opposed defining taxable income as more closely approximating economic income cited favorable treatment of the same industry in Canada as a reason preferential U.S. proposals should not be eliminated.

The range of possible METRs is not bounded by zero. If investment allowances under an income tax are more generous in present value terms than expensing, the METR will be negative. This occurred in the United States during the early 1980s. The combination of accelerated depreciation and the investment tax credit was estimated to be roughly equivalent to expensing in real present value terms at the rate of inflation in 1981; it thus became more generous than expensing when inflation declined.

In the case of debt finance, the combination of expensing (or its equivalent) and debt finance results in negative METRs. Even if we account for taxes paid by lenders, the aggregate METR will be negative if, as is common, lenders are in lower marginal tax brackets than borrowers. Negative METRs cause special reason for concern when no clear external benefits to investment exist, because they imply that the private (after-tax) return to an investment is higher than the social return (indicated by the before-tax rate of return).

To dramatize the adverse effects of negative METRs, we might note that with a METR of minus 100 percent—hardly an unusual figure in the upside-down world of negative METRs—an investment that would yield only 5 percent before tax would yield 10 percent after tax.[17] With a

[15] See U.S. Department of the Treasury, *Blueprints for Basic Tax Reform*.

[16] Where multinational corporations are involved, the validity of this statement may depend on the tax regime in the home country of the parent—that is, on whether there is a territorial system or a worldwide system, and, in the latter case, on the treatment of income retained by the subsidiary and the creditability of foreign taxes.

[17] A METR of minus 90 percent is reported for equity-financed investment in vehicles in a world with price stability in U.S. Department of the Treasury, *Tax Reform for Fairness, Simplicity, and Economic Growth* 2 (Washington, 1984), 156. Debt finance would make many negative METRs much higher in absolute value.

statutory rate of 50 percent, such an investment would compete favorably with a fully taxed project yielding 20 percent. Of course, for a country to be indifferent between investments yielding 5 percent and 20 percent is pure folly.

Negative METRs could not exist under a logically consistent Simplified Alternative Tax. Expensing, the ultimate investment allowance, reduces the METR on equity-financed investment only to zero; a negative METR cannot occur. Nor can debt-finance make the METR negative, since interest expense is not deductible. Nor are these results dependent on the rate of inflation; the zero METR is independent of the rate of inflation. (I should note here that first, a logically consistent income tax also would not have the defects that characterize most actual systems and second, it is possible that a defective version of the Simplified Alternative Tax that produced negative METRs could be enacted; for example, by allowing investment incentives or interest deductions in addition to immediate expensing. Which of the two systems is more likely to constrain METRs to be positive cannot be settled a priori.)

Pros and Cons of the Alternatives

Economists commonly extol the economic virtues of a consumption-based tax. Under certain restrictive circumstances, such a tax does not distort the allocation of capital between current consumption and saving for future consumption. While these special circumstances will almost certainly remain unrealized, these potentially important advantages will nonetheless likely be approximated.[18]

A consumption-based tax is also considered superior to the income tax because of its horizontal equity. Under certain circumstances, the present value of tax that will be paid over the lifetime of an individual is independent of when the individual's income is earned and when it is spent.[19] Moreover, if gifts and bequests are taxed to the transferee with no deduction for the transferor, the tax base is the lifetime endowment of the taxpayer, arguably a better measure of taxpaying ability than either consumption or annual income.[20] Nonetheless, opponents of the Simplified Alternative Tax commonly cite its effects on vertical equity, noting that elimination of tax on income from marginal investment would greatly reduce the progressivity of taxation.[21] Whether taxing gifts and bequests

---

[18] See also David F. Bradford, "The Case for a Personal Consumption Tax," in *What Should Be Taxed: Income or Expenditure?* (Washington, 1980), 75–113.

[19] *Ibid.*

[20] See Aaron and Galper, *Assessing Tax Reform.*

[21] Richard A. Musgrave, "Short of Euphoria," *Economic Perspectives* vol. 1, no. 1 (Summer 1987), 59–71.

would offset the distributional effect of eliminating tax on the marginal return to capital deserves further attention.

My own view is that intertemporal neutrality and horizontal equity are not the primary attractions of a consumption-based direct tax, especially given its potentially adverse effects on vertical equity.[22] (Taxation of gifts and bequests, considered by many to be an important component of any scheme for a consumption-based tax with acceptable vertical equity, may even largely eliminate intertemporal neutrality advantages.) Much more important are the simplifications of the tax law that might be possible under the Simplified Alternative Tax.

Since all quantities relevant for measuring the tax base occur in current monetary values, there is no need to deal with timing issues and no need for inflation adjustment. There is also no need to distinguish between the purchase of capital assets (which are only depreciable under an income tax) and other expenditures (which can be deducted immediately). The existence of bearer bonds and the political and technical difficulties of enacting withholding on interest would be irrelevant, since tax would in effect be collected by forbidding interest deductions. I have argued elsewhere that these administrative advantages (and others) make the Simplified Alternative Tax a potentially attractive alternative for both the United States and for developing countries.[23]

Nor does it seem that any increase in savings that might result from switching to a consumption-based tax would justify such a switch by a small closed economy; presumably in such an economy the level of investment would not be determined primarily by domestic saving, except under quite stringent and effective exchange controls.[24] On the other hand, the Simplified Alternative Tax may prevent tax-induced outflows of portfolio capital, some of which are motivated by tax evasion.

[22] I would favor movement to a consumption-based direct tax only if gifts and bequests were included in the tax base of the recipient and no deduction were allowed for such transfers. A detailed discussion of this point is beyond the scope of this paper, but see "Implementing Direct Consumption Taxes in Developing Countries" or McLure, "The 1986 Act."

[23] See Charles E. McLure, Jr., "Lessons for LDCs of U.S. Income Tax Reform" in *Tax Reform in Developing Countries* (Durham, N.C., 1989); or McLure, "The 1986 Act."

[24] One can hardly avoid reference to the work in Martin Feldstein and Charles Horioka, "Domestic Saving and International Capital Flows," *Economic Journal* 90 (June 1980), 314–29; and Martin Feldstein, "Domestic Saving and International Capital Movements in the Long Run and the Short Run," *European Economic Review* 21 (Mar.-Apr. 1983), 129–51, which indicate a surprisingly close relation between domestic saving and investment across countries. In "A Few Good Taxes," *New Republic* (30 Nov. 1987), 14–15, Lawrence Summers suggests that the result reported may reflect government policies to prevent unacceptable capital flows, rather than a lack of international mobility of investment funds.

CONVENTIONS OF INTERNATIONAL TAXATION

The "rules of the game" for taxing income flowing between countries can set the stage for what follows. The ways in which common practice departs from those rules—especially those departures involving taxation more generous than expected—are important.[25]

In principle, income might be taxed where it originates, under the "source" principle, or where its recipients owe tax allegiance, under the "residence" principle. Countries that tax only income originating within their jurisdiction are said to follow the "territorial" approach; those that tax all the income of their residents, regardless of source, follow the "worldwide" approach.[26]

Economists have traditionally favored the worldwide approach. Basing taxation on the residence of the taxpayer and including worldwide income in the tax base seems necessary to achieve horizontal equity among taxpayers. Moreover, this approach contributes to capital-export neutrality, at least in principle. If the same tax will be due regardless of where capital is invested, taxation does not affect the allocation of the world's capital stock among competing countries.

By comparison, economists have traditionally had little good to say about the economic effects of source-based taxation, commonly the favorite of business. By producing a level playing field in the taxing nation, source-based taxation produces capital-import neutrality; but economists agree that this form of neutrality is insubstantial. Rather, source-based taxation distorts the allocation of the world's capital stock toward low-tax jurisdictions. On the other hand, use of the source principle can be seen as a compromise with reality. Many countries—especially less-developed countries (LDCs)—may simply be unable to enforce a residence-based tax.

The choice between source and residence as the basis for taxation clearly can have important implications for the distribution of tax base between source and residence countries. Developing countries, being capital importers, have commonly favored the source principle.[27] They argue, with considerable academic support, that they are entitled to tax

[25] For a more complete discussion, see Charles E. McLure, Jr., "U.S. Tax Laws and Capital Flight from Latin America," in *InterAmerican Law Review* 20 (Spring 1989).

[26] See Peggy B. Musgrave, *United States Taxation of Foreign Investment Income: Issues and Arguments* (Cambridge, Mass., 1969). In his chapter in the present volume, Fernando Sánchez Ugarte applies this analysis to the tax system of Mexico.

[27] For a statement of the case for source-based taxation in Latin America, see Aldolfo Atchabahian, "The Andean Subregion and Its Approach to Avoidance or Alleviation of International Double Taxation," in *Fiscal Harmonization in the Andean Countries* (Amsterdam, 1975), 7–33.

the income produced within their boundaries.[28] Developed countries, however, have commonly favored the residence principle, reflecting their status as capital exporters.

Unless all countries adopt the same approach, there will be gaps and overlaps when taxing income from foreign investment. As a practical matter, the country of source gets first crack at the income, and residence countries must adapt, either by exempting foreign-source income (that is, adopting the territorial principle), by allowing a credit for foreign taxes paid, or by allowing a deduction for foreign taxes, which provides only partial relief from double taxation.[29] Especially important for this discussion is the fact that the United States allows foreign tax credits for taxes paid to host governments. (Canada allows credits for foreign taxes paid on portfolio income, but exempts foreign-source income from direct investment. See Brean for a description.)[30] Moreover, it taxes income of foreign subsidiaries only when the income is repatriated as dividends. Brean argues that it is reasonable to assume a zero residence-based tax on foreign-source income in the United States.[31]

Capital-importing countries commonly tax income earned in a domestic trade or business under the same tax regime, whether it is earned by "true" residents or by foreigners operating through branches or domestically chartered subsidiaries. Remittances of interest, dividends, and perhaps branch profits (as well as other forms of income) are commonly subject to additional withholding taxes. Such withholding taxes are generally creditable under the laws of countries that allow foreign tax credits, up to the domestic tax that would be due on the income.

In order to reduce the source country's taxation of such income, developed countries attempt to negotiate foreign tax treaties under which such withholding taxes are reduced to below the standard rate. This has long been the subject of controversy between developed and developing countries, which see little to be gained from such treaties, and there are relatively few treaties between countries at greatly different stages of development.[32] The existence of such treaties creates the phenomenon of

[28] Peggy B. Musgrave, "Interjurisdictional Coordination of Taxes on Capital Income," in Sijbren Cnossen, ed., *Tax Coordination in the European Community* (New York, 1987), 197–225.
[29] See, for example, *U.S. Taxation of Foreign Investment Income* or G. C. Hufbauer, "A Guide to Law and Policy," in *U.S. Taxation of American Business Abroad* (Washington and Stanford, Calif., 1975), 1–6.
[30] D. J. S. Brean, *International Issues in Taxation: The Canadian Perspective* (Toronto, 1984).
[31] *Ibid.*
[32] The differences in viewpoints are captured in the very different provisions of the OECD and UN Model Treaties.

"treaty-shopping," the channeling of investment through countries with which there are favorable treaties in order to avoid withholding taxes.[33]

Many developed countries unilaterally reduce or eliminate taxes on interest (and perhaps other forms of income) paid to foreigners. The United States, for example, taxes no bank interest paid to foreigners, taxes portfolio interest only under special circumstances, and does not tax capital gains realized by foreigners, other than those on real estate.[34]

Various interpretations can be given to this phenomenon. It may simply reflect the view that income should be taxed only at residence. In this view, the field is simply vacated so the residence country can tax the income involved. This interpretation seems altogether too charitable, since one does not ordinarily expect tax provisions that could be used to gain concessions from others to be unilaterally given away. Moreover, this view reveals an attitude toward residence countries that is either un-realistic or cynical. Many LDCs, especially those in Latin America, do not attempt to tax on a worldwide basis, and those that do make the attempt are almost certainly not successful.[35] For the United States to exempt the income involved gives foreign investors an untaxed alterna-tive to taxable investment at home.

A more accurate interpretation includes the desire to attract investment from abroad and the competitive pressures to exempt income on such investment to avoid putting domestic borrowers at a disadvantage in world capital markets. The rationale for such a policy is well stated in Brean:

International markets for portfolio capital are broad, competitive, and highly efficient. As a result, national policies to restrict capital outflows or to limit capi-tal inflows generally impose national costs with relatively little consequences for international capital markets. . . . The efficiency of international capital markets causes the interest on foreign portfolio investment to be a poor choice for a tax base. A withholding tax on interest paid abroad drives up the gross-of-tax yield required by foreign lenders and, in the process, it pushes up the level of all do-mestic interest rates. . . . [I]nterest-sensitive private decisions, notably investment decisions, are affected negatively by the increase in the cost of capital.[36]

In some cases, exempting interest paid to foreigners is an explicit decision to try to attract portfolio capital from abroad. Clear evidence of this purpose can be found in the report of the Fowler task force submitted to

---

[33] See Milka Casanegra de Jantscher, "Tax Havens Explained," *Finance and Develop-ment* vol. 13, no. 1 (Mar. 1976), 31–34.

[34] See McLure, "U.S. Tax Laws and Capital Flight," for a survey of U.S. practice in this area.

[35] *Ibid.*

[36] Brean, *International Issues in Taxation*, 41.

President Johnson in 1964: "revision of U.S. taxation of foreign investors is one of the most immediate and productive ways to increase the flow of foreign capital into this country."[37] Similarly, when dealing with the large gap in its taxation of portfolio interest paid to foreigners caused by its treaty with the Netherlands Antilles, the United States, in 1984, repealed withholding on almost all such interest, rather than simply repealing the treaty.[38] This raises another important variable in the equation. Many European countries do not tax interest earned on bearer bonds, presumably in response to domestic pressures.

Such policies have a variety of undesirable effects. First, they attract funds into the country and provide generous treatment for the income involved. LDCs that can ill afford to lose capital, and yet are unable to implement the residence principle, are thus victimized by the "beggar-thy-neighbor" tax policies of developed countries such as the United States. Capital formation, economic development, tax revenues, and equity are all reduced in the country from which capital is attracted. Nor is this only a matter of academic concern; in a recent discussion of tax reform in Mexico, Gil Díaz offers the following analysis:

[T]here is no doubt that the Mexican economy has been open to international currency and financial transactions. It also shares a large border with the largest capital market in the world. . . . As a result, *financial interest income cannot be taxed*. If a tax is applied to interest, it will have to be grossed up to maintain the net-of-tax interest rate. In this case, the tax is borne by credit users, most likely smaller firms and less wealthy individuals without access to international credit markets. The tax will also affect domestic financial intermediaries, making them smaller in size than they would otherwise be. (emphasis added)[39]

Second, these policies invite residents of the taxing country to channel investments through foreign countries and take advantage of the preferential treatment their own governments accord foreign-earned income. Evidence exists that residents of the United States were channeling flows of funds through treaty countries for reinvestment in the United States even before the 30 percent tax on portfolio interest was eliminated.[40]

[37] "The Task Force on Promoting Increased Foreign Investment in United States Corporate Securities and Increased Foreign Financing for United States Corporations Operating Abroad," reprinted in *Legislative History of H. R. 13103, 89th Congress, 2d session, Foreign Investors Tax Act of 1966* (Washington, 1967).

[38] See Alan Winston Granwell, "Repeal of the 30 Percent Withholding Tax on Interest Paid to Foreigners," *Tax Management International Journal* 13 (1984), 306–11

[39] As further evidence on this score, it might be noted that Leopoldo Solis, in his *Economic Policy Reform in Mexico: A Case Study for Developing Countries* (New York, 1981), 75, describes an interesting episode in which the Central Bank of Mexico sided with opponents of elimination of bearer bonds, citing fear of capital flight to the United States.

[40] See Allaire Urban Karzon, "International Tax Evasion: Spawned in the United States

In the extreme case, there would be relatively little investment directly in one's own country; either one would actually invest elsewhere on a tax-exempt (or tax-preferred) basis or one would use foreign mailboxes to evade taxes while investing at home. In either situation the result is similar: tax-induced capital flows that exist only to avoid or evade domestic taxation. As Bird has noted, "An international tax system that places the main burden of taxing portfolio investment on the countries in which investors reside rather than those in which they earn their money is a system that both encourages excessive international capital flows and undermines the domestic taxation of capital in general."[41] Karzon has expressed the same sentiment in even stronger terms:

[T]he historical United States . . . treaty policy . . . fosters international tax evasion by favoring residency-basis taxation over source-basis taxation for portfolio income. . . . [O]rientation toward residency country taxation of portfolio income should be reappraised, and a return to source-country taxation should be reconsidered. . . . The merit of source-country taxation lies in its simplicity of administration and certainty of tax collection. . . . [T]his shift might enhance rapport with developing countries, long advocates of source taxation.[42]

POTENTIAL SOLUTIONS

Richard Bird calls for a new international order for taxing income flowing across national boundaries. In this he distinguishes between two different problems: the taxation of income from direct investment and the taxation of income from portfolio investment.[43] Most of the following discussion relates to the taxation of portfolio income—despite Bird's warning that "reform of the taxation of international portfolio investment, although more needed by most criteria than that of direct investment, seems likely to prove more difficult."[44]

The situation described above creates problems for all three countries of North America. For Canada and Mexico there is the possibility that domestically owned portfolio capital will be invested in the United States

and Nurtured by Secrecy Havens," *Vanderbilt Journal of Transnational Law* vol. 16, no. 4 (Fall 1983), 757–832, and Richard A. Gordon, "Tax Havens and Their Use by United States Taxpayers—An Overview," a report to the Commissioner of Internal Revenue, the Assistant Attorney General (Tax Division) and the Assistant Secretary of the Treasury (Tax Policy), 12 Jan. 1981.

41 Richard M. Bird, "Shaping a New International Tax Order," *Bulletin* of the International Bureau for Fiscal Documentation 42 (July 1988), 292–303.

42 Karzon, "International Tax Evasion."

43 For further discussion of this important distinction, see Brean, *International Issues in Taxation.*

44 On this, see Bird, "Shaping a New International Tax Order"; and Charles E. McLure, Jr., *Economic Perspectives on State Taxation of Multijurisdictional Corporations* (Arlington, Va., 1986).

rather than at home. For the United States, there is the risk of tax evasion by residents using foreign addresses to invest at home.

The Income Tax Approach

One strategy is to improve implementation of the worldwide approach under the income tax. This plan seems more or less hopeless, especially for Canada and Mexico. After all, the United States does follow the worldwide approach, arguably has one of the best tax administrations in the world, and yet cannot even prevent evasion of U.S. taxes by its own citizens using foreign addresses; it is hard to believe its two neighbors could do better. For the same reason there seems to be little hope that exchange-of-information agreements would do much good. If the United States, which has access to some of the relevant information, cannot tax its own residents, it will probably be unable to provide enough useful information for the governments of Canada or Mexico to tax theirs.

A potentially more promising alternative would be for the United States to repeal the exemptions for both bank and portfolio interest. This would considerably reduce the problems faced by all three countries, but it would not eliminate them. As long as there are untaxed alternative investment outlets in the rest of the world, tax-induced capital flows may be a problem. Unilateral repeal is most attractive as a way to raise revenues and deal with the specter of Americans using offshore addresses to earn tax-free U.S. income.[45] There does not, however, appear to be much support for such action.

Finally, the United States will probably continue to be reluctant to repeal existing exemptions, except as part of a multilateral effort to deal with the problem. This is especially true when one considers the U.S. balance-of-payments position and its explicit use of exemptions to attract the capital needed to finance its balance-of-payments deficits.

It is reasonable to believe that a new international order for taxation of income flowing across national borders is desirable. But not much evidence exists that this view is widely held. Indeed, there would be substantial opposition to eliminating the preferential treatment now accorded portfolio income by source countries. Bird notes that:

The nontaxation of such flows is politically popular with three powerful (if unspoken) allies: business enterprises seeking cheaper capital, the financial institutions that run the system, and the increasingly large group of tax minimizers (evaders or avoiders, as the legal niceties may be) who supply the money. Change

[45] It is interesting, though perhaps not indicative of the direction policy might have taken under a Democratic administration in 1989, that Lawrence Summers, said to be an adviser to Governor Michael Dukakis, advocated taxing capital income earned in the United States by foreigners in his article "A Few Good Taxes."

will not come easily or soon in the face of such opposition. But it must, in the end, occur—perhaps through the reassertion of the source principle—if anything like the present income tax is to continue to exist in this increasingly integrated world.[46]

Moreover, the continued availability of treaty-shopping—the use of tax treaties by residents of third countries—implies that one may continue to invest in the United States on a tax-preferred basis, even if current exemptions were repealed by all nations (unless an agreement is arrived at on the problem of treaty-shopping). Of course, it is one thing to agree to tax all income originating within one's borders; it is quite another to assist third-party countries in preventing abuse of the treaty by their residents.

In short, there is little hope that a solution will soon be found to these problems within the framework of the traditional income tax. Given the interest that has been expressed in consumption-based taxation, it is natural to ask whether the Simplified Alternative Tax holds out more hope.

The Simplified Alternative Tax

If adopted by all countries, the Simplified Alternative Tax would clearly eliminate the problems discussed above. Income from portfolio investment would be taxed where it originates without deductions for interest and dividends. (It would thus be inappropriate to tax the income on a residence basis when received, because this would both create double international taxation and be inconsistent with the basic structure of the Simplified Alternative Tax, which exempts all interest and dividend income.) Tax havens and treaty shopping would thus be things of the past, at least as far as portfolio investment is concerned.[47]

Of course it can be argued that the elimination of tax-induced capital flows and tax havens has been purchased at a high price: the elimination of taxation of the marginal income from capital and all that means for vertical equity.[48] Moreover, some countries would presumably refuse to

[46] Bird, "Shaping a New International Tax Order."

[47] Income from inframarginal investments would continue to be taxed at source under the business part of the Simplified Alternative Tax. Dividends resulting from foreign direct investment would be exempt in the parent company's country of residence under the general exemption of intercorporate dividends. If such dividends were to be taxed, it seems likely that foreign tax credits would be allowed. James B. Davies and France St-Hilaire, in their *Reforming Capital Income Taxation in Canada: Efficiency and Distributional Effects of Alternative Options* (Ottawa, 1987), 66, note that it is illogical for a small open economy to allow credits for taxes paid to foreign governments.

[48] See "Implementing Direct Consumption Taxes in Developing Countries" for an extended discussion of this topic.

forbid interest deductions for the same reason that they levy no withholding tax on interest paid to foreigners: such a policy would raise the
cost of borrowing by their nationals. For these and other reasons, universal adoption of the Simplified Alternative Tax seems unlikely. Thus it
seems worthwhile to inquire about the effects on international capital
flows and investment a country could expect if it acted alone to adopt
the Simplified Alternative Tax.

Since the METR under the Simplified Alternative Tax is zero, domestic
investment of national capital would be accorded the same treatment as
tax-preferred foreign investment. This should result in greater incentives for domestic investment, except in those cases in which tax incentives for investment under the income tax are even more generous than
the Simplified Alternative Tax. (Of course, the elimination of negative
METRs inherent in the adoption of the Simplified Alternative Tax would
help prevent unproductive domestic investment in that case.) The potential benefits from eliminating the disincentive for domestic investment
are among the relatively neglected advantages of the Simplified Alternative Tax.[49]

A potentially crucial question for many countries contemplating adoption of the Simplified Alternative Tax is whether the tax and any withholding tax accompanying it would be creditable against the income tax
of the United States (and other countries that employ foreign tax credits).
The potential importance of this question is obvious. The burden of
taxes that are credited is, in effect, paid by the government of the capital-
exporting country rather than by the taxpayer; thus the taxes have no
adverse effect on foreign investment in the country. Taxes that are not
credited, however, are paid by the taxpayer and can reduce foreign investment. Presumably the creditability issue would be important primarily for businesses under the Simplified Alternative Tax.

Whether the tax would be eligible for foreign tax credit in the United
States is not clear. In order to prevent credit being taken for gross receipts
taxes, severance taxes, and other non-income taxes (especially those levied by oil-rich nations), the United States only credits taxes paid on net
income. If the emphasis is placed on income, the Simplified Alternative
Tax might seem not to qualify, since its structure is consistent with a
consumption tax, not an income tax. On the other hand, the tax is clearly
a tax on the net proceeds from business, since deductions are allowed for
all expenses other than interest. At the operational level, the question is
whether disallowing interest deductions would render the tax ineligible

[49] For an exception that recognizes this advantage, see Davies and St-Hilaire, *Reforming Capital Income Taxation.*

for credit. The immediate expensing of capital assets is sufficiently generous to overwhelm the effect of forbidding interest deductions on average; the net effect of the two provisions is a zero marginal effective tax rate. Thus there is at least some possibility that the tax would be creditable.

Of course, because the METR under the Simplified Alternative Tax is zero, the only source of net revenues from the tax is the return on inframarginal investment.[50] Therefore there may be a tendency for countries to want to supplement the tax with a withholding tax on remittances to foreigners. This raises the second question of whether the withholding tax is creditable. This is also unclear, but there is reason to believe that the creditability of the withholding tax depends on the creditability of the Simplified Alternative Tax itself.[51]

Finally, it is worth noting that the creditability issue may not be as important as it first appears. Recall that the United States employs what is called the "overall limitation" on the ability to credit foreign taxes against U.S. taxes; this means that all foreign-source income of a given type and all creditable taxes levied by foreign governments on that type of income are lumped together when calculating the foreign tax credit limit. Recent changes in U.S. law have reduced the ability of many American firms to obtain full credit for taxes paid to foreign governments. Thus "excess foreign tax credits"—foreign taxes paid in excess of what can be credited—are more common than before.[52] To a company with excess foreign tax credits, it may make relatively little difference whether the taxes levied by a particular country are creditable.[53]

CONCLUDING REMARKS

This paper is a preliminary look at a relatively small piece of the investment strategies and fiscal harmonization puzzle. In particular, I concentrated on whether it makes sense for the three countries of North America to consider shifting to a system of direct taxation based on con-

[50] See David G. Hartman, "The Welfare Effects of a Capital Income Tax in an Open Economy," working paper 1551 (Cambridge, Mass., National Bureau of Economic Research, 1985). Hartman suggests that under certain circumstances, tax revenues may constitute an important part of incoming investment benefits.

[51] See *Taxation of Income in Colombia.*

[52] See Ugarte, "Taxation of Foreign Investment in Mexico." Ugarte notes that tightening U.S. rules for creditability will increase the extent of international double taxation.

[53] See also Brean's contention, in *International Issues*, 46, that "zero residence tax liability is a reasonable approximation to the present tax treatment of both U.S. foreign direct investment and Canadian direct investment abroad" and the conclusion of James B. Davies and France St-Hilaire, in *Reforming Capital Income Taxation*, 66, that "reductions in Canadian CIT (corporation income tax) cannot be opposed on the simple grounds that they will only result in an increase in payments to the U.S. Treasury."

sumption rather than income. There are good administrative reasons for considering such a shift, especially in a world in which inflation is expected and administrative talent—the patience to deal with complex provisions that are manageable, if only at a price—is scarce.

A consideration of international aspects of the question adds to the advantages of the Simplified Alternative Tax, especially for Mexico and Canada. Adoption of such a tax by Mexico would probably help reduce pressures for tax-induced capital flight. Its adoption by Canada would likely increase national welfare by attracting capital. Adoption of the Simplified Alternative Tax by the United States might have smaller domestic benefits than either Mexican or Canadian adoption, but the spillover of benefits to those two countries—and to others facing capital outflow to the United States—might well be important.

Direct Investment Strategies and the Canada-U.S. Free Trade Agreement

A. E. Safarian

M ANY CANADIANS are ambivalent about foreign-owned firms in Canada. They believe economic or political problems are associated with them, and consequently favor some degree of government control. Canadians are also aware of the economic benefits that such firms can bring, hence are reluctant to see them leave and may favor efforts to attract them.

What will Canada gain and give up with regard to foreign direct investment by the terms of the proposed free trade agreement with the United States?[1] That question presents at least two related issues. The first is how the proposed agreement affects the Canadian government's power to influence business decisions on flows of direct investment and activities of existing subsidiaries. The second concerns the effects of free trade itself on the behavior of existing foreign-owned firms.

The first section of this chapter outlines the investment provisions of the agreement and the effects on Canadian and U.S. policies. Canada

---

[1] The first section of this chapter is based on my article, "Investment Aspects of the Canada-U.S. Free Trade Agreement," in Murray G. Smith and Frank Stone, eds., *Assessing the Canada-U.S. Free Trade Agreement* (Halifax, N.S., 1987). The second section draws in part on my article, "The Relationship Between Trade Agreements and International Direct Investment," in David W. Conklin and Thomas J. Courchene, eds, *Canadian Trade at a Crossroads: Options for New International Agreements* (Toronto, 1985), 206–19. Useful analyses of the topics covered here can be found in David F. Burgess, "The Impact of Trade Liberalization on Foreign Direct Investment Flows," in *Canada-United States Free Trade* (Toronto, 1985), 193–99; Bernard M. Wolf, "The Reaction of U.S.-Based Multinational Enterprises to Free Trade Between Canada and the United States: Impediments to Empirical Verification," paper delivered to the Fourth International Congress, North American Economics and Finance (Montreal, July 1986), mimeo; and Asim Erdilek, Potential Impact of a Bilateral Free(r) Trade Agreement on U.S. Direct Investment in Canadian Manufacturing, working paper no. 1986–5 (Cleveland, Case Western Reserve University, 1986).

clearly made the larger concessions in this area, not so much in current policies as in possible future policies. We note, however, that Canada retains quite substantial powers to influence investment and firm behavior, provided it avoids more obvious forms of discrimination. In the second part, I examine the likely response of new direct investment and existing subsidiaries to the agreement, particularly in the case of manufacturing. Although there will be some divestment from Canada, there are substantial offsets—opportunities to rationalize production in Canada for export; competitive responses to free trade; third-country investments; and increased investment outside manufacturing.

GOVERNMENT POLICIES AND THE AGREEMENT

How will the agreement affect what Canada and the United States are now doing to regulate foreign direct investment? How will it affect their power to undertake policy on such investment in the future?

Major Investment Provisions

Briefly, the provisions on foreign investment are as follows:[2] "National Treatment" will be provided with certain exceptions for each other's investors. National treatment means that foreign-controlled firms are treated no less favorably than domestically-controlled firms in similar situations. This applies to measures affecting the establishment, acquisition, sale, and operation of business enterprises. More particularly, each party agrees that (1) it will not require that minimum levels of equity be held by nationals, (2) it will not require forced divesture, (3) there will be fair standards for expropriations and compensation, and (4) it will not impose export, local-content, local-sourcing, or import-substitution requirements on each others' investors. Some exceptions are provided for Crown corporations; for example, limitations can be placed on foreign ownership when such corporations are sold to private owners.

However, *all* existing laws, regulations, and published policies and practices not conforming to these obligations can be retained. That includes a long list in each country. Canada, for example, limits or prohibits foreign ownership in a variety of media, the energy sector, some types of transport, and uranium production. In the United States there are limitations on foreign ownership of broadcasting, land, and various aspects of transportation, among other sectors.[3]

---

[2] The provisions are from External Affairs Canada, *The Canada-U.S. Free Trade Agreement* (Ottawa, 1987), chaps. 14, 16, 17, and 20, and Article 2005.

[3] For a fuller list, see Organization for Economic Cooperation and Development (OECD), *Controls and Impediments Affecting Inward Direct Investment in OECD Member Countries* (Paris, 1987).

Canada agrees to raise progressively the review-exemption level for direct U.S. acquisitions of Canadian-owned firms from the current level of $5 million to $150 million in gross assets, measured in constant dollars. Review of indirect acquisitions, namely those where the parent firm's ownership changes, will be phased out.

The "cultural industries" are excluded from the investment chapter, both with regard to national treatment and the new limits to the review process. The right to trade-remedy actions in such industries is retained, however, with regard to future policies. Canada agrees to purchase such businesses at a fair value where divestiture is required.

Canada agrees to give U.S. firms national treatment with respect to ownership of Canadian financial institutions. In particular, this will end the 25 percent limit on foreign ownership of Canadian bank assets (although not the 10 percent limit for any one owner, domestic or foreign) and the limit on the total domestic assets of foreign bank subsidiaries. The United States agrees to give Canadian financial institutions the same treatment as U.S. institutions if the Glass-Steagall Act, which limits bank ownership of securities firms, is ended.

A number of other service industries are covered by applying principles similar to those in the investment chapter, namely provision for national treatment, right of establishment, right of commercial presence, transparency of policies, and provisions for dispute settlement.

The Effect on Present Policies

The first question is how the agreement will change what the two countries are now doing with respect to investment. As noted above, some sectors are now partly or wholly closed to foreign ownership in each country, and there are various forms of fiscal discrimination as well. There will be little change in these respects outside of financial services, because existing laws, regulations, and published policies and practices are exempted from national treatment. These exemptions include the Canadian ownership objectives in petroleum, gas, and uranium and the entire cultural sector as defined in the agreement. These sectors continue to be subject to present regulations on acquisitions and subject to a new rule on compensation for divestitures.

The United States has no comparable process for foreign investment review, thus Canada clearly made the concessions on this issue. Except for acquisitions of middle-sized firms, however, Canada has given up rather little in actual practice. This is true not only with respect to what Investment Canada has been doing since its inception but also with respect to the way the Foreign Investment Review Agency (FIRA) operated in its last two years or so.

FIRA's regulations and operations were significantly eased after 1982, except in the energy sector and cultural industries. In that year, the ceiling for small business investments was raised from 100 employees and $2 million in gross assets or planned investments to 200 employees and $5 million. New business proposals or direct acquisitions below these figures involved fewer data requirements and faster approval processes. In the previous decade, over 85 percent of all reviewable applications involved assets below $5 million. Other measures were also taken after 1982 to clarify and facilitate the review process.

The Investment Canada Act, which came into force June 30, 1985, was designed to encourage and facilitate investment in Canada, in contrast to the widespread perception regarding FIRA operations before 1982. Under Investment Canada only notification, not review, has been required for all new businesses (regardless of size), for all direct acquisitions with assets under $5 million, and for most indirect acquisitions with assets under $50 million. However, new businesses and smaller acquisitions in designated sectors such as the cultural industries have remained subject to review. Investment Canada has not rejected any of the acquisitions it reviewed.

The change to Investment Canada exempted from review the great majority of the number of cases reviewable by FIRA. Under the Canada-U.S. Free Trade Agreement, review of indirect acquisitions will be phased out entirely. This review has been used to some effect in the petroleum and cultural industries; in these two sectors the existing provisions have been retained. As for direct acquisitions, about two-thirds of total Canadian-controlled assets will still be reviewable when the new threshold on these is introduced. In effect, U.S. acquisitions of the 500 or so larger firms will continue to be reviewed.

Where Canada will change its current practice is in the $5 million- to $150 million-sized businesses. Although Investment Canada has rejected no acquisitions proposals involving firms of this or any other size group, it has often required commitments before allowing an acquisition. Under the FTA this will no longer be possible. Many of the firms in this size sector have experienced exceptionally rapid growth in recent years.

The existing benefit criteria for larger acquisitions will continue to apply under the FTA, except for those on foreign trade and stock equity. These criteria include the effects on competition and international competitiveness, employment of nationals, a range of research and productivity issues, and conformity with federal and provincial laws. Canada had already stopped making import requirements a condition of investment in response to a 1983 GATT ruling. It is doubtful that export requirements would survive a challenge under section 301 of the current

U.S. Trade Act, which targets such performance requirements imposed on foreign investors. Presumably, however, Canada can continue to negotiate product mandates, R & D, and technology-transfer commitments with larger firms, even though these could later affect trade flows.

The United States, in turn, has given up the right to review Canadian multinationals in the event such a review process is introduced against other countries. In the late 1970s, some congressional committees demanded such a review process, partly in response to acquisitions of U.S. firms by investors in Middle Eastern oil-exporting countries. An interdepartmental committee was established to advise the U.S. government on policy for inward direct investment and sensitive cases, but to date it falls short of being a review agency. The idea of a review agency is being revived in some quarters in response to the recent increase in foreign acquisitions of U.S. firms. The Exon-Florio amendment to the Trade Act of 1988 authorizes the President of the United States to reject a foreign takeover of a U.S. firm for national security reasons. This amendment, whose scope is not yet clear, includes Canada.

During the FTA negotiations, the U.S. government attempted to free direct-investment flows, reduce the limitations on existing subsidiaries, and constrain future government restrictions. This effort met with some success. However, one way to look at the FTA is that it allows Canada to continue to review larger acquisitions by U.S.-controlled firms, while guaranteeing Canadian multinationals both greater export access to the United States and, except in specified sectors, full security to invest and to operate there. Export access and investment access are largely complementary functions, as we will underline in the next section.

The liberal position taken by Canadian governments toward inward direct investment in the last four or five years is part of a worldwide trend. This trend reflects a variety of pressures and opportunities such as the economic adjustments posed by growing internationalization, a process in which multinationals often play a major role. In addition, Canada had other reasons for moving from negotiating commitments from such firms to providing a more attractive setting for both foreign- and domestically-owned multinationals. One reason is that foreign control of Canadian industry has fallen steadily from about 36 percent in 1970 to about 26 percent today.[4] Second, multinationals have concentrated their investments in fewer markets during the last decade or so, with the United States the major recipient. Competition for such investments by

[4]Statistics Canada, *Canada's International Investment Position, 1968–1970* and subsequent issues. By another measure, the degree of foreign ownership and equity in corporations that are 50 percent or more held abroad fell from 37 percent in 1971 to 24 percent in 1983. See Statistics Canada, *Corporations and Labour Unions Returns Act*, part 1, 1985.

Canada and other countries has increased correspondingly. Third, Canadian-owned multinationals have come of age quickly. The accumulated stock of overseas investment by Canadian multinationals, expressed as a percentage of the accumulated stock of investment in Canada by foreign multinationals, has risen from 20 percent in 1974 to at least 60 percent today and is increasing rapidly.

Canadian governments have often expressed concerns about direct investment that are common among host or recipient countries. The changes just noted have led Canadian authorities to emphasize some of the concerns of an important home country for multinationals, particularly the need for a more stable or less restrictive investment environment for such firms. (This will be achieved by the FTA.) A second concern has been that portion of Canadian direct investment in the United States that is attracted there, at least in part, to avoid actual or threatened protectionist measures. Home countries usually prefer that their firms export rather than invest abroad. In effect, the FTA reduces the incentive for protection-induced direct investment in the United States, while guaranteeing a more stable investment climate for other more important types of direct investment.

We conclude, therefore, that Canada has conceded little in terms of current policy practices on inward direct investment. U.S. acquisitions of smaller and medium-sized Canadian firms will not be reviewable. Canada explicitly retains the power to review acquisitions of the largest Canadian firms and also retains current policies that favor Canadian ownership in particular industries, with the major exception of financial services. At the same time, Canada gains more assured access to the United States for its firms, except in those sectors where the United States already restricts foreign ownership.

The Effect on Future Policies

The significance of the investment-policy changes to which Canada agreed depends on what has been secured from the United States throughout the FTA. It depends also on which of the changed policies could have been sustained and what one thinks of their value. For example, Canada forfeits the power to use import-duty waivers to attract foreign direct investment into the automobile industry; yet perhaps this practice would have been subjected to a countervailing-duty test in the United States before long.[5] As for the value of past policies, those who believe the policies were wrong in their assumptions about the effects of multinationals or that they were counterproductive in practice will not regret that his-

[5] Paul Wonnacott, *U.S. and Canadian Auto Policies in a Changing World Environment* (Toronto and Washington, 1987) concluded such a test was likely before long.

tory cannot be repeated in quite these ways.[6] Whatever one thinks of the particular measures used in the past, however, the fact remains that there are some valid concerns about both domestic and foreign multinationals. If past experience is any guide, these concerns and many more dubious claims will become politically irresistible at fuller employment and when resource profits soar. What happens then? What happens if new and unpredictable developments raise strong calls for intervention? While Canada made limited concessions in terms of current practice, it has agreed to some potentially significant changes in policies. For example, except in several sectors noted earlier, Canada will not be able in the future to review new inward direct investments, or indirect acquisitions where the foreign parent's ownership changes. Again, with the exceptions noted earlier, review of direct acquisitions will not be possible for the large number of smaller firms with assets under $150 million in constant dollars.

In such circumstances, the agreement requires that governments find ways to deal with these issues that do not discriminate by nationality of ownership. While many Canadians believe the contrary, strong evidence exists that the economic performance of foreign-owned firms is generally not inferior to that of domestically-owned firms once other determining variables are taken into account.[7] The FTA should encourage governments to consider the underlying sources of the problems rather than to concentrate on foreign-owned firms, as has often happened in the past. Moreover, where necessary the agreement would require that remedies apply to all firms that qualify, whether owned in Canada or the United States, whether multinational or uninational. The discipline this imposes could be salutary, or at least no worse than what happens now.

More specifically, Canada retains quite formidable powers to intervene with regard to investment. It retains the power to review larger acquisitions on a reduced set of criteria. Presumably, Canada can operate the review mechanism in low gear, as at present, or tighten up its application at some future time if it wishes. One observes that pattern even in the European Economic Community, although because it is a common market, the EEC has more limitations on discrimination against EEC investors than those proposed in the Canada-U.S. Free Trade Agreement.[8]

[6] My own evaluations of the major policies used in Canada are mostly negative, for reasons explained more fully in A. E. Safarian, "Government Control of Foreign Business Investment" in *Domestic Policies in the International Economic Environment* (Toronto, 1985).

[7] See Safarian, "Government Control of Foreign Business Investment."

[8] For operation of investment policies in countries in the European Economic Community, see A. E. Safarian, *Governments and Multinationals: Policies in the Developed Countries* (Washington, 1983).

In the 1986 Competition Act, Canada finally has what may turn out to be an effective set of civil law proceedings to deal with mergers and monopolies—now called abuse of dominant position—that substantially lessen competition. There are many interesting links between competition policy and investment-review policy, of which only three will be noted. First, an effective competition policy on mergers and monopolies removes a need for investment review. Countries such as the United States, United Kingdom, and the Federal Republic of Germany, all of which lack investment review agencies, have used competition policy to review, and discipline if necessary, some international mergers or monopolies.[9]

Second, the freer trade that the free trade agreement will bring will itself lead to increased international competition in a considerable number of industries, thereby limiting any tendency of domestic and multinational firms for anticompetitive behavior. Third, the FTA will likely increase not only new investment but also mergers, acquisitions, joint ventures, and other forms of domestic and foreign business activity as firms attempt to specialize production for export and otherwise penetrate each other's markets. While studies indicate that the overall economic effects will be favorable, the competitive effects in any particular industry are difficult to predict. This point will be taken up again when the competitive adjustments to free trade are considered.

Despite national treatment, each country can treat investors from the other differently to the extent necessary for prudential, fiduciary, health and safety, or consumer-protection reasons. Such treatment, although different, must be equivalent in effect to the treatment given its own investors (Art. 1602:8).

Canada retains the power to use a wide variety of across-the-board fiscal policies that will have a substantial impact on investment, so long as these policies do not discriminate by nationality of ownership. For example, the review agencies used the criterion of whether the investment would stimulate net exports. Some current tax-reform proposals have the same effect, but do not discriminate between firms by country of ownership. Indeed, within the investment chapter of the FTA, the two countries reserve the right to apply new taxes and subsidies that do not involve

[9]Grant L. Reuber and Thomas A. Wilson, "Merger Policy Proposals: An Evaluation," in *Canadian Competition Policy* (Toronto, 1979), argued a decade ago that the Foreign Investment Review Act should be rescinded and any elements considered essential should be integrated with a revised Competition Act. The efficiency gains test in the 1986 act is generally quite different from the criteria used by Investment Canada. The size tests are also different. Pre-merger notifications involve two size tests; the parties to the merger and their affiliates have assets or sales revenues in Canada exceeding $400 million; and the assets being acquired have a value or sales revenue exceeding $35 million.

"arbitrary or unjustifiable discrimination between investors of the parties or a disguised restriction on the benefits accorded to investors of the parties" (Chap. 16, Art. 1609). Time will tell what this means in practice, and the proposal is hedged by the dispute-settlement mechanism; it does appear to allow more leeway than simply applying across-the-board measures.

Canada more or less retains its present powers to engage in a wide range of industrial policies, subject only to the investment and trade provisions of the free trade agreement. Of course, if such policies are trade distorting, they will be subject to U.S. trade law as they are now. Only a strong code on subsidies binding both parties would have changed this, and the agreement contains no such code—at least not yet.

EFFECTS ON NEW AND EXISTING DIRECT INVESTMENTS

In recent years, the Canadian federal government has gone to great lengths to persuade multinational enterprises that Canada warmly welcomes their investments. Competition for such foreign direct investment has become commonplace among governments desperately attempting to increase jobs, tax revenues, and technical capacities and to reorganize entire industrial sectors. One concern is that the FTA will doom efforts to attract investment. Indeed, some argue that with Canadian protection reduced or eliminated, many manufacturing firms might withdraw from Canada. That was the central point, for example, in a report prepared for the Ontario government.[10] This concern deserves attention, considering that Canada's share of direct-investment inflows to thirteen developed market economies fell from 16 percent in the mid-1970s to 3 percent in the late 1970s and was negative in the early 1980s. Canada's contributions to outflows rose from 2 percent to 6 percent and 9 percent over this period.[11]

What is ultimately of interest here, however, is the multinational firm's response to the FTA. Many other economic variables and policies can affect investment by such firms. One needs to look at new investment and acquisitions abroad and the ongoing activities of existing subsidiaries in each country. At least three types of multinationals should be considered: U.S. multinationals with subsidiaries in Canada, Canadian multinationals with subsidiaries in the United States, and third-country multinationals with subsidiaries in either country. This analysis focuses largely on

[10] Jack Baranson, *An Assessment of the Likely Impact of a U.S.-Canadian Free Trade Agreement upon the Behaviour of U.S. Industrial Subsidiaries in Canada (Ontario)*, (Toronto, Ministry of Industry, Trade, and Technology, 1985).
[11] Safarian, "Government Control of Foreign Business Investment."

156   A. E. SAFARIAN

manufacturing rather than on primary products, since concerns about
divestment center on the former. Finally, it should be emphasized that the
objective of a free trade agreement is better defined as to increase economic efficiency and real incomes through a larger and more secure market, rather than to promote foreign direct investment.

U.S. Investment and the Canadian Manufacturing Sector

Canada has long relied on tariffs and other barriers to imports to persuade domestic and foreign-owned firms to manufacture here. Why
should they do so in the face of an agreement that will eliminate tariffs
and also limit the extent to which governments can use other barriers to
imports and similar inducements to invest here? Indeed, why should
there not be a gradual exodus of a considerable number of existing foreign-owned subsidiaries, particularly those that have benefited from such
policies?

There is no doubt that the FTA will cause some existing subsidiaries
and some Canadian-owned plants to close down. Other firms that might
have established here because of tariffs will not do so. However, the size
of these divestments will not likely be nearly as large or worrying as some
have suggested, the results are not all bad for Canadians, and offsetting
increases in investment will probably exceed these decreases by a considerable margin.

New investment decisions. There are a number of reasons for doubt-
ing the pessimistic predictions. First, well-substantiated evidence on how
multinationals decide to enter new markets clearly suggests that, while
tariffs and other forms of protection have played a role in attracting direct investment into manufacturing, other variables are usually more important. Three points on trade and factor mobility will suffice for present
purposes. First, direct investment theory involves no necessary link with
tariffs or other barriers to trade. Multinationals must decide on which
form of organization to use in serving foreign markets—that is, whether
to trade, license, or joint venture with independent parties, or whether to
do all these things through controlled subsidiaries. Multinationals favor
such subsidiaries in many types of activities or markets where they increase profits—for example, by slowing the loss of information to competitors or by making it easier to transfer technology—quite apart from
whether protection exists.[12]

[12]The literature on the choice between subsidiary, trade, and mixed forms of organiza-
tion is summarized in Richard E. Caves, *Multinational Enterprise and Economic Analysis*
(Cambridge, Eng. and New York, 1982), chaps. 1 and 2; and Alan M. Rugman, *Inside the
Multinationals: The Economics of Internal Markets* (New York, 1981).

Second, conclusions drawn from trade theory that trade and factor movements are substitutes has long since been challenged.[13] The idea of trade and investment as complements gained further ground once one allowed for product differentiation and for specialization and exchange within the international firm.[14] Among the more careful empirical demonstrations have been those by Lipsey and Weiss indicating that exports by U.S. firms were higher as the output of the U.S. firm in that area increased—strongly so for intermediate goods but also for finished products.[15]

Third, while it has long since been demonstrated that tariffs are a determinant of direct investment, the evidence seems equally conclusive that other variables are more important in the typical case. These other variables include the size and growth of markets, costs of production and distribution, the nature of the competition involved, government attitudes to business as expressed in a variety of fiscal and regulatory policies (including protection), and perhaps exchange-rate variations.

The many empirical tests of these determinants vary greatly in quality and coverage. Some certainly suggest that the extent of domestic protection had a considerable impact on the investment decision, particularly for earlier periods in the developed countries and for a number of developing countries still. In many such tests the variables reflecting protection are swamped by other variables, notably size and growth of markets.[16] There are at least four studies concentrating on Canadian direct investment in the United States, only one of which appears to give protection a significant weight in the investment decision.[17] It should be added that protection played a larger role for many existing subsidiaries when they were established in Canada, often many decades ago, than it does today.

[13] See Douglas D. Purvis, "Technology, Trade, and Factor Mobility," *Economic Journal* vol. 82, no. 327 (Sept. 1972).

[14] For primary products, of course, this view had long since been accepted.

[15] Richard E. Lipsey and Merle Y. Weiss, "Foreign Production and Exports in Manufacturing Industries," *Review of Economics and Statistics* 63 (1981), 488–94; Lipsey and Weiss, "Foreign Production and Exports of Industrial Firms," *Review of Economics and Statistics* 66 (1984), 304–308.

[16] Caves, *Multinational Enterprise and Economic Analysis*, 40–43 gives the case for tariffs as a determinant of direct investment. About a score of such tests are discussed in Gary C. Hufbauer, "The Multinational Corporation and Direct Investment," in *International Trade and Finance* (London and New York, 1975), 177–82. Still others are covered in Organization for Economic Cooperation and Development, *Investment Incentives and Disincentives and the International Investment Process* (Paris, 1983) and OECD, *Recent Trends in International Direct Investment* (Paris, 1987), 206.

[17] These studies are summarized in Alan M. Rugman, *Outward Bound: Canadian Direct Investment in the United States* (Toronto and Washington, 1987), chaps. 2 and 3. Rugman takes a stronger view of what the tests have to say about the effects of protection on direct investment.

Behavior of existing firms. A second point concerns the fate of the large number of existing subsidiaries in Canada under a free-trade regime. It is well known that many of these subsidiaries have unit costs greater than those in U.S. plants. There is concern, therefore, that the parent firm's strategy would dictate halting or reducing the activities of some subsidiaries, specifically those sometimes referred to as "tariff factories," and supplying the Canadian market from the United States. This might happen, for example, where the Canadian market was a relatively small part of the North American market or where production was at a higher constant unit cost in the relevant range. Canadian-owned uninational or multinational firms could face similar problems as Canadian protection is reduced.

The pessimistic predictions are also subject to several qualifications, as has been underlined in a range of studies. First, market access under a free trade agreement is enhanced in *both* directions, at least potentially. With some exceptions, U.S. tariffs will go to zero and remain there, some nontariff barriers for goods and services will be reduced or eliminated, and the application of trade laws will be clearer and more stable than previously.[18] How far actual access will increase will depend on the competitive reactions of the firms involved. In principle, however, it is possible for firms to gain export access as well as meet enhanced import competition. Second, where sunk costs are substantial, the ability of firms to divest fully or early will be limited—a point emphasized in various studies such as Bishop and Crookell's.[19] Third, however, to the extent that exit or entry can occur with regard to a product, plant, or firm, it is important to note that all of the determinants of direct investment noted earlier—markets, costs, competition, government policies, and the exchange rate—can change with free trade, and many change in ways favorable to investment in Canada.

More specifically, the major published studies of what would happen in Canada with freer trade generally conclude that under the FTA, Canada will be a competitive source for a wide range of manufactures.[20] The

[18] This leaves open the questions of just how far potential access has been increased and what was the balance of concessions from each party.

[19] Paul M. Bishop and Harold Crookell, "Specialization and Foreign Investment in Canada," in *Canadian Industry in Transition* (Toronto, 1986).

[20] Two of the more comprehensive sets of studies are in Richard G. Harris and David Cox, *Trade, Industrial Policy, and Canadian Manufacturing* (Toronto, 1983), and in further work summarized in Richard Harris, "The Economic Impact on Canada of Changing Trade Barriers Between Canada and the United States," working paper DP87-6 (Toronto, University of Toronto, 1987) and by Sunder Magun et al., "Open Borders: An Assessment of the Canada-U.S. Free Trade Agreement," discussion paper 344 (Ottawa, Economic Council of Canada, 1988), and Magun et al., "Impact of Canada-U.S. Free Trade on the

overall effects on income, investment, and overall employment in manu-facturing are expected to be positive. The studies also note labor-adjust-ment costs for some industries in transition while specialization is being developed, although employment changes resulting from free trade are relatively small overall.

These studies conclude that significant gains from freer trade occur because the rationalization of production takes place mainly within firms and industries rather than among them, thus minimizing the adjustments involved for labor, capital, and communities. In particular, the studies depend on the Eastman-Stykolt model of concentrated industry with high levels of tariffs and unexhausted economies of scale.[21] This model predicts that the pressure on prices from reduced tariff protection will likely lead to fewer and more profitable product lines, but possibly increased output as well. If the industry subject to increased international competition is characterized by monopolistic competition, increased specialization is also predicted but total output could fall.[22] Briefly, real income can be raised by increased or more stable market access where scale economies or product differentiation exist, and also in other circumstances such as when some industries need to cover substantial research costs. The experience of the 1970s, when substantial adjustments were forced on Canadian industry by increased international competition and supply shocks, would appear to confirm predictions based on an Eastman-Stykolt model, including rationalizing investment and increased export-import penetration.[23]

Competitive adjustments to free trade. Up to this point, it has been assumed that market access will be improved by the FTA, since tariff and nontariff barriers are to be removed or reduced and the application of trade-remedy laws and procedures has been somewhat constrained. Ac-tual market access will depend, however, on the nature of competition in the industry. If a potential exporter is looking at a foreign industry with high entry barriers, for example, he may find his foreign competitors

Canadian Economy," discussion paper 331 (Ottawa, Economic Council of Canada, 1987). Doubts about the size of bilateral free trade gains have been expressed by Fred Lazar, "Survey of Ontario Manufacturing," *Canadian Public Policy*, vol. 14 (Toronto, 1988), and R. Wigle, "Between a Rock and a Hard Place: The Economics of Canada-U.S. Freer Trade," *Canadian Public Policy* 14 (Toronto, 1988).

[21] H. C. Eastman and S. Stykolt, *The Tariff and Competition in Canada* (Toronto, 1967).

[22] Richard E. Caves, "Market Structure, Seller Competition and Adjustment to Interna-tional Disturbances," working paper 87–5 (Toronto, University of Toronto, 1987), 4–8.

[23] John R. Baldwin and Paul K. Gorecki, "Trade, Tariffs, Product Diversity, and Length of Production Run in Canadian Manufacturing Industries 1970–1979," discussion pa-per 247 (Ottawa, Economic Council of Canada, 1983); Caves, "Market Structure, Seller Competition and Adjustment to International Disturbances."

prepared to protect their market shares with a wide variety of tactics. They can try to forestall entry to their market by building extra capacity, or by investing more in R & D or product differentiation. These and other techniques signal increased barriers to entry or increased competition after entry, both of which could scare off the potential entrant. There is now a substantial, though still controversial, body of literature on the role of government in promoting strategic trade policy in circumstances of this kind, including some work on export-promotion policies appropriate to small countries undergoing liberalization.[24]

For present purposes this literature suggests, first, that in such circumstances firms may react in ways that increase foreign direct investment and technology and marketing contacts in both directions. Rather than attempting to gain a share of the tariff-free market with exports, it may be less disturbing or more effective to enter the foreign market by acquiring an existing firm. It may be still less risky to arrange a licensing arrangement or joint venture with a foreign firm. Of course, these and other tactics are also open to the foreign firm. It might decide that the best way to deal with an efficient exporter to its market is to buy it out, or try for a license or other arrangement. All of these techniques are likely to involve trade between the parties, reinforcing my earlier point about the often complementary nature of trade and investment.

Second, the FTA allows Canada to continue to review acquisitions of larger firms by U.S. interests while Canadian firms are free to make acquisitions in the United States. In each case there are exceptions, such as existing sectoral restrictions on direct investment, and of course in each country there are nondiscriminatory laws and regulations on mergers and acquisitions. U.S. firms, including their subsidiaries in Canada, are more constrained than Canadian firms from engaging in actual or threatened takeovers as part of their strategy for penetrating the other market. What this means in practice depends on how Canadian authorities use the existing review process and how far they are challenged in the process. In some countries, the existence of a review process has played a significant role in the way the takeover game has been played.[25]

Country of ownership and the adjustment process. One might protest that some of the major studies noted earlier consider the manufacturing sector without distinguishing firms' country of ownership. The foreign-owned firm may react differently than those owned domestically to the

[24] Respectively, *Strategic Trade Policy and the New International Economics* (Cambridge, Mass., 1986), and Richard G. Harris, *Trade, Industrial Policy, and International Competition* (Toronto, University of Toronto, 1985).
[25] For example, *Governments and Multinationals*, 20–24.

changes discussed earlier. In particular, the speed of adjustment may differ, though it is not clear a priori which type of firm will adjust more quickly. The existence of plants abroad and better international information systems could speed adjustment for the foreign-owned sector, while less independence in subsidiaries' planning could slow change.[26] There is considerable material on this subject in other contexts; for example, Europe's experience with trade and investment when the European Common Market was established and plant closure data in various countries.[27] Only studies relating to Canada will be discussed here.

One of the most inclusive studies examined the responses of all manufacturing firms to the trade opportunities of the 1970s—a period of significant declines in tariff protection. Both import and export penetration of manufactures increased in this period, as the specialization argument suggests. The study also found that foreign ownership did not exacerbate the lack of specialization and scale that plagued many manufacturing firms.[28]

There may be a difference in how larger and smaller subsidiaries adjust to freer trade. A study of the twenty-one largest Canadian-owned multinationals and the seventeen largest U.S. subsidiaries in Canada suggests their reactions to bilateral trade liberalization will be very similar. Specifically, they expect to adjust readily to new trade regimes, and they regard trade and investment as largely complementary to, rather than substitutes for, each other.[29] A study of a matched sample of thirty smaller U.S.-owned subsidiaries and Canadian-owned firms found that about half had become more specialized in response to trade liberalization under GATT. It appeared also that the foreign-controlled firms in the sample responded more slowly to trade liberalization.[30] A more extensive study concluded that smaller subsidiaries adjusted relatively slowly to changes in the international environment, while multinationals were in a strong position to rationalize production because of intrafirm and intraindustry trade.[31]

[26] On the first point, see Caves, "Market Structure, Seller Competition," 11–12. On the second point, see Bishop and Crookell, "Specialization and Foreign Investment."

[27] Lawrence G. Franko, *The European Multinationals: A Renewed Challenge for American and British Big Business* (Greylock, 1976); Organization for Economic Cooperation and Development, *Structural Adjustment and Multinational Enterprises* (Paris, 1985), 46–50.

[28] John R. Baldwin and Paul K. Gorecki, "Trade, Tariffs, Product Diversity, and Length of Production Run in Canadian Manufacturing Industries: 1970–1979," discussion paper 247 (Ottawa, Economic Council of Canada, 1983), 54–65, 109–116.

[29] Rugman, *Outward Bound.*

[30] See Donald J. Daly and Donald C. MacCharles, *Canadian Manufactured Exports: Constraints and Opportunities* (Montreal, 1986), especially pages xix and 77.

[31] Donald C. MacCharles, *Trade among Multinationals: Intra-Industry Trade and National Competitiveness* (London and New York, 1987), 133–39, 159–66.

Another study covering twenty-three businesses or divisions of thirteen firms considered in detail the options open to foreign-owned firms in Canada as import tariffs decline and pressures to specialize increase.[32] The options considered were to continue with the present degree of product diversity, to import in place of Canadian production, to rationalize production between the Canadian and U.S. affiliates, or to rationalize production while developing world product mandates. The last of these options develops in the subsidiary the skills needed for product renewal in international markets. There is evidence that increased specialization in response to international competition has been underway for some time; rationalization of production occurs in products sensitive to price and quality while product mandates usually emphasize quality and technology, and the foreign-owned businesses studied were generally more interested in specializing than divesting.[33]

Caves studied the experience of manufacturing industries from 1970 to 1979, distinguishing concentrated and unconcentrated industries. He found that tariff reductions led to rationalizing investments, as already noted. He relates this process to "the relative ubiquity of product or spatial differentiation, its effect amplified by the prevalence of foreign subsidiaries."[34] Although multinationals did not affect international transmission of price disturbances, they did speed quantity disturbances.

Another study examines the processes by which multinationals in Canada adjust to several types of pressures, including tariff reduction. It does not find multinationals more likely than other firms to shift operations to low-cost foreign sources, or, given falling domestic demands, to sell or close a plant. In many sectors, employment in Canada has fallen relative to that of U.S. parents, but this is less so where Canadian trade barriers have been reduced most. There is less agreement, however, on the rationalization patterns of multinational and uninational firms.[35]

Although these studies would not support the more pessimistic views about the adjustment processes in international firms, they do point to significant adjustment problems for some. Further work on this topic is clearly needed.

[32] "Specialization and Foreign Investment in Canada."
[33] Bishop and Crookell, "The Reaction of Multinational Enterprises to Sectoral Free Trade" (Toronto, York University, 1984) mimeo, 15–20 examines at length the circumstances in which rationalization would be pursued as distinct from mandating. Alan Rugman and Sheila Douglas, in their article "The Strategic Management of Multinationals and World Product Mandating," *Canadian Public Policy* 12 (June 1986), 321–28 doubt that the scope for mandating is large.
[34] Caves, "Market Structure, Seller Competition."
[35] Economic Council of Canada, *Managing Adjustment: Policies for Trade-Sensitive Industries* (Ottawa, 1988), 14–18.

Effects on Other Types of Direct Investment

The Canada-U.S. Free Trade Agreement will likely lead to increased investment in Canadian natural resources by both foreign and Canadian multinationals. Most studies show that Canada already has a comparative advantage in a number of resource and primary-manufacturing industries. The removal of even small barriers to exports—or the reduced threat of such barriers—should significantly increase investments to process such products further, wherever transport costs and other barriers to competition allow export. As for the service industries, some such as banking prefer or even require subsidiaries or branches rather than trade when they go abroad. The removal of actual or potential barriers should increase foreign direct investment in such industries.

In the past decade or so, Canada has become an important exporter of business capital. Manufacturing plays a smaller role on the outflow side, and marketing and management skills are often more important than technological advantages. Moreover, as noted earlier, there are several determinants of direct investment, and protection is usually not the most important. Nonetheless, U.S. protectionism has helped persuade some Canadian firms to locate in the United States instead of exporting from Canada.[36] To that extent, freer trade will keep new investments in Canada. But one should not expect the FTA to lead to any substantial divestment of Canadian firms already in the United States. Instead one should expect, based on the experience of other trading areas, much greater competition for new investment within the rules of the agreement.[37]

Finally, what about investment in Canada or the United States by third-country firms? Many such firms would hesitate today to produce in Canada for the combined Canadian-U.S. market simply because export access to the larger U.S. market could be blocked by government policy. The FTA should reduce or, in some cases, even remove this concern. In addition, any trade diversion because of the agreement could increase investments by third-country firms in the combined Canadian-U.S. market. It would be surprising if those who promote direct investment in Canada do not also endorse this potentially enlarged market area for Canadian-based firms.

CONCLUSIONS

Fears of a major exodus of foreign-owned firms and capital from Canada in response to the bilateral free trade agreement with the United

[36] See Rugman, *Outward Bound* for studies of the nature and determinants of Canadian direct investment in the United States.

[37] Stephen E. Guisinger et al., *Investment Incentives and Performance Requirements: Patterns of International Trade, Production, and Investment* (New York, 1985), chap. 1.

States appear to be exaggerated. Some divestment will occur, but the offsetting gains in manufacturing will be substantial. They include rationalization by U.S. firms already engaged in secondary manufacturing in Canada so as to take advantage of the large and more secure U.S. market; gearing up by Canadian-owned secondary manufacturing firms for the same purpose; expanded investment in primary-resource processing; and, possibly, expanded third-country investment in the enlarged Canada-U.S. market. It seems unlikely that all these gains will result in net divestment. The investment that remains, moreover, will not levy a permanent tax on consumers in the way that tariff-induced investments often do. Finally, once one accounts for the competitive reactions to the threat of market entry, direct investment in both the United States and Canada may well increase for a time.

It should be added that both retrospective and prospective tests of what happens to the manufacturing industry with freer trade are mostly better than tests of changes in the direct investment sector.[38] What happens, then, if the analysis presented here should prove to be wrong and there is a massive divestment of capital from Canada because of free trade? Several adjustments would occur to limit the damage.[39] The value of the Canadian dollar would fall, increasing the cost of transferring funds out of Canada and probably making Canada a better location for export. Undoubtedly some sources in the United States would be unhappy with this development. Given its origin, however, they could hardly argue that it reflected an attempt by the Canadian government to depreciate the exchange rate. Moreover, such a fire sale of foreign-owned assets would tempt other investors to try to operate the assets or parts of them, perhaps in conjunction with a technology or marketing license negotiated with the former owners. Such sales have often occurred in recent years when foreign and Canadian multinationals have restructured their domestic and foreign operations.

In contrast to this pessimistic scenario, there is the possibility of increased direct investment during the FTA's transition period. This could lead to an increase in foreign ownership of Canadian industry for a time, although this would depend also on the agreement's general effect on investment in Canada. In the longer term two developments should resist any tendency for the share of foreign ownership to rise. First, Canadian-owned firms with one plant or a few plants would be less likely to merge with multinationals, since they can achieve more efficient scale and some

[38] "The Reaction of Multinational Enterprises to Sectoral Free Trade."
[39] For further discussion of these points, see "Impact of Trade Liberalization"; R. Wonnacott, *Canada's Trade Options* (Ottawa, 1975), 101–103; and Eastman and Stykolt, *Tariff and Competition in Canada*, chap. 4.

related administrative functions independently in the enlarged market. Second, with increased efficiency the capital-output ratio would fall in some sectors, thus reducing reliance on foreign capital to finance investment. While direct investment is not closely associated with capital scarcity, it also could lessen the degree of foreign ownership to the extent that capital and technical change go together. Moreover, for a variety of international and domestic reasons, Canada's share of world direct investment has fallen sharply over time, as has the degree of foreign ownership of Canadian industry since about 1970.

Canadian governments retain quite extensive powers to influence investment, and substantial divestment is unlikely. Two caveats should be added, however, to put this discussion of direct investment in context. First, the capacity to attract new investments—to revitalize old industries and capture new ones—depends on a range of market, cost, and government-policy variables that go well beyond the scope of this paper. A free-trade environment is only one important aspect of a policy designed to assure more competitive Canadian industries and more secure access to Canada's largest foreign market. It will not succeed itself in attracting new investments over time if other policy variables are damaging to investment. Second, while evidence suggests the adjustments will not be severe, some sectors and workers will be under considerable competitive pressure for a time. One of the more important tests of the economic desirability and political feasibility of free trade is precisely whether convincing arrangements exist to assist people in coping with the changes that will come with it.

Taxation of Foreign Investment in Mexico: The North American Perspective

Fernando Sánchez Ugarte

A LL THREE North American countries—Canada, Mexico, and the United States—have either undergone or are in the process of undergoing major tax reforms. Their approach to this reform has been similar: to broaden tax bases and reduce nominal tax rates. The Canadian and U.S. reforms have sought to broaden the tax base by eliminating tax incentives and reducing both personal and corporate rates and deductions. While reforms in both countries have been revenue neutral, the greater share of the overall tax burden has been shifted from individuals to corporations.

In contrast, tax reform in Mexico has so far concentrated on the corporate sector. Mexico has broadened its tax base by forbidding deductions for the inflationary component of nominal interest payments, and has reduced corporate tax rates to levels similar to those in the United States and Canada. In this manner, Mexico has tried to increase corporate revenue and thus the share of the corporate income tax (CIT) in its total tax revenue.

Notwithstanding these similarities in tax-reform approaches, the new tax systems pose several problems for the flow of investment across the region. On the one hand, U.S. legislation has adopted a more inward-oriented approach, severely limiting the scope of the foreign tax credit. On the other hand, the drastic rate reductions in Canada and the United States left Mexico with relatively high personal tax rates. This disparity created distortions in the system for withholding taxes on dividends.

The ongoing process of tax reform in the three countries created both the need and the opportunity to look at how tax policy affects the intra-regional flow of investment. Furthermore, the need to restore the flow of capital from north to south, which has been hindered by the foreign debt crisis, calls for a review of the way these countries tax foreign investment.[1]

INCOME TAXES AND FOREIGN INVESTMENT

Most countries tax income according to the residence principle; income obtained by residents is taxed in the country of residence regardless of where the income was generated. On the other hand, most countries also apply the source principle; the tax on nonresident income is withheld by the source country.

The application of both principles would give rise to double taxation of income if the countries did not provide unilateral relief.[2] The system most widely used to avoid double taxation gives a tax credit for income tax paid abroad. Generally, the foreign tax credit is limited to the amount of the tax that would have been levied on the income if it had been received in the home country.

A few countries, following the French tradition, use the territorial principle of taxation. Under this principle, income generated abroad is exempt from taxation in the home country. Regardless of the principle applied, most countries withhold taxes at source on the income paid to nonresidents.

Table 1 summarizes the basic rules of taxation under the small-country assumption and principle of home-country taxation according to residence.[3] When the corporate tax rate in the host country is lower than the corresponding rate in the home country, dividends should be taxed at an effective tax rate equal to that in the home country. Earnings of incorporated affiliates should be taxed at the same corporate income tax rate that applies to national corporations. On the other hand, when the corporate tax rate in the host country is higher than that in the home country,

[1] For further preliminary reading on taxation and foreign investment, see Peggy B. Musgrave, "United States Taxation of Foreign Investment Income: Issues and Arguments" (Cambridge, Mass., Harvard Law School, International Tax Program, 1969); Dennis G. Hartman, "Tax Policy Foreign Direct Investment," working paper 689 (Cambridge, Mass., National Bureau of Economics Research, June 1981); George F. Kopits, "Taxation and Multinational Firm Behavior: A Critical Survey," *Staff Papers* vol. 23, no. 3 (Washington, International Monetary Fund, 1976); Thomas Horst, "American Taxation of Multinational Firms," *American Economic Review* vol. 67, no. 3 (June 1977); and Arturo M. Fernández-Pérez, "Taxation in Small Open Economies," Ph.D. diss. (University of Chicago, Mar. 1986).

[2] Tax treaties are bilateral measures taken to avoid double taxation. They contain clauses that either credit foreign taxes or exempt foreign investment income. These treaties also limit the extent to which a given country can tax income received from foreign investment.

[3] In these conclusions, I have expanded Fernandez's theory in *Essays on Taxation in Small Open Economies* to include the issue of tax deferral.

TABLE I

Rules for Taxing Foreign Investment Income

Type of income	$t_c^a < t$	$t_c^a > t$
Remittances		0
Dividends	$t_d^a = \dfrac{t - t_c^a}{1 - t_c^a}$	
Other	$t_r^a = t$	$t_r^a = t$
Earnings of incorporated affiliates	t_c^a	t_c^a

NOTE: t = tax rate; t_c^a = corporate tax rate in host country; t_d^a = tax withheld by host country on dividends; t_r^a = tax withheld by host country on other remittances. "Other" income includes branch earnings, interest, royalties, and fees. A proper adjustment must be made in the tax withheld on gross income to ensure that the effective tax rate on net income is t.

dividends should be taxed at the same rate as domestic corporate earnings. In both cases, all other remittances should be taxed at the same effective rate as in the home country.

Two situations may arise with regard to tax incentives. When the home country does not grant tax sparing, only tax incentives that promote reinvestment of earnings are effective. This rules out the use of tax holidays and exemptions, and suggests the use of accelerated depreciation, investment tax credit, and investment expensing (which was shown to be more effective because of its neutrality).

When the home country grants tax sparing, tax holidays and exemptions given by the host country can effectively encourage new investments. Other tax incentives should then be used to promote the reinvestment of earnings.

INCOME TAXES AND FOREIGN INVESTMENT
IN MEXICO, PARTICULARLY INVESTMENT
FROM THE UNITED STATES AND CANADA

Mexico, like many developing countries, must foster foreign investment to complement domestic savings. During the 1970s, foreign savings in Mexico grew rapidly, predominantly taking the form of indirect foreign investment. During the 1980s, however, the reduced inflow of new foreign loans has made the country rely on a growing, but still vastly insufficient, amount of direct foreign investment.

Before 1988, taxation had not been an important issue in foreign investment decisions. This lack of concern over the fiscal system occurred because indirect foreign investment, which had traditionally been taxed at a lower rate, prevailed over other forms of investment. After the loan market dried up and tax reforms were enacted in Canada, the United States, and Mexico, taxation began to be a concern for foreign investors.

In this section, I will first look at the recent evolution of foreign investment in Mexico. I will then analyze the way Mexico taxes all forms of foreign investment, looking at how the Mexican tax system interacts with the systems in Canada and the United States. The section will continue with an assessment of whether Mexican tax rates are too high and thus discourage foreign investment. The conclusion derived here is that while corporate income tax rates are competitive, personal income tax rates are higher than those in Canada and the United States. Finally, I discuss how the structure of foreign investment in Mexico, dominated by a tax-exempt public-sector foreign debt, deteriorates the ability of the Mexican tax system to generate tax revenues.

Recent Foreign Investment in Mexico

During the 1970s, gross capital formation in Mexico averaged 22.6 percent of GDP (see Table 2). In the present decade, gross capital formation has averaged 23.4 percent of GDP. Investment in 1980 and 1981 reached about 29 percent of GDP, the highest level ever in Mexican history (see Fig. 1). Eliminating these two outliers from the analysis results in an average of 21.7 percent of GDP for the period 1982–1987. In the 1980s, investment relative to GDP is only slightly lower than the 1970s average.

The balance between private- and public-sector investment and the financing of these investments have changed dramatically over the period of analysis. During the 1970s, about 90 percent of gross investment was fixed-capital formation; during the 1980s, the share of fixed capital had dropped to 82 percent (see Fig. 2). The share of public-sector savings rose steadily from one-third in 1970 to 49 percent in 1978 (see Table 3). During the 1980s, the share of public-sector investment has fallen back to one-third (see Fig. 3).

The structure of investment financing has changed dramatically from 1970 to 1987. Depreciation has financed between one-fourth and one-fifth of total investment, while the remainder is financed with both domestic and foreign savings. A clear correlation emerges between public and external savings: when public-sector savings contract, external savings expand. For instance, foreign savings varied from 4.9 percent of GDP in 1970 to 10.4 percent in 1987. Public-sector savings financed more than 50 percent of total investment in 1988 (see Table 4), as opposed to only about 17 percent in the previous decade. In the 1970s, private-sector savings were relatively stable, financing from 40 to 50 percent of total investment. After 1988, however, the share of private-sector savings dropped to about one-third. This tendency seems to be reversing

TABLE 2
Capital Formation, 1970–78
(Billions of Pesos)

	1970	1971	1972	1973	1974	1975	1976	1977	1978
Gross capital formation	101.0	99.2	114.7	147.7	208.6	360.6	305.6	422.4	551.6
Gross fixed investment	88.7	88.1	107.1	133.3	178.9	235.6	288.4	363.3	492.4
Change in inventories	12.3	11.1	7.6	14.4	19.7	25.0	17.2	59.1	59.2
Finance of gross capital formation	101.0	99.2	114.7	147.7	208.6	260.6	305.6	422.4	551.6
Fixed capital consumptions	23.8	25.5	29.8	35.3	46.7	59.7	75.9	106.7	136.2
Savings:	77.2	73.7	84.9	112.4	161.9	200.9	229.7	315.7	415.4
Foreign savings (net loans from the rest of the world)	13.4	11.0	10.9	16.3	33.0	46.2	45.4	37.3	61.3
Domestic savings:	63.8	62.7	74.0	96.1	128.9	154.7	184.3	278.4	354.1
Public sector savings	15.9	22.5	23.6	21.0	20.0	23.1	17.6	85.9	145.3
Private sector savings	47.9	40.2	50.4	75.1	108.9	131.6	166.7	192.5	208.8
Gross domestic product	444.3	490.0	564.7	690.9	899.7	1100.0	1371.0	1849.3	2337.4

AS PERCENTAGE OF GDP

	1970 %	1971 %	1972 %	1973 %	1974 %	1975 %	1976 %	1977 %	1978 %
Gross capital formation	22.7	20.2	20.3	21.4	23.2	23.7	22.3	22.8	23.6
Fixed capital consumption	5.4	5.2	5.3	5.1	5.2	5.4	5.5	5.8	5.8
Savings:	17.4	15.0	15.0	16.3	18.0	18.3	16.8	17.1	17.8
Foreign savings	3.0	2.2	1.9	2.4	3.7	4.2	3.3	2.0	2.6
Domestic savings	14.4	12.8	13.1	13.9	14.3	14.1	13.4	15.1	15.1
Public sector	3.6	4.6	4.2	3.0	2.1	2.1	1.3	4.6	6.2
Private sector	10.8	8.2	8.9	10.9	12.1	12.0	12.2	10.4	8.9
Inflation tax	0.39	0.44	0.53	1.84	1.63	0.96	2.47	1.78	1.34
Real interest rate of internal debt	0.24	0.27	0.30	0.27	0.25	0.29	0.31	0.29	0.29

TABLE 2 (*continued*)

Capital Formation, 1979–87

(Billions of Pesos)

	1979	1980	1981	1982	1983	1984	1985[a]	1986[a]	1987[a]
Gross capital formation	796.0	1202.7	1702.6	2000.8	3472.2	6216.8	10477.6	17663.7	40686.4
Gross fixed investment	718.5	1032.9	1509.4	2098.8	2972.3	5163.6	8395.4	13695.0	33388.0
Change in inventories	77.6	169.8	193.1	−98.0	499.9	1053.2	2082.2	3968.7	7298.4
Finance of gross capital formation	796.0	1207.7	1702.6	2000.8	3472.2	6216.8	10477.6	17663.7	40686.4
Fixed capital consumptions	178.4	236.6	327.9	528.1	992.8	1692.2	2644.1	4588.9	11119.0
Savings:	617.6	966.1	1374.7	1472.7	2479.4	4524.6	7833.5	13074.8	29567.4
Foreign savings (net loans from the rest of the world)	110.7	151.7	289.2	−90.6	−734.9	−720.8	−294.7	282.6	−6970.0
Domestic savings:	506.9	816.5	1085.5	1563.3	3214.3	5245.4	8128.2	12792.2	36537.4
Public sector savings	223.4	325.2	175.8	182.5	1775.3	3555.1	4453.4	6786.4	15561.0
Private sector savings	283.5	489.3	909.7	1380.8	1439.0	1690.3	3674.8	6005.8	20976.4
Gross domestic product	3067.5	4226.5	5874.4	9417.1	17141.7	28748.9	45419.8	77778.1	191700.0

AS PERCENTAGE OF GDP

	1979 %	1980 %	1981 %	1982 %	1983 %	1984 %	1985[a] %	1986[a] %	1987[a] %
Gross capital formation	25.9	28.1	29.0	21.2	20.3	21.6	23.1	22.7	21.2
Fixed capital consumption	5.8	5.5	5.6	5.6	5.8	5.9	5.8	5.9	5.8
Savings:	20.1	22.6	23.4	15.6	14.5	15.7	17.2	16.8	15.4
Foreign savings	3.6	3.3	4.9	−1.0	−4.3	−2.5	−0.6	0.4	−3.6
Domestic savings	16.5	19.5	18.5	16.6	18.8	18.1	17.9	16.4	19.1
Public sector	7.3	7.6	3.0	1.9	10.4	12.4	9.8	8.7	8.1
Private sector	9.2	11.4	15.5	14.7	8.4	5.9	8.1	7.7	10.9
Inflation tax	1.79	2.56	2.23	7.88	3.68	2.36	2.29	3.18	5.26
Real interest rate of internal debt	0.32	0.35	0.42	0.57	0.51	0.52	0.52	0.58	0.71

SOURCES: National Accounts, National Institute Public Finance Statistics, S.H.C.P. Presidential Report, 1985, 1987.
[a] Estimated figures.

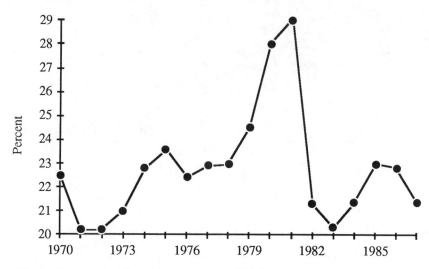

Fig. 1. Gross capital formation as percent of GDP.

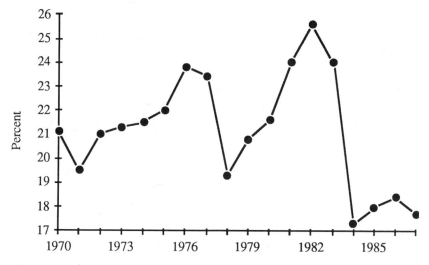

Fig. 2. Fixed capital formation as percent of GDP.

TABLE 3

Public Investment as Percentage of Total Investment

1970	32.92	1980	43.16
1971	25.77	1981	43.37
1972	32.03	1982	44.28
1973	38.78	1983	41.25
1974	37.95	1984	39.26
1975	41.89	1985	35.50
1976	38.87	1986	33.77
1977	39.83		
1978	45.10		
1979	43.77		
Average		Average	
1970–1979 =	37.69	1980–1986 =	40.08

SOURCES: National Accounts, National Institute of Statistics, Geography, and Information. President's Annual Report to Congress, 1985 and 1987. Public Finance Statistics, Mexican Ministry of Finance.

TABLE 4

Structure of Investment Finance

(*as percentage of investment*)

	Capital consumption	Savings	Foreign savings	Domestic savings	Public sector savings	Private sector savings
1970	23.8%	76.2%	13.2%	64.0%	15.8%	48.2%
1971	25.7	74.3	10.9	63.4	22.8	40.6
1972	26.1	73.9	9.3	64.5	20.7	43.8
1973	23.8	76.2	11.2	65.0	14.1	50.9
1974	22.4	77.6	15.9	61.6	9.5	52.1
1975	22.8	77.2	17.7	59.5	8.9	50.6
1976	24.7	75.3	14.8	60.5	5.8	54.7
1977	25.4	75.0	8.8	66.2	20.2	45.8
1978	24.6	75.4	11.0	64.0	26.3	37.7
1979	22.4	77.6	13.9	63.7	28.2	35.5
1980	19.6	80.4	12.4	67.6	27.0	40.6
1981	19.3	80.7	16.9	63.8	10.3	53.5
1982	26.4	73.6	−4.7	78.3	9.0	69.3
1983	28.6	77.4	−21.2	92.6	51.2	41.4
1984	27.3	72.7	−11.6	89.3	57.4	27.3
1985[a]	25.1	74.9	−2.6	77.5	42.4	35.1
1986[a]	26.0	74.0	1.8	72.2	38.3	33.9
1987[a]	27.4	72.6	−17.0	90.1	38.2	51.4

SOURCES: National Accounts, National Institute of Statistics, Geography, and Information. President's Annual Report to Congress, 1985 and 1987. Public Finance Statistics, Mexican Ministry of Finance.
[a]Estimated figures.

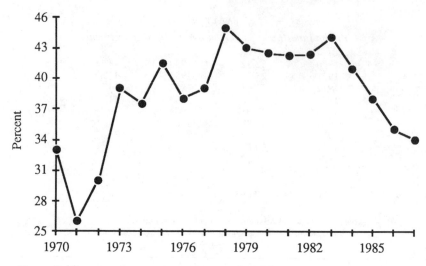

Fig. 3. Public sector investment as percent of total investment.

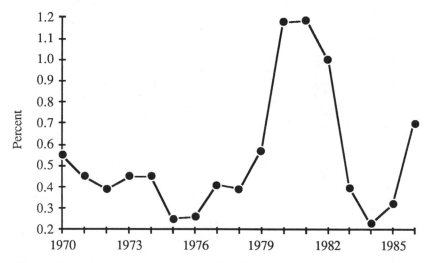

Fig. 4. Direct foreign investment as percent of GDP.

TABLE 5

Foreign Investment from the United States: 1973–1987

(*in current millions of dollars*)

	Direct foreign investment			
	Accumulated (1)	Accumulated from U.S.A. (2)	Percent (2/1)	New DFI from U.S.A.
1973	4,359.5	3,335.0	76.5	219.8
1974	4,721.7	3,640.4	77.1	279.3
1975	5,016.7	3,516.7	70.1	206.8
1976	5,315.8	3,838.0	72.2	215.9
1977	5,642.9	3,931.3	69.7	229.6
1978	6,026.2	4,206.3	69.8	267.5
1979	6,836.2	4,758.0	69.6	563.6
1980	8,458.8	5,836.6	69.0	1,119.6
1981	10,159.9	6,908.7	68.0	1,156.7
1982	10,786.4	7,334.8	68.0	426.0
1983	11,470.1	7,601.4	66.3	266.6
1984	12,899.9	8,513.4	66.0	912.0
1985	14,628.9	9,840.2	67.3	1,436.6
1986	17,053.1	11,046.6	64.8	1,206.4
1987[a]	20,930.3	13,716.2	65.5	2,669.6
Average annual growth rate:				
73–76	6.83%	4.79%		−0.59%
77–82	13.83%	13.28%		13.16%
83–87	16.25%	15.90%		77.89%
73–87	11.86%	10.63%		19.52%

SOURCE: General Direction of Foreign Investment, Mexican Secretariat of Commerce and Industrial Development (SECOFI).
[a]Preliminary figures.

itself; in 1987, private-sector savings financed about 50 percent of total investment. Foreign savings have been the most erratic component of investment financing in Mexico, reaching as high as 4.9 percent of GDP in 1981, and as low as −4.9 percent of GDP two years later.

Most of foreign savings have taken the form of debt financing. Direct foreign investment was well below 1 percent of GDP during the 1970s (see Fig. 4). Even though direct foreign investment has increased dramatically to about 2 percent of GDP in 1986–87, the foreign debt, which has experienced some real amortization, is still so large that it dominates the balance.

Although the United States has traditionally been the main source of direct foreign investment for Mexico, its share has declined from 77 to about 65 percent of the total (see Table 5). At the same time, the United States holds only about 25 percent of the foreign debt.

TABLE 6

Foreign Investment from Canada: 1973–1987

(*in current millions of dollars*)

| | Direct foreign investment | | | |
	Accumulated (1)	Accumulated from Canada (2)	Percent (2/1)	New DFI from Canada
1973	4,359.5	95.6	2.2	n.d.
1974	4,721.7	108.9	2.3	n.d.
1975	5,016.7	145.5	2.9	n.d.
1976	5,315.8	106.3	2.0	n.d.
1977	5,642.9	118.5	2.1	n.d.
1978	6,026.2	108.5	1.8	n.d.
1979	6,836.2	109.4	1.6	n.d.
1980	8,458.8	126.9	1.5	n.d.
1981	10,159.9	132.1	1.3	n.d.
1982	10,786.4	140.2	1.3	n.d.
1983	11,470.1	162.3	1.4	22.1
1984	12,899.9	194.8	1.5	32.5
1985	14,628.9	229.7	1.6	35.1
1986	17,053.1	270.3	1.6	40.6
1987[a]	20,930.3	289.6	1.4	19.3
Average annual growth rate:				
73–76	6.83%	3.60%		—
77–82	13.83%	3.42%		—
83–87	16.23%	15.58%		−3.33%
73–87	11.86%	8.24%		—

SOURCE: General Direction of Foreign Investment (SECOFI).
[a]Preliminary figures.

TABLE 7

Mexican Debt with United States and Canada

(*Balance to December 31, 1988, in millions of dollars*)

Year	United States	Canada	Year	United States	Canada
1977	10,677.0	779.0	1983	22,036.6	3,835.1
1978	7,722.0	1,996.0	1984	24,964.2	3,658.6
1979	8,630.0	1,845.0	1985	22,408.2	3,898.1
1980	8,079.4	2,359.1	1986	20,742.0	4,215.2
1981	15,530.5	3,130.9	1987	20,499.7	4,618.5
1982	18,891.3	3,199.8			

SOURCE: General Credit Office, Mexican Ministry of Finance.

Canada's share of outstanding foreign investment has always been relatively small, but it is declining even further. Its share of investment in Mexico fell from 2.2 percent in 1973 to 1.4 percent in 1987 (see Table 6). At the same time, Canada holds only about one-fourth the amount of Mexican debt held by the United States (see Table 7).

Taxation of Foreign Investment in Mexico

The Mexican income-tax law applies both the residence and the source principle. Further, foreign investment legislation makes establishing a subsidiary the preferred form of organization for direct foreign investment. Hence, the typical foreign investor in Mexico operates through a subsidiary and complements this operation with technical assistance and patent agreements, as well as with loan contracts from either the parent in the home country or another subsidiary abroad.

This typical setup results in a different tax treatment for each type of income remitted abroad. Profits are first taxed at the corporate level when they are generated; distributed profits are subsequently deducted from corporate taxable income and a 50 percent tax is withheld on distribution.

As of 1987, Mexico uses two tax bases to calculate the amount of tax paid. The new tax base is fully adjusted for inflation, so that depreciation is calculated at real, not historical, values. Only the real component of interest paid is deductible—real interest received is taxed. The traditional tax base is only partially adjusted for inflation and assets are partially revalued based on the corporation's level of indebtedness. Interest paid is fully deductible, while interest earned is fully taxed.

The tax rate is 38 percent on the new base and 42 percent on the traditional base. Taxes are calculated on both bases and a proportion of each is paid so as to add up to 100 percent. The proportion paid on the new base increases by 20 percent each year, while that paid on the old base is reduced by the same proportion. By 1991, only the new base will exist—with an effective tax rate of 38 percent.

The CIT allows for dividends paid to individuals or corporations to be deducted. A 50 percent tax, the highest personal tax rate, is withheld on dividends paid to individuals or foreigners. No tax is withheld on dividends paid to corporations, but these payments are considered taxable income. The deduction of dividends allows full integration of the personal and corporate tax systems. Hence, distributed corporate profits are not doubly taxed, and the effective level of taxation of corporate income is determined at the individual level. Consequently, dividends paid by

Mexican corporations are effectively taxed by Mexico at 50 percent—the amount of tax withheld at source.

In addition to the corporate taxes mentioned above, profits, as determined under the rules of the traditional tax base, are subject to a 10 percent profit sharing to workers (PSW). The PSW is not a true tax. Even though PSW is mandatory, it is received by employees of the paying corporation. Some of this benefit is expected to be perceived by workers as part of their salary so that wages paid by the corporation could be reduced. The appropriate way to analyze the PSW is to consider it a 10 percent tax on profits with an x percent firm-specific subsidy to the use of labor. The firm-specific rate of subsidy to the use of labor will depend on the capital-labor ratio used by the firm.

Since only the new tax base accurately measures corporate profits, and the old base will vanish in 1991, one can safely assume that the new system determines investment decisions at the margin. Thus the effective tax rate on corporate profits is 35 percent (see Fig. 5). To this, one should add the effect of the PSW, which, as mentioned above, increases the effective rate of taxation. The PSW is determined according to the traditional tax calculations, so that interest paid is deductible on a nominal basis.

Distributed profits, however, are subject to a 50 percent withholding tax, and benefit from a full dividend deduction at the corporate level. Since the PSW is not deductible by the paying corporation, the effective tax on distributed profits abroad is 57.7 percent.

Payments made abroad in accordance with approved technical assistance (and royalty contracts associated with technical assistance) are subject to a 21 percent withholding tax. Otherwise, 42 percent is withheld on approved royalty payments. Payments made abroad, which are not approved, will not be considered a deductible corporate expense (see Fig. 6).

Interest paid abroad is subject to a withholding tax at source that varies from 0 to 42 percent. Interest paid on Mexican government foreign debt, publicly placed bonds, and bankers' acceptances are exempt from taxation, as are those loans from foreign sources that promote exports in their home countries. Interest paid on commercial bank loans is subject to a 15 percent withholding tax, while all other loans are subject to a 42 percent withholding tax. Because most of Mexican foreign debt is owed by the government, most of the interest paid abroad goes untaxed. The average effective tax rate on private-sector loans is about 9 to 10 percent, since most of these loans are held by banks and many of the other loans are tax-exempt.

Before 1986, a U.S. parent corporation was allowed a tax credit on the

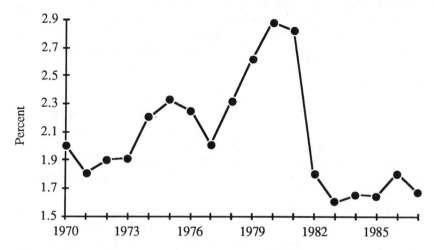

Fig. 5. Corporate income tax revenue as percent of GDP.

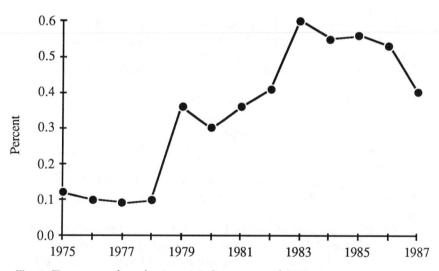

Fig. 6. Tax revenue from foreign capital as percent of GDP.

global foreign source income. In addition, dividends were allowed an indirect credit for the CIT paid abroad. The possibility of globalization allowed for pooling of high- and low-tax income, as well as pooling of remittances from high- and low-tax countries. The pooling of foreign income from all sources in order to determine the foreign tax credit allowed by U.S. legislation made double taxation very unlikely. A U.S. investor with investments in Mexico and other countries could, first of all, combine remittances in interest and dividends. The combined effective rate resulting from doing this could be below 46 percent—the U.S. corporate income tax rate at that time. Moreover, the investor could pool income generated in Mexico with that received from other countries, many of which could have lower effective rates. This strategy would guarantee that income received from abroad was effectively taxed at the U.S. tax rate and no double taxation occurred.

The 1986 U.S. Tax Reform Act severely modified the rules of the game. First of all, the CIT rate was lowered from 46 to 34 percent, with a consequent reduction in foreign tax credit. Second, the U.S. Congress severely limited pooling of high- and low-tax income when determining foreign tax credit. According to the new rules, foreign source income cannot be globalized; it must be separated into high- and low-tax sources so that the foreign tax credit of each base cannot exceed the tax that the same income would have paid in the United States. These two changes in U.S. legislation make it more likely that double taxation will arise.

Are Mexican Tax Rates Too High?

In general, then, income-tax rates in a host country should be similar to those in the home country. When tax rates in the host country exceed those in the home country, foreign investment is discouraged and double taxation may arise. When the opposite scenario occurs, the host country is undertaxing foreign investment; an increase in the level of taxation by the host country will increase tax revenue but not affect foreign investors' economic behavior.

The above rule does not apply, however, to reinvested profits. Because of deferral, the CIT rate in the host country determines investment decisions. Hence, the investor will compare the CIT rate paid in the host country against that which would be paid in the home or alternate host country. Due to the limited scope of this paper, I will only compare the host's CIT rate with that of the home country.

As a result of the new U.S. limitations on foreign tax credit, information on taxation on each type of income in both the home and the host countries must be known in order to assess the adequateness of tax rates in the host country. A comparison will be made between Mexico, Canada, and the United States, with Mexico the host country and the two other nations home countries.

After the tax reforms in Mexico, the United States, and Canada, corporate tax rates are quite similar in all three countries. In both Canada and the United States, corporate profits are taxed by the federal and the provincial or state governments. In Canada, provincial corporate tax rates range from 10 to 20 percent, the average rate being about 15 percent. Adding the federal tax rate of 28 percent for large businesses to the provincial rate results in an aggregate rate of 43 percent. In Canada the federal and provincial governments tax manufacturing industry and small businesses at lower rates (see Table 8).

In the United States, however, states tax corporate income at rates ranging from 0 to 12 percent. The state corporate income tax can be deducted from federal corporate taxable income. Considering that the typical state corporate tax rate is about 6 percent and the federal tax rate is 34 percent, the aggregate corporate tax rate is 38 percent.

In Mexico, states do not tax corporate income. The federal corporate income tax rate, in the new system, is 35 percent, as mentioned before. The new federal corporate income tax rate, which affects investment financed with retained profits, is lower than comparable rates in either Canada or the United States. This assertion is qualified, however, because corporate profits in Mexico are subject to PSW. Since PSW is not deductible from the tax base and profits are only 90 percent of total profits, the effective tax rate is equal to 38.9 percent (35/90). Perhaps this latter rate should be compared with the aggregate corporate rates derived earlier for Canada and the United States.

Dividends in Canada and Mexico increase when the corporate and

TABLE 8

Tax Rate Comparison, 1988: Mexico–Canada–United States

(*in percent*)

	Mexico	Canada	USA
Reinvested earnings	35 + 3.9 = 38.9	28 + 15 = 43	34 + 6 = 40
Dividends:			
Corporate	35 + 3.9 = 38.9	28 + 15 = 43	34 + 6 = 40
Personal	57	60.1	57.0
Withholding taxes:			
Interest	15	28	30
Dividends	57	25	30
Royalties	21	25	30

personal income-tax systems are integrated. In Mexico, dividends paid are deducted from corporate profits, so that the effective rate, once the effect of PSW is accounted for, is 57 percent at the highest personal income tax rate (50 percent). In Canada, however, dividends receive a 25 percent credit so that the effective tax rate is 60.1 percent at the highest personal tax rate (29 percent).

In the United States, dividends are subject to the classical system of taxation; profits are taxed first at the corporate level and then at the personal level after dividends are distributed to shareholders. This classical system taxes dividends twice. The effective tax rate on dividends is 58.6 percent, at the highest personal tax rate of 29 percent, once state personal and corporate income taxes are taken into account.

Thus Mexico has the lowest personal dividend tax rate in North America. Mexico, a host to foreign investment, withholds a tax of 50 percent of dividends distributed abroad. If the dividend were received by an individual, the 50 percent withheld could be fully credited against the personal dividend tax in both Canada and the United States. However, most Mexican subsidiaries have a corporate parent abroad; the 50 percent withheld in Mexico must be credited against a 35 percent corporate tax in the United States or a 28 percent tax in Canada. The Mexican tax cannot be fully credited because both countries limit foreign tax credits to the amount foreign income would have been taxed in the home country.

U.S. or Canadian foreign investment in Mexico from a corporate parent, then, will probably be taxed twice. Two qualifications should be made to this conclusion, however. First, both tax rates and tax bases should be considered when looking at the possibility of crediting foreign taxes. The value-added tax (VAT) in Mexico could increase the chance that dividend-withholding taxes are credited abroad. Second, some countries globalize foreign income and tax credits, so that low-tax countries and/or sources of income can be pooled with high-tax countries and/or sources. The possibility of pooling was largely reduced in the United States after its tax reform. It is thus highly unlikely that the Mexican withholding tax can be fully credited in the United States—it is more likely to be credited in Canada.

Indirect foreign investment introduces quite different problems. In Mexico, interest paid abroad is subject to a withholding tax rate that varies from 0 to 42 percent depending on the interest-payment recipient. There is obviously no possibility of taxing this tax-exempt interest twice. Similarly, there should be little or no threat with respect to interest that pays the 15 and the 21 percent withholding tax, since corporate tax rates in both Canada and the United States are well above those levels. Nevertheless, a possibility of double taxation arises with respect to bank loans. Since a bank is a financial intermediary, profits on a given loan constitute only a small fraction of the total interest paid. Hence, the 15 percent Mexican withholding or total-interest tax could equal or exceed the bank's profit margin. In this case, it is difficult to credit the total interest paid, because the borrower's home country only considers the bank's profit margin.

Notice that this problem arises only because the bank is a financial intermediary. If a foreign corporation makes a loan to a Mexican corporation, the profit of the former would be most of the interest paid by the latter, so that the 21 percent Mexican withholding tax could be credited in the home country. The bank cannot fully credit the Mexican tax because the bank's profit margin is small relative to total interest paid.

Consider what would happen if instead of a loan, the flow of funds to Mexico took the form of direct foreign investment. Clearly, profits would pay a tax at the corporate level and there would also be a withholding tax when dividends were remitted abroad. Dividends paid would cause a corporate-level deduction that would nullify the CIT. Mexico would collect taxes on this income because the income was generated in Mexico: profits of foreign-owned corporations are part of the GDP.

Most of Mexico's foreign debt is government-owned and tax-exempt. The Mexican government pays about 5 to 7 percent of its GDP as interest abroad. If these interest payments were subject to taxation at the 15 percent rate, Mexico could collect about .75 percent of GDP, or about 40 percent of the amount collected through the CIT. Because of the tax exemption on Mexico's foreign debt, the country is foregoing collecting taxes on a large chunk of income generated within. It should be recognized that Mexico and other debtor nations have narrowed their income-tax bases by the amount their sovereign foreign debt has grown.

Most nations recognize the right of a country to tax domestically generated income. This rule is implicit in most double-taxation treaties and in the principle of foreign tax credit in countries that follow the residence principle. There is no reason why interest income should be taxed differently.

THE ROLE OF DEVELOPING COUNTRIES IN PROMOTING FOREIGN INVESTMENT

In general, the level of effective taxation on foreign investment is determined by the level of taxation in the home country. Tax policy by the developing country can do little to promote new foreign investment, other than keep consistent the level of taxation in developing and capital-exporting countries. A positive, secure investment climate with opportunities for profit are the most important factors for foreign investors, and the developing country has policy options that can achieve these factors. Hence, there is no need for developing countries to engage in costly tax-incentive programs to attract new foreign investors; these will likely be ineffective unless tax-sparing clauses are signed with specific capital-exporting countries.

On the other hand, the corporate income-tax rate in the host country was shown to be a determinant in a corporation's decision to reinvest profits. Remittances should be taxed at an effective rate equal to that in the host country and the corporate tax can be adjusted to promote re-investment of earnings. Expensing all of the reinvested profits is a policy equivalent in efficiency to removing the corporate tax, but it does not incur as large a revenue loss. In all instances, developing countries should not attempt to discriminate against domestic investment; this policy would probably result in a distorted allocation of resources. Tax policy should not attempt to discriminate against foreign capital either, as this is likely to result in countervailing measures by capital-exporting countries.

In conclusion, developing countries have a very limited role in promoting foreign investment. On the one hand, a pressing need for tax revenue always exists for these countries. They should be entitled to tax foreign investment but should do so judiciously. Certainly, tax revenue is an important by-product of foreign investment. Tax policy in capital-exporting countries, however, can either promote or discourage foreign investment. Both the foreign tax credit and tax deferral assist the flow of capital investment to developing countries, and result in a fair distribution of tax revenue between the home and the host country. Any attempt to reduce the scope of either the foreign tax credit or tax deferral will reduce incentives to invest abroad and result in a decreased flow of capital to developing countries.

CONCLUSIONS AND RECOMMENDATIONS

Investment in Mexico has declined from its 1982 levels. Consider, however, that during the period 1979–1981, Mexico had the highest level of investment ever. More pronounced than the decline in total investment is the change in its financing structure. The inflow of financial funds from abroad has declined dramatically. Increases in direct foreign investment have not been able to compensate for the huge drop in loans from abroad.

Canada, Mexico, and the United States have undergone major tax reforms that could significantly alter the flow of capital among the three nations. It has been shown that CIT rate levels in the three countries are very similar as a result of tax reforms that have lowered them significantly. However, profit sharing to workers in Mexico could pose a problem because of its magnitude and because it is not a creditable tax in the home country.

Both Canada and the United States have substantially reduced their personal income tax rates, but Mexico has been slow to follow their lead. The higher level of personal taxation in Mexico, however, does not itself pose a problem to foreign investment. Because Mexico has integrated personal and corporate income taxes and does not tax income at the state level, personal dividends are taxed at rates similar to those in Canada and the United States.

Mexico's dividend tax, though, is withheld at a higher rate than normally could be credited by a corporation in Canada or the United States. One solution to this problem would be to lower the Mexican withholding rate when dividends are paid to corporations abroad, so that the tax could be credited by the parent company in the home country. But this problem is not currently of major consequence to the flow of foreign investment to Mexico. The relevant rate for profit reinvestment is the CIT rate in the host country; the dividend rate guides the decision regarding new investment.

Bank lending, however, is a serious problem that affects indirect foreign investment. Most home countries do not allow banks to pass the foreign tax credit on to the actual recipient of interest income in the home country. Hence, the bank cannot, in general, fully credit the Mexican withholding tax because the home-country tax generated by the bank only corresponds to that associated with the bank's profit margin. This situation has forced Mexico to exempt most of its foreign debt, and has meant that a significant fraction of its GDP escapes taxation altogether. Mexico should have the right to tax, at a reasonable rate, income generated within its boundaries. Home countries must let the bank pass the benefit of the foreign tax credit on to the ultimate recipient of interest income.

In conclusion, tax policy should be harmonized within the countries of the North American region in order to generate an adequate and efficient flow of investment across borders. To do so, each nation should recognize the right of the country where income is generated to tax that income. This policy will not only provide for a fair distribution of tax jurisdictions, but will also allow an economically efficient flow of capital among the three countries.

PART IV
Intellectual Property and Technology Transfer

Intellectual Property: A National Perspective

Yehuda Kotowitz

T HE PURPOSE of this paper is to analyze some aspects of national policies with respect to intangible property, in particular, the strength of innovation property rights to encourage innovation. These rights can be enforced by private actions such as secrecy and advertising or by public policy (for example, patent and trademark protection).

The problem may be approached from a global welfare point of view by evaluating the optimal degree of property rights enforcement to maximize global welfare, or from the more narrow national or interest-group-welfare point of view. I shall concentrate on the latter and try to identify the interests of innovators and their home country and complementary factors in different countries and consumers.

We must concentrate on the long-term, or equilibrium, results rather than on short-term considerations. It is obvious that in the short run, once innovation is in place, consumers and complementary factors benefit if property rights are weak because imitators may then utilize the innovation at no cost. However, in the long run lower profitability due to weak property rights will cause a decline in innovation, an effect that may make everyone worse off.

In addition, if public property rights are weakened, private actions by innovators to protect their property rights (such as secrecy and advertising) may be more costly and have undesirable side effects, such as diversion of research and development (R & D) to innovations that are easy to protect by secrecy, the elimination through licensing of gains from trade in innovations, and so on.

We shall concentrate on the question of optimal patent life from the point of view of individual countries (or groups of countries). However, the analysis is qualitatively valid for other innovation-promoting instruments such as trademarks, compulsory licensing and royalties, taxes on technology transfer, and R & D subsidies.

Not surprisingly, the results depend on a variety of special circumstances. We shall look at the following country and industry characteristics: country size; the structure of the innovation industry; the structure of production; supply of complementary factors; ownership of the innovation industry; location of R & D; and type of innovation.

Before proceeding with this analysis, I will review briefly the nature of innovation and its costs and benefits from a global point of view, ignoring distributional issues. This discussion will be a yardstick for the succeeding evaluations of national policies.

THE NATURE OF INNOVATION

The literature generally identifies three types of innovation: (1) minor process innovation, (2) major process innovation, and (3) product innovation. Each of these leads to a somewhat different configuration of net benefits. I will illustrate each under conditions of competitive production and perfectly elastic factor supplies.

A Minor Process Innovation in a Competitive Industry

A minor process innovation is one that reduces costs only slightly in an industry that is competitive prior to the innovation. The situation is illustrated in Figure 1 where C_0 denotes costs prior to the innovation, and C_1 costs after the innovation. The maximum royalty the innovator can charge for licensing all producers in the industry equals the total cost saving due to the innovation, at the pre-innovation level of output. This is because the innovator faces competition, or at least potential competition, from unlicensed firms using the old technology and hence cannot raise the price above that which prevailed prior to the innovation.

During the period over which the innovator can exercise a monopoly on this innovation, consumers do not benefit because the price of the product is the same. Other factors of production, however, may benefit or suffer to the extent that the innovation changes relative demand and supply for factors of production and according to the supply elasticity of these production factors.

After the monopoly over the innovation ends, competition will drive the price of the product down to C_1, eliminating the monopoly profits of the innovator. The reduction in price will therefore increase consumer surplus by the full cost savings of the innovation, which equals the monopoly profit plus the area abd (which represents the gain in consumer surplus from the increased output at the lower price).

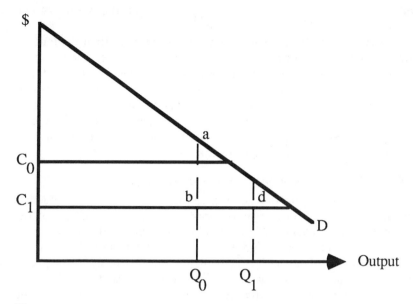

Fig. 1

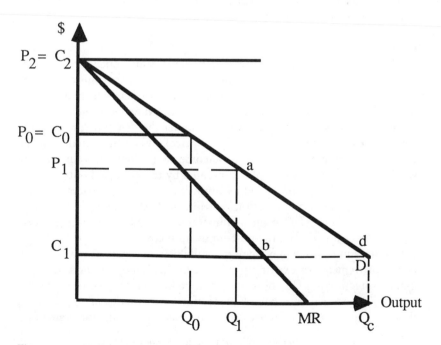

Fig. 2

This consumer surplus, which benefits society more than the innovator, is at the heart of the patent-system dilemma. An increase in the scope and period of protection to the innovator increases the private benefits to the innovator and his incentive to innovate, but decreases—or rather, postpones—the greater social benefits. Thus optimal patent protection requires that such protection stop short of a perpetual patent. The incentive effects of additional patent protection must be balanced against the loss in consumer surplus that arises from it.

A Large Process Innovation in a Competitive Industry

A large process innovation is assumed to lower the costs of production sufficiently below those prevailing prior to the innovation, so that the optimal royalty payment falls short of the cost savings due to the innovation. This can be seen in Figure 2: when costs fall from C_0 to C_1, maximum industry profits occur at P_1, which is lower than C_0. In this case, the gain to the inventor falls short of the cost decrease due to the innovation. Some of the gain accrues to consumers who benefit from the lower price even during the period of the patent monopoly. Thus the excess of social benefits over private benefits in this case is greater than in the small innovation case.

Product Innovation

When a new and superior consumer product is introduced, Usher demonstrated that the product will confer a net consumer surplus even when it is monopolistically priced.[1] Thus the benefits to society from a product innovation equal the monopoly profits of the innovator plus the consumer surplus (represented by the area under the demand curve for the new product and above the monopoly price). When the patent expires, consumer surplus will increase to encompass the monopoly profit and the additional consumer surplus generated by the increased output.

It is useful to think of a product innovation as a large process innovation in which the pre-innovation cost intersects the demand function at zero output. This relationship is illustrated in Figure 2, where the pre-innovation cost is C_2 and the post-innovation cost is C_1.

Product innovations may involve totally new products or major or minor improvements of existing products. In this sense, patent and trademark protection are clearly related. Where innovations are not substantial enough to generate patent protection, trademarks may be useful, though imperfect, substitutes. Thus the basic rationale for trademark

[1] Usher, "The Welfare Economics of Invention," *Economica* 31 (1964), 279–87.

protection is similar to that of patent protection. There are, however, significant differences between patents and trademarks. Trademarks require continuous expenditure on quality control, advertising, and so on, to maintain their value. Trademarks also allow reputation in one product to be at least partly transferred to other products. These properties of trademarks require longer periods of protection than the more product-specific patents need.

An important difference between product and process innovations is that process innovations are frequently easier to protect with secrecy. Hence patent protection may not be as important in this case except for licensing. Furthermore, from an international point of view patent protection in producing countries is particularly important for process innovations, while for product innovations patent protection in the consuming countries is especially important. It is difficult to ascertain which process created a product, or part of a product, that is imported. Even determining the product's origin may be difficult.

Note that if factor supplies to the industry are inelastic, some of the benefits to consumers are transferred to these factors, with a correspondingly higher price in the post-patent period and smaller social benefits. If supply is perfectly inelastic, no reduction in price occurs in the post-patent period. The factor in limited supply appropriates the inventor's profits. This appropriation of profits reduces the social benefits of the innovation.

MARKET STRUCTURE OF THE INNOVATION INDUSTRY

The market structure of the innovation industry is critically important in determining optimal patent protection. A detailed analysis of the optimal patent life for individual projects was developed by Nordhaus for the case of small process innovations under monopoly in innovation.[2] He found that the optimal patent life varies considerably, depending on the parameters of the function relating R & D to cost savings, and on the elasticity of product demand. In particular, the optimal patent life is shortened as the elasticity of demand and the profitability of invention rises, so that patent life should be shorter for industries that have elastic demand and in which technological conditions favor invention. However, departures from optimal patent life do not affect welfare significantly, so that a patent life of 5 years and one of 1,000 years are almost

[2] W. D. Nordhaus, *Invention, Growth, and Welfare: A Theoretical Treatment of Technological Change* (Cambridge, Mass., 1969); W. D. Nordhaus, "The Optimal Life of a Patent," *American Economic Review* 62 (1972), 428–31.

equally efficient. Therefore the social losses due to a uniform patent life are insignificant. However, for high elasticity of demand and relatively large or important inventions, the efficiency of the patent system is quite low relative to an ideal system of lump-sum taxes and subsidies. Thus the patent system is efficient for small inventions where demand is relatively inelastic, but inefficient for larger inventions where demand is elastic, regardless of the patent life (within broad limits).

Two major conclusions emerge from Nordhaus's analysis. First, a fixed patent life is not optimal in theory, although it may be unavoidable in practice. If we are to err on one side, the analysis suggests too long a patent life is better than too short a patent life. For run-of-the-mill innovations, the losses from monopoly are small compared to the gains from invention. The best way to prevent abuse is to ensure that trivial inventions do not receive patents.

Second, the complications arising from risk, drastic inventions, imperfect product markets, and "inventing around" patents generally make advisable a longer rather than shorter patent life.

These conclusions, however, critically depend on the assumption of monopoly in innovation. Lack of competition in innovation eliminates the common-pool problem and any welfare losses that arise due to competition for the rents. A longer patent period, which raises rents to successful innovators, is required to induce sufficient innovation. These rents are part of the welfare gain from innovation.

Similar results were obtained by Dixit and Stiglitz for product innovation, where R & D expenditure are product specific.[3] In their models, there is no competition for any specific innovation, although there is competition among inventors in general. Hence, no rents to successful innovators are dissipated by unsuccessful competitors.[4] Competition in innovation, however, tends to dissipate such rents via the common-pool problem that arises from competition in innovation. The patent system, by creating large rents for the successful innovator, leads many competitors to invest in the hope of capturing the rent. If there are no barriers to entering the innovation industry, expected excess profits in any line of endeavor are expected to be zero. Thus during the patent period there may be no social benefits from the innovation.

The results are similar for other appropriation methods. To the extent that they guarantee excess profits to successful innovators, they generate

[3] Avinash K. Dixit and Joseph E. Stiglitz, "Monopolistic Competition and Optimum Product Diversity," *American Economic Review* 67 (June 1977), 297–308.
[4] These results are therefore more applicable to trademarks than to R & D.

excessive investment to capture such profits. The degree of such potential overinvestment and possible waste is directly dependent on the convexity of the overall innovation process—that is, on the difference between the average and the marginal product of R & D. As firms invest in R & D until the average product equals the marginal resource costs, the excess of average over marginal product leads firms to invest in projects in which the marginal product is smaller than the marginal resource costs. This effect makes the patent system as well as other similar rent-generating mechanisms socially inefficient in generating optimal research effort.

When allowance is made for the common-pool problem, the optimal patent life is drastically reduced. Kotowitz found optimal patent life to be relatively short (one to five years for minor process innovations).[5] The results are similar for product innovations. Optimal patent life for product innovations is only slightly longer than that prescribed for similar minor innovations, except for low-profitability and low-probability projects, where product innovations require a significantly longer optimal patent life. This is because during the patent consumers benefit from marginal product innovations but not from small process innovations. Marginal process innovations, which require very long patents to make them profitable even to one innovator, confer almost no benefits on society at large, because the present value of the small benefits the project generates is drastically reduced by postponement. However, even for marginal projects with long patent life for product innovation, some benefits are available to consumers during the patent, justifying a longer patent life.

In general, the results of these studies indicate that the lower the expected profitability and the higher the degree of uncertainty, the longer the optimal patent life for a project. As well, product innovations generally require a longer patent life than process innovations with equal profitability and probabilities. Thus there is a large variance in optimal project-specific patent life.

However, from a practical point of view, it is necessary to design a fairly uniform patent system to minimize transaction costs and an undesirable degree of government bureaucratic discretion in administering the patent system. Indeed, as pointed out by Wright, the patent system's

---

[5] Yehuda Kotowitz, *Issues in Patent Policy with Respect to the Pharmaceutical Industry* (Ottawa, 1986). Kotowitz used the R & D models from N. Gallini and Yehuda Kotowitz, "Optimal R & D Processes and Competition," *Economica* 52, pp. 321–34; and Partha Dasgupta and Joseph Stiglitz, "Uncertainty, Industrial Structure, and the Speed of R & D," *Bell Journal of Economics* 11 (Spring 1980), 1–28.

major advantage over the alternatives is that it requires little government information to operate.[6]

The optimal average patent period must take into account the social benefits and costs associated with a given patent period for very different circumstances. A patent period too long for a given project can waste resources and lower social benefits by postponing competitive use of the innovation. However, if the patent period is too short, insufficient investment in the relevant project results, and some worthwhile projects will not be undertaken, or will attract too few firms, reducing the probability of innovation.

In contrast to the monopoly inventor case, social welfare is very sensitive to an inappropriate choice of patent length. Patent periods that are too long generate considerable resource waste. Such waste tends to be greatest for more profitable and hence more socially desirable projects. Thus a policy of long patent life may be reasonably efficient under monopoly conditions but inefficient under competitive conditions. Kotowitz finds in this situation that inframarginal projects dominate the picture.[7] The resulting optimal life is heavily biased toward a patent life appropriate for high-profitability projects. Indeed, many of the lowest-profitability projects are eliminated. The reason is obvious: inframarginal projects involve large social welfare, postponement of which is more detrimental than the relatively low social benefits conferred by the marginal projects.

Trademarks will likely yield different results. Although investment competition for trademark benefits will probably persist, the degree of uncertainty and duplication will likely be lower for trademarks than for major innovations. Investments in trademarks are also more likely to be brand-specific. The optimal degree of protection for trademarks will therefore in all likelihood closely resemble that we can expect for the monopoly model.

COUNTRY AND SECTORAL INTERESTS

The policy difference under conditions of monopoly and competition in innovation is exacerbated when individual country interests are considered.

In general, it pays for individual countries to free ride on everyone else's R & D. A country may extend a weak patent protection, or even no patent protection at all, to anyone without violating the Paris conven-

[6] Brian D. Wright, "The Economics of Invention Incentives: Patents, Prizes, and Research Contracts," *American Economic Review* 73 (Sept. 1983), 691–707.

[7] Kotowitz, *Issues in Patent Policy.*

tion. Thus, while resident innovators benefit from foreign patents, resident producers and consumers may appropriate the benefits of foreign innovation at no cost. The effect on global innovation incentives is small if the country is small. The reduction in innovation incentive to residents is also likely to be small, because residents can still benefit from patent rights elsewhere.

If competition in innovation prevails—leading to zero profits—the identity of inventors does not matter. All R & D expenditure induced by local patent protection generates only normal profit, so no net benefits accrue to innovators. The only relevant social welfare is that of local consumers and/or producers, depending on the nature of the innovation and the patent protection. Unless the country is very large, local patent protection must fall significantly short of what would be the socially optimal one, globally speaking, even when patent protection in the rest of the world is too weak.[8]

If patent protection in the rest of the world is long, for example, fourteen to seventeen years, then countries that account for less than about 20 percent of global consumption should provide no patent protection. This conclusion is not surprising; current patent protection in the rest of the world is much too long if competition in innovation prevails. There would be significant overinvestment in R & D with very low marginal returns. The reduction in incentives to invest in R & D caused by lowered patent protection has very little effect on innovation, so the transfer of benefits from innovators to local producers and consumers is simply distributive and can therefore be accomplished with little effect on global welfare.[9]

The situation is markedly different if monopoly in innovation prevails. Under monopoly, the marginal productivity of R & D is likely to be high even with relatively long patent periods elsewhere. So free riding using short local patent periods may significantly hurt local consumers and producers in the long run, and thus becomes a less-appealing option. Moreover, innovators might select their nation of residence according to how much profit they can keep. Thus, patent policies of innovating and non-innovating countries are likely to diverge drastically.

[8] For product innovations: $\phi = \Psi^*(1 - \Psi/4c)$; see *Issues in Patent Policy*, where $\phi = 1 - e^{-2t}$ defines the strength of local patent protection; t = length of patent protection; $\Psi = 1 - e^{-2T}$ and T = length of patent protection elsewhere; Ψ^* is globally optimal Ψ and c = consumption in the country or world.

[9] Of course, retaliation by others will reduce global patent protection. If everyone pursued this policy, patent protection will fall short of the globally optimal one. If there are n equal size countries, all will choose $\phi = \Psi_p/(1 + \Psi_p n/4)$, which is much too weak.

The extent to which monopoly exists worldwide is debatable. There are few industries dominated by one or a few firms worldwide, and even those are subject to potential competition from innovators in related industries. However, there are several cases where such conditions may exist.

First, if a monopoly exists in the final product market, a monopoly may exist in the innovation market because of the "learning by doing" effect. Also, the incentive of outsiders to innovate for a monopoly is weak because, unless the innovation is sufficiently drastic to allow independent entry, the innovator must sell the innovation to the monopolist. In the resulting bilateral monopoly, the innovator has a poor bargaining position. The benefits to the existing monopoly are greater than those that might accrue to outside investors. Hence, most R & D investment is undertaken by the monopolist, even where such investment is very profitable.

Worldwide monopolies are uncommon, but local monopolies or worldwide oligopolies are prevalent. Although in oligopoly innovation rivalry may occur, it seldom eliminates all excess profits. As well, cross-licensing and other agreements may modify innovation competition, so the results approach those of the monopoly model. It is, however, important to note that in such cases patent protection may not be important, except to the extent that it facilitates cooperation among cartel members. The factors that generate the production monopoly are sufficient to generate monopoly in innovation and protect the monopolist from imitation. This effect is most strong for process innovations, particularly minor ones.

An important exception may arise, however, when the monopoly in production and innovation depends on ownership of an important patent, which then supports any further innovations. In addition, in the aerospace and some joint-venture industries, significant economies may exist in R & D such that there are very few competitors, even when there are excess profits.

Berkowitz and Kotowitz investigate two cases depending on the residence of the innovator.[10] Where innovators are local, they demonstrate that the optimal local patent protection is at least as long as that adopted in the rest of the world, unless patent life in the rest of the world is excessive. This is true because the marginal benefits to innovators and local consumers exceed the losses to local consumers as long as the world patent period is suboptimal. Only when the world patent period is op-

[10] M. Berkowitz and Y. Kotowitz, "Patent Policy in an Open Economy," *Canadian Journal of Economics* vol. 15, no. 1 (Feb. 1982), 1–17; Kotowitz, *Issues in Patent Policy.*

timal do local benefits just offset local losses from consumer surplus postponement.

Thus when patent protection in the rest of the world is insufficient, monopoly countries have an incentive to compensate and increase patent protection beyond the globally optimal one.

The situation is different for countries that do not produce many innovations. If the product is supplied competitively, prices in the country in question fall by the full cost saving caused by a minor innovation. Hence, the only relevant benefits are those to local consumers. The situation is similar to the competitive case, except for the marginal incentive effects generated by lengthening local patent protection. The R & D brought forth by a given increase in profitability under competition is smaller. But the marginal productivity of such investment may be higher than under competition at the same world patent life. The resulting optimal patent life is similar to that of the competitive case. For small countries (or groups of countries), no patent protection is optimal.

THE LOCATION OF R & D AND PATENT OWNERSHIP

So far, we have ignored the issue of the location of R & D. In the absence of taxes and subsidies, and where the supply of inventive resources is infinitely elastic, only the ownership of the innovation matters. However, matters change with taxes and subsidies.

Research and development is typically heavily subsidized. First, all R & D expenditure is written off for tax purposes.[11] This tax treatment effectively subsidizes R & D at a level proportional to the corporate tax rate. Thus it becomes appealing to conduct R & D in high-tax jurisdictions, but transfer any profits from successful R & D to low-tax jurisdictions. This transfer can be done by registering patent rights in such jurisdictions or by charging low royalties to subsidiaries in low-tax jurisdictions. Because the product is intangible, if no licensing agreements with outside producers exist, it is very difficult to police the relevant transfer prices. These considerations must modify significantly the welfare calculations. In the competitive case, subsidies contribute to potential resource waste when patent protection is excessive, but in addition, may transfer some profits from successful innovations to foreign governments via increased tax revenues.

The results are similar, though perhaps stronger, for the monopoly case. When one considers the tendency of foreign corporations to trans-

---

[11] Advertising expenses, which are important for trademark promotion, are treated similarly.

fer patent ownership and profits to parent companies or to lower-tax jurisdictions, it is clear that offering shorter patent protection to foreign
corporations is desirable. Berkowitz and Kotowitz point out that: "Local patent protection only exacerbates what is an undesirable situation,
where local government subsidizes research by foreign companies reap-
ing only a small fraction from the resulting inventions. The insistence on
the performance of research in local subsidiaries of foreign companies is
misguided, unless governments can insure that patent rights (and appropriate royalties) reside in the local subsidiary."[12]

SUPPLY OF R & D FACTORS

All of the foregoing conclusions were based on the assumption that the
supply of R & D factors, or complementary R & D or production factors, is infinitely elastic. The analysis thus assumes partial equilibrium—
that the innovation sector is small and that resources can be transferred
easily between it and other sectors. This assumption may not be valid
even in the long run. It is therefore important to reevaluate the result
assuming an inelastic supply of innovative resources.

This new assumption transfers rents from innovation to scarce factors.
Increased patent protection increases rents without generating any significant increase in R & D. The results resemble those found when increasing the convexity of the innovation process in the monopoly case.
From a global point of view, increasing patent protection postpones the
increase in consumer surplus without generating additional innovation.
Hence, a shorter patent period is called for. However, the conflict of interest between high-innovation and low-innovation countries remains.
Low-innovation countries prefer a short patent life and high-innovation
countries prefer a longer one.

The situation is quite different in the competitive case. Although competition among innovators dissipates their rents, the rents are transferred
to the scarce factors rather than dissipated in the form of additional unproductive R & D.

Thus the rents to scarce factors must be included in the calculus. This
changes the competitive model to resemble a monopoly one, albeit with
very low elasticity of supply for innovations. As we have seen, such a case
leads to short optimal patent life from a global point of view but exacerbates the conflict between low- and high-innovation countries.

Under these conditions, the location of R & D becomes important. If
a low-innovation country succeeds in forcing more R & D into its own
territory (for example, Canada and its pharmaceutical industry) while

[12] Berkowitz and Kotowitz, "Patent Policy," 14.

importing the scarce resources, some of the rents associated with innovation may be transferred to the country. Whether this transfer can offset the tax effects and the costs of attracting these resources is certainly questionable.

SOME EFFECTS OF THE CANADA-U.S. FREE TRADE AGREEMENT

A major effect of the FTA is expected to be a rationalization of production—namely, increased specialization, whether by comparative advantage or a random selection of intraindustry trade. It is expected that some subsidiary production will be eliminated or replaced with a marketwide narrower product-line mandate.

However, some of these patterns may be disrupted by differential patent protection. Consider, for example, a U.S. firm producing in the United States and exporting to Canada. A process innovation reduces industry costs, but due to patent protection in the United States, prices remain unchanged. If no patent protection exists in Canada, it may pay someone to utilize the innovation in Canada by manufacturing locally for local consumption and possible export to other non-patent countries. The desired effects of rationalization may be thwarted. Tariff protection is replaced by lack of patent protection. The U.S. firm could supply the Canadian market at lower prices, but this would require barring reimportation into the United States.

If rationalization does occur because of the FTA, will it resolve some of the conflicts associated with patent policy? Some argue that such rationalization will lead to a more even distribution of innovations across countries, and hence remove the conflicts.

It is reasonable to assume that innovation is more likely where significant production occurs. In particular, through "learning by doing," innovations in any industry are more likely to arise in countries that produce a significant share of industry output. If this relation is nonlinear, then as productivity in innovation rises with production, innovation will tend to increase in smaller countries due to the rationalization of production due to the FTA.[13]

However, while rationalization may reduce the patent-policy conflict, it will not eliminate the problem. Free riding still exists. Small countries, regardless of inventive intensity, still stand to benefit much more than large countries by free riding on the innovation of others. Hence, the conflict can only be resolved through negotiations. As small countries are likely to benefit more than large countries from free trade agreements, a trade appears possible. It is clearly in the interest of all countries to set

[13] I am not aware of any empirical evidence on this question.

patent protection at the globally optimal level, while allowing for equitable distribution of rents.

SUMMARY AND CONCLUSIONS

My objective was to analyze intellectual property protection from a national-interest point of view. The economic rationale for such property rights is to attract resources for producing intellectual property. Innovators, the intellectual property "resources," are attracted by the promise of potential profits: property rights to their innovations. The problem arises from the "public good" nature of intellectual property: once it exists, it is relatively easy to copy or imitate. Property rights to it may severely restrict its use, and thus its societal benefit. Hence, property rights are a relatively inefficient tool for eliciting resources and ensuring full use of the results.

Other public instruments such as subsidies, however, require too much direct intervention, a task that governments have shown themselves incapable of accomplishing efficiently. Moreover, private methods of protecting property rights, such as secrecy, appear to be even more inefficient. Thus it appears that the public protection of intellectual property must be used, in spite of its deficiencies.

The analysis reveals that the degree of protection that is optimal varies considerably, depending on the industry's market structure and on whose interests are considered. Under competition in innovation, globally optimal patent protection is relatively short—less than five years. Under a monopoly, however, a long patent life is desirable. Similarly, even under competitive conditions, strong protection for trademarks may be warranted.

This distinction appears to become even sharper when viewed from a national perspective. There is a fundamental conflict between countries that generate significant innovations and those that do not. Although all countries have an incentive to eliminate patent protection in their jurisdictions and free ride on the innovations of others, this incentive is particularly strong for consuming countries. If innovation industries are competitive, this conflict is not serious. A short patent period is optimal for everyone. However, under conditions of monopoly in innovation, or an inelastic supply of innovative resources, this conflict is enhanced. Innovation-producing countries press for maximum patent protection to encourage innovation and increase their share of benefits from innovation. Innovation-consuming countries prefer weaker patent protection, not only to free ride on innovation efforts elsewhere, but also to protect themselves against the monopoly power of the innovating countries.

This conflict emerges in the opposing policies of developed and underdeveloped countries toward the protection of intellectual property rights. It appears that this conflict is based on the belief that a significant degree of monopoly power in innovation exists, either at the enterprise level or for individual countries. Our analysis suggests that such an assumption may not be warranted; lower levels of patent protection may be desirable even for innovation-producing countries.

Industrial Modernization, Technological Development, and Industrial Property: Mexico Vis-à-vis the Challenges of the New Technological Revolution

Mauricio de María y Campos

MEXICO'S CURRENT national context is one of uncertainty, but also one of determination to take whatever steps are necessary to modernize and survive as an independent country.

Although some causes of Mexico's uncertainty will be short-lived, Mexico seems at present to face overwhelming challenges—a situation to be expected in light of the seriousness of the problems that have faced the country since 1982. These problems include a foreign-earnings and foreign-debt crisis, a sharp decline in world oil prices, severe earthquakes in 1985, and a sharp downturn in the stock market in 1987. Mexico's determination to take concrete steps to deal with these difficulties produced responses ranging from the Plan for Economic Restructuring to the Economic Solidarity Pact.

Fortunately, Mexico is achieving significant successes in stabilizing the national economy and reducing inflation, improvements that guarantee Mexico will face a much-improved national picture in the near future. However, not all of the factors that are sources of uncertainty and instability in Mexico today are of short duration and easily resolved. Much of the uncertainty can be attributed to the fact that in Mexico, as in all other countries, changes are in motion that are without precedent, which present novel problems and options to developing countries. These nations are often unable to offer an adequate response because they are simply emotionally unprepared. As Michael Blumenthal noted in a recent issue of *Foreign Affairs*, accelerated change can produce uncertainty in a developing country such as Mexico, with its scarce resources and burdensome external debt—a debt owed abroad but that is also a cost to be carried by Mexican society. The situation is thus doubly problematic.[1]

What exactly is happening? The factors of change are many. Nevertheless, one very decisive factor has undoubtedly characterized the 1970s and the 1980s: the worldwide scientific and technological transformation, which is occurring so rapidly that the political, social, economic, and cultural weave of a country is sometimes not able to incorporate it. This situation generates tensions, inappropriate or misguided responses, and sometimes even social paralysis.

Of what does this technological change consist? What are its effects in countries like Mexico? How does the theme of industrial property fit within this framework? What steps could Mexico take to address these challenges most effectively? What is the role in all this of relations among Mexico, Canada, and the United States?

THE NEW TECHNO-INDUSTRIAL REVOLUTION
AND ITS IMPLICATIONS FOR MEXICO

Recent scientific and technological trends are multiple and diverse. However, advances in the field of microelectronics have clearly held center stage. The printed circuit board and microprocessor have revolutionized communications and transportation, and their impact has been felt strongly in production and marketing methods, education, health care, and recreation. Even more notably, the printed circuit board and microprocessor have transformed information into a basic resource of modern life—one that crosses geographic, political, and social barriers and has generated a world that is increasingly in touch and interdependent, despite sometimes acute disparities in income distribution.

The interface between electronics and biotechnology, the development of new materials, and the incorporation of new properties into traditional materials are processes transforming agriculture, food production, health, and care of the environment, as well as trade flows. Current discussions within GATT about services are one result of technological changes in the management of information and in international transactions of intangible goods, where the United States and other developed countries already concentrate a major share of their workers and income.

The global economy has entered a new phase in its development, the importance of which must not be underestimated. Changes underway at the international level have accorded industrialized countries a new com-

[1] W. Michael Blumenthal, "The World Economy and Technological Change," *Foreign Affairs*, 66, no. 3 (1988), pp. 529–50.

parative advantage through introducing worldwide a new generation of processes, products, organization forms, and industrial structures. These new developments have allowed industrialized countries to optimize their abundant resources: technology, organization, capital, and information. On the other hand, these changes have allowed developed countries to maximize their comparative advantage by substituting production factors, while developing countries still rely on the same factors on which they initially based their development: abundant raw materials, energy resources, and manpower.[2]

Newly developed materials offer alternatives to traditional materials. Examples include the use of fiberglass in place of copper in telephone cables and the use of composites and ceramics in automobile manufacture. Similar substitutions are being introduced through biotechnological advances; sugar's replacement by industrial glucose is but one example.[3]

Some of these developments, such as those occurring in the automobile and aeronautics industries, were driven by the search for lighter, more energy-efficient materials. Each success in this area meant a further reduction in the demand for oil.[4]

These trends pose a dual dilemma for developing countries such as Mexico: there is a structural reduction in demand and prices for raw materials, and the production of new materials carries implicit technological challenges that developing countries are in a poor position to address.

Regarding the impacts on demand and prices, a recent study revealed that Mexico's 1986 exports earned only what they would have if marketed in 1980. Export earnings for 1986 totaled $16 billion, whereas at 1980 prices they would have generated $27 billion. Import prices, meanwhile, continue to increase. If imports to Mexico had also been priced at 1980 levels, imports would have amounted to $9.1 billion, rather than the $11.4 billion actually spent on imports in 1987. If both imports and exports had been realized at 1980 prices, Mexico's 1986 trade surplus would have been nearly $17 billion, rather than the registered $4.6 billion.[5]

[2] Mauricio de María y Campos, in *Mexico and the United States: Face to Face with New Technologies* (Washington, Overseas Development, 1987).

[3] John Senell, "The Dual Challenge: Managing the Economic Crisis and Technological Change," in *Growth, Export, and Jobs in a Changing World Economy*, U.S. Third-World Policy Perspectives, no. 9 (Washington, Overseas Development Council, 1988).

[4] Eric Larson, Marc Ross, and Robert Williams, "Beyond the Era of Materials," *Scientific American* (June 1986).

[5] Héctor Hernández Cervantes, "Retos y perspectivas de la reconversión industrial," in *Reconversión Industrial en América Latina* (Mexico City, Fondo de Cultura Económica, 1987).

Clearly this difference cannot be attributed entirely to the introduction of energy-saving technologies or the replacement of traditional raw materials with innovative substitutes. However, over the long term, these factors are proving to be strong explanatory variables for structural changes in demand and prices.

Probably the new technologies' strongest impacts in countries with accelerated demographic growth occur in the labor market. New technologies carry with them increasing reliance on robots and automation, both of which decrease dependence on an unskilled work force in the production process. Moreover, the new technologies cannot economically be made labor intensive, given the demands that the international market makes in terms of quality, flexibility, and technology interface.[6]

An automobile assembly plant built recently by the Ford Motor Company in Hermosillo, Sonora, evidences the impact of the new technologies. The number of jobs initially opened at the plant fell by approximately 60 percent as the plant turned increasingly to robotization.

A similar situation emerges in Mexico's in-bond assembly plants, the *maquiladoras*. Even though total employment in the *maquilas* has doubled over the last six years, worker productivity has increased at an even higher rate, again as a result of increased automation.[7]

In effect, despite the fact that salaries on Mexico's northern border average only one-eighth of those on the U.S. side of the frontier, Mexico's comparative advantage is threatened by labor-saving innovations—a threat confirmed by two recent studies in the electronics and apparel industries.[8]

The technological revolution has allowed industrialized countries to consolidate in product areas where they have traditionally dominated in order to gain control of traditional sectors that were believed lost to developing countries (such as the textile industry) and in order to develop new products that confer an advantage in innovative fields such as microelectronics, telematics, biotechnology, and new materials, the most notable of these being superconductors.[9]

Rapid technological change is fostered by the growing internationalization of investment, production, and services—a result of the revolu-

[6] Manuel Castells and Laura d'Andrea Thyson, "High Technology Choices Ahead: Restructuring Interdependence," in Senell, *Growth, Export, and Jobs.*

[7] "Evolución reciente de la industria maquiladora," study prepared for the Department of Industrial Promotion and Regional Development (Dirección General de Promoción Industrial y Desarrollo Regional) (Mexico City, Ministry of Trade and Finance (SECOFI), 1987).

[8] Castells and Thyson, "High Technology Choices Ahead."

[9] Y Campos, *Face to Face with New Technologies.*

tion in informatics—as well as by changes in the geographic distribution of economic power and technological excellence. In this sense, perhaps the most important change is the one affecting the technological prominence that the United States has enjoyed over the last fifteen years. While the United States continues to invest more in absolute terms in science and technology than do its industrialized counterparts, this investment has declined to 2 percent of U.S. Gross National Product (GNP), which is a percentage below that of other developed countries.[10] The result is clear. As a recent study notes, not only has Japan taken the lead in introducing new products and processes to the world market, the qualitative value or importance of Japanese patents is far superior to that of the U.S. patents, a fact that undermines the timeworn image of Japan as a nation of imitators.[11]

It should come as no surprise, then, that the economic development of the West is evolving as a power triangle comprising the United States, Japan, and Europe, and that the upcoming years will likely reveal a world that is increasingly interdependent but comprising four blocs, the fourth being the Soviet Union.

Especially important in defining the new distribution of economic power are the policy decisions being adopted by European Economic Community (EEC) countries as they bring their regulations and procedures in line with one another and remove all internal obstacles to forming an economic community of nations by 1992. Their decision for unity reflects Europe's hopes of competing with the United States and Japan. The resolution assumes a tremendous technological effort, both to train human resources and to build a research and development (R & D) infrastructure that will guarantee levels of productivity and competitiveness typical of industrialized countries.[12]

Unfortunately, large multinational corporations, which are based in the developed countries, have two strong incentives for restricting developing countries' access to new technologies. The first incentive stems from the transnationals' concern about the short life cycle of the emerg-

[10] Robert Reich, "The Economics of Illusion and the Illusion of Economics," *Foreign Affairs*, 66, no. 3 (1988), pp. 516–28.
[11] William J. Broad, "By One Measure, Japan Overtook the United States in Inventions in the 1970s," *New York Times* (May 1988).
[12] For a general overview, see coverage in the *New York Times* during May 1988. For a focus on the telecommunications sector, see the article by Terry Dodsworth, *Financial Times* (11 May 1988); for the automobile industry, see various papers prepared for the International Policy Forum, hosted by the International Motor Vehicle Program of the Center for Technology, Politics, and Industrial Development of the Massachusetts Institute of Technology, and held at Villa d'Este, Lago Como, Italy, 15–18 May 1988.

ing technologies; the second is the increasing price tag for R & D. These two factors, along with the emergence of new competitors in Latin America and particularly along the Pacific Rim, have led multinationals to adopt a deliberate policy of limited access.[13]

Multinationals' strategy of limited access results in two negative consequences for developing countries. The developing countries are discovering that transnational companies are less willing to license their new technologies, and with licensing declining, the transnationals are increasingly relying on an export strategy or, when this option is not open to them, direct investment in foreign markets. This situation is not new to Mexican firms, which have felt its effects in recent years, especially in advanced technologies. The impact of the transnationals' strategy is increasing with each lowering of Mexico's trade barriers.[14]

Perhaps the most severe repercussion of the multinationals' policy of restricting access to new technologies is the pressure that major international companies in technology-intensive sectors have brought to bear on their governments. These governments, in turn, redirect the pressure onto the developing countries that are most advanced in the area of intellectual property, and demand they respect intellectual property rights and patents to the letter.[15] This strategy, originally introduced by chemical companies, particularly pharmaceutical firms from Organization for Economic Cooperation and Development (OECD) countries, has become more entrenched since the end of the 1970s in response to the success that Japan and the more advanced developing countries have had in copying, reproducing, and improving original technologies.[16] Over the past five years, the hard-line pursuit of this strategy has encompassed the following actions:

- New fields have been brought under strict protection, including industries producing electronics, biotechnology, and innovative materials.
- Large companies have increasingly emphasized product patents and

---

[13] Castells and Thyson, "High Technology Choices Ahead."

[14] Benito Bucay, presentation at the National Meeting on Industrial Modernization of the Institute of Economic/Political Research, of the Institutional Revolutionary Party (PRI) (San Luis Potosí, Mexico, April 1988).

[15] Eduardo White, "El problema de las patentes en el sector farmacéutico," prepared for the meeting of the Regional SELA, the pharmaceutical industry in Mexico (Mexico City, May 1988).

[16] Organization for Economic Cooperation and Development (OECD), "The Newly Industrializing Countries: Implications for OECD Industries and Industrial Policies," (Paris: OECD, 1988); United Nations Industrial Development Organization, "La evolución de las patentes sobre medicamentos en los países desarrollados," taken from a document prepared by F. Lobo (Caracas, Venezuela, May 1988); The President's Commission for Industrial Competitiveness (Washington, Government Printing Office, 1985).

improvements on process patents and insisted that the more advanced developing countries adopt legislation consistent with this focus.

▪ Business has lobbied both to increase the term and extent of the privileges that patents provide their holders and to eliminate obligatory licensing.

▪ Efforts have been made in international forums to harmonize legislation on patents, trademarks, and author rights worldwide.

▪ Mechanisms for exercising pressure on policymakers and legislators have proliferated, while traditional mechanisms have been rejected in an effort to concentrate on bilateral negotiations and the multilateral mechanisms that govern foreign trade, such as the Uruguay Round of the General Agreement on Tariffs and Trade (GATT).

Within this strategy, U.S. companies and the U.S. government have clearly played a leadership role, especially since the passage of the 1984 Trade Law and the Uruguay Round. The consensus on the leadership status of the United States is clear in the ongoing discussions between the U.S. executive and legislative branches concerning the U.S. executive's proposal on trade and competitiveness.[17]

The strategy of limiting access to technology is perfectly understandable from the perspective of the developed countries, including the United States, which is struggling to protect its productivity, competitiveness, and balance of trade. The irony is that the industrialized countries are pursuing this strategy at the very moment that Mexico and other countries of the developing world are struggling with economic crisis, when their costs of servicing the foreign debt is stunting all internal growth, when their financial and investment resources are in precipitous decline, and when their governments and companies are forced to reduce investment in science and technology.

Moreover, the proposals now on the negotiating table suggest that the patent law is natural and universal; that it transcends national differences and therefore deals fairly with everyone. In reality, the patent law confers monopoly privileges on companies acting in a world that is increasingly asymmetric in economic and technological terms.

A source of conflict thus emerges in the differing national viewpoints. What developed countries and their industries view as a legitimate effort to defend their technological property against imitative, or even disloyal, practices is commonly perceived by observers in developing countries as a new type of protectionism now applied to the diffusion of technological know-how—in effect, a barrier to creative activity in developing countries.

[17] White, "El problema de las patentes."

MEXICO'S RESPONSE TO THE
TECHNO-INDUSTRIAL REVOLUTION

Clearly the implications of the new technological-industrial revolution are broad and significant. Mexico cannot afford to remain marginal to this process. Rather, it must adopt policies consistent with these changes—and it must do so soon if it hopes to define its own role in the new international context, consolidate its past achievements, and advance toward new stages of social development. Mexico can learn from the experiences of other countries, but it should not imitate a borrowed pattern; it must follow its own path at the national and regional levels.[18]

To pursue an independent direction implies, once again, a dual challenge: to overcome the accumulated residues left by late arrival to the process of technological change, and to address the new international technological revolution effectively despite the economic crisis. Mexico must exert the tremendous effort necessary to transform its productive and organizational structures and its work processes if it is to become a more central player within the new global economic structure.

Mexico has not been idle during recent years, despite the severity of its difficulties. The country has begun a process of economic restructuring, reduced the public-sector debt, transformed the traditionally negative trade balance into a net surplus, rationalized the government's role in the economy, and brought itself into the international economy by opening its domestic market to imports, joining the GATT, and replacing its former resistance to foreign investment with a policy that selectively promotes such investment.

Mexico's process of restructuring, or modernization, is intended to raise the country's levels of productivity and international competitiveness and allow it to take advantage of the export opportunities presented by the international market. Unfortunately, Mexico's economic crisis, which began in 1982, has since then caused Mexico to severely cut productive investment, the crucial factor in technical progress. The crisis has also prevented the government from allocating adequate resources to support R & D activities, both in research institutions and in centers of higher learning. Expenditures in technological R & D, as well as the budget allocated to the National Science and Technology Council (CONACYT), have been cut significantly in real terms since 1986.[19]

[18] Mauricio de María y Campos, "Los retos de la modernización ante el cambio científico y tecnológico," paper presented at the meeting of World Economic Change and Modernization, organized by the Institute of Political and Economic Studies of the PRI (Mexico City, 16 March 1988).

[19] *Ibid.*

Given their very limited resources, industrial firms and research centers have been forced to focus on survival, rather than on pursuing innovative research. Their concerns lie more with their financial difficulties than with production or technology issues. The result of this focus is visible today: a serious lag in technological development.

Mexico's economic crisis has also provoked serious delays in the preparation of human resources, particularly technical personnel. Both in number and quality, the professionals who have recently been employed in various productive and academic activities fall far short of meeting the country's requirements. Moreover, the need for this type of personnel is increasing with the pace of structural change, and the lack of trained human resources will prove an ever more serious problem in the future.

Some sectors, however—the automobile industry, electronics, pharmaceuticals, textiles, and the food and beverage industry—have made important productive investments directed toward improving their companies' export profiles, and these investments have produced a surplus in Mexico's trade balance. Factors contributing to this success include the country's current macroeconomic and sectoral policies, as well as the fact that Mexico—because of its geographic location and social stability—offers a particularly attractive and suitable location for industries such as automobile assembly and electronics. Mexico is an ideal manufacturing site, thanks to its productive and cheap labor force, its proximity to U.S. markets, and its ability to rapidly incorporate modern administrative practices.

THE FUTURE CHALLENGE: EQUITABLE GROWTH, MODERNIZATION, AND TECHNOLOGICAL DEVELOPMENT WITHIN AN UNCERTAIN INTERNATIONAL CONTEXT

Over the next decade, Mexico must face a two-edged challenge: (1) to regain the path of sustained growth and higher levels of production, investment, and job creation within a framework of macroeconomic stability and social justice, and (2) to follow through with the structural changes and economic modernization that are already underway, relying primarily on Mexican resources and efforts within an international context characterized by caution and growing protectionism.

In the area of technology the challenge is formidable, since growth and modernization will depend principally on Mexico's own technological efforts. These efforts are seriously restricted by current limitations on financial resources, despite the fact that an increase in foreign direct investment would somewhat alleviate the domestic shortfall. Moreover,

Mexico must overcome inertia and deeply rooted patterns of technological passivity in order to construct a dynamic technological strategy that surpasses strictly technical considerations.

Mexico needs to consolidate its efforts in technology development with attainments in administration, marketing, and informatics so that the combination leads to more efficient production, higher product quality, and especially, more added value. Achieving this aim will require that Mexico design production processes that are more efficient than any currently available, give free rein to creativity, and develop new products and designs that can efficiently satisfy modern-day social demands. The Mexican entrepreneur must recognize, at last, that developing new technologies is not only an essential factor in ensuring his survival and ability to offer a comparative advantage; it can be and should be an activity that proves highly profitable over the long term.

Mexico's large firms, spurred by international competition, will find themselves increasingly able to incorporate foreign technological changes and create their own technological capacities and strengths. The sector that will be most challenged is small and mid-sized industry, the backbone of Mexican industry in terms of both employment and its promotion of regional development. This sector will find it must incorporate technological change even more judiciously than must the larger firms.

Fortunately, flexible systems are available today that help incorporate new processes and improve those goods manufactured using small-scale production processes. This technology is very complex and requires training highly skilled individuals to exploit these systems effectively. However, there are also other more easily attained goals. These include the dissemination of information, a process that facilitates a small industry's access to shared regional information networks, enhances communication among similar sectors and companies, and counteracts the disadvantages accruing traditionally to small-scale production.

It is important to remember that the concept of economies of scale is not always applicable to the new technologies. A more appropriate concept might now be "efficient production capacities for specific products."

Given the multiple challenges outlined above, Mexico must pursue a realistic and pragmatic strategy for technological development over the upcoming years—a strategy linked to national goals and Mexico's social needs, available resources, and comparative advantages. Such a strategy must satisfy the specific needs of the productive sector. Broad acceptance and implementation of the plan depends on an effective alliance among entrepreneurs, the state, and the scientific-technological community. The strategy cannot be unfocused or indiscriminate: Mexico's shortage of human and financial resources, the elevated costs for R & D, and international realities all require that it be specific and selective.

In shaping this strategy, Mexico can benefit from the experiences of other countries, even though it will need to define and follow its own national course. A particularly relevant model that should not be overlooked, despite its limitations and peculiarities, is that offered by Japan and the four "tigers" of the Pacific Rim—Taiwan, Korea, Singapore, and Hong Kong. These countries were able to achieve sustained and internationally competitive industrial development by following sectoral-technology policies designed by companies and governments working in concert. Their policies were directed toward specific goals and toward designing their own terms for comparative advantage within a dynamic international economy.

Japan is probably the best-known case. Throughout the 1950s and 1960s, Japan encouraged selective and regulated importation of technology to priority sectors. But even more important to its success was the fact that Japan also induced companies to invest in technological R & D at a cost four times greater than the cost of purchasing foreign technology.[20]

The fact that such an approach has now been adopted by other countries—not only developing countries, but also several European countries and even the United States—in strategic sectors such as electronics, aeronautics, and biotechnology obviously introduces the possibility that some international friction may arise. Nevertheless, several recent events indicate that, despite the risk of international frictions, this type of strategy will become increasingly prevalent.[21]

The U.S. government now finances about 50 percent of U.S. industry's costs for technology R & D through direct supports, government purchase programs, and fiscal incentives. Although some sectors, such as the automobile industry, are controlled solely by market mechanisms, other sectors involved in breakthrough technology enjoy increasing support.[22]

We find a similar situation in Europe, although the level and type of support, as well as the sectors that benefit, vary from country to country. In Great Britain, about sixty different programs provide companies with technological support. Mexico and other developing countries will have to adopt similar programs if they are to compete in the international

[20] Terutomo Ozawa (personal communication).

[21] See, for example, recent frictions between Japan and the United States over semiconductors, or the Airbus-Boeing-McDonnell Douglas case in aeronautics.

[22] U.S. Government Printing Office, *Economic Report of the President* (Washington, 1988).

market. Unfortunately, these support structures must be created and activated under conditions of comparative disadvantage.

Mexico should also review the experiences of Italy, West Germany, and the Scandinavian countries. These countries have shown that it is not necessary to reject the industrial occupations that are already established in and well-adapted to a country, but rather it is important to raise these occupations to a level of international excellence. Even though conventional wisdom argues that Mexico must jump aboard the technological train soon, it should not do so heedlessly. First, the country must seek the best way to do what it does well, with ever-increasing efficiency and creativity.

Several countries severely criticized Italy for not diversifying its production, but rather persisting in its focus on clothing, furniture, and shoes. Nevertheless, with time Italy developed new technologies and products in these production areas and invested in fashion and design with such success that it stimulated exports, generated more added value, and realized healthy profits. Italy simultaneously disseminated at other production levels the technologies for the industrial design and manufacture of those capital goods needed by its consumer goods industries. These capital goods now constitute another of Italy's export products.[23]

Because of the important position that technological change holds in current international economic relations, and because of Mexico's urgent need to consolidate a national technological base, Mexico's policy for science and technology must include directing more of its financial resources toward technology over the next few years. Underpinning this effort must be a strategy that can maintain a balance between primary and applied research and that will foment linkages between the needs of society and those of the productive sector.

The public effort to be undertaken is immense in light of today's scarcity of resources. But even more overwhelming is the need to stimulate private programs that can satisfy the needs for skilled personnel and other resources for research, development, and technological adaptation within productive and service entities, within groups of companies, and within regions. The public sector must support such efforts through basic infrastructure and direct support as other countries have done, but Mexico's private sector will have to shoulder a growing share of the responsibility and provide a larger portion of the necessary investment.

---

[23] Phillipe Lorino, "Nuevos retos industriales en el Europa Occidental," in *La reconversión industrial de América Latina y el nuevo contexto internacional* 2 (Mexico City, Fondo de Cultura Económica, 1987).

OPTIONS FOR TRADE AND TECHNOLOGY RELATIONS
AMONG MEXICO, CANADA, AND THE UNITED STATES:
COOPERATION OR DEEPENING CRISIS?

Mexico's ability to continue its process of structural change could be in jeopardy if the country cannot attain within the next few years acceptable growth in GNP, investments, and employment. Growth in these areas will only be realized if there is a reduction in the country's foreign debt burden, an increase in financial resources, and an expansion of the external market.

Trade

It is obvious that the external market will play a key role in this structural change, especially when we consider that Mexico's past industrial strategy stood on just one leg. It would be a tragedy if protectionist attitudes in developed countries, and especially in some sectors of the United States, were to close the door to Mexican products just when Mexico is making unprecedented strides in manufactured exports and its business sector is becoming outwardly focused.

Even so, the foreign market alone cannot provide the support Mexico needs. Although Mexico's export opportunities are plentiful and the country can theoretically increase exports many times over before exhausting the full range of openings offered by the international markets, many factors suggest that exploiting the external market will not be an easy task. Among these factors are the following considerations: First, Mexico must still dedicate a significant share of its total resources to servicing its external debt. Second, the industrialized countries are themselves in a period of slow growth. And finally, competition in the international market is growing as more and more countries seek ways to increase exports or decrease their negative trade balances (as is the case with the United States). These considerations suggest that the external market will not resolve Mexico's financial and foreign-exchange difficulties, much less allow the country to stimulate investments at the level needed to increase and restructure its existing industrial plant.

A first step for developing countries should be to resume growth at a rate equal to that of the international economy. To do this, they must reactivate their slumping domestic markets. Obviously each country holds the ultimate responsibility for stimulating its own domestic economy, and this process must be undertaken gradually and selectively. Nevertheless, international economic cooperation is indispensable at this juncture. The current situation requires bold but pragmatic changes, in which genuine cooperative efforts should dominate. Over the long term, these efforts will yield reciprocal benefits far greater than any gains industrialized countries could achieve by pursuing a policy of "beggar thy neighbor."

Cooperation would involve more than access to markets and an adjustment in the developing countries' foreign debt burden. It should also stimulate growth, expanding employment, improvements in industrial productivity, and a stable economic and social context conducive to structural change and technological advance.

Much of the accelerated technological change that has occurred in developed countries over the last decade nullifies the comparative advantages developing countries have traditionally held—advantages based on cheap labor, energy resources, and other abundant national resources. These technological changes reduce the maneuvering space available for industrial strategies that are founded on exports. Instead, the arena of international competition favors countries like those of the Pacific Rim, which during the 1960s and 1970s were able to diversify their productive structure, master the art of exporting, and develop their own technologies.

Countries like Mexico, which postponed a broad restructuring of their protected industries and their sources of non-industrial earnings and focused instead on oil and a handful of industries, must now restructure at a less propitious moment, when the technological gap has widened, foreign debt has escalated, and the outlook in the international economy is relatively gloomy. Although Mexico enjoys an advantage because of its geographical proximity to the United States, the asymmetry between these two countries and the absence of synchronous policies have hindered the emergence of a level of cooperation that would provide reciprocal benefits.

During the last five years, Mexico has implemented many of the adjustments it previously postponed. All present indicators suggest that it is the United States' turn to adjust its economic policies in order to overcome its budget deficits, trade deficit, and production problems, which are negatively affecting its international competitiveness.

In developing countries like Mexico, the adjustment formulas employed have been conventional ones proposed by the International Monetary Fund or the World Bank. But what formula will serve the most powerful country in the world? What will be the effects on U.S. trade and financial flows, which are entangled in this economic web? Will the country's rate of growth decline? Will the cost of servicing the U.S. debt held by Japan and other creditors rise? Will protectionist threats become entrenched?

Mexico has a special interest in the future economic evolution of the United States; the United States should have a particular interest in Mexico's economic future as well. First and foremost, the two countries are neighbors, with a 2000-mile common border, but beyond this, they have practical economic reasons to be concerned about each other's prospects. These reasons have led Mexico to explore opportunities for extending its commercial, technological, and financial relations with Canada, especially in light of the border this country shares with the United States and the free trade agreement recently signed by the United States and Canada.

Until 1981, Mexico was the United States' second most important trading partner. In this relationship, the United States enjoyed an enduring and significantly advantageous position. The United States, in turn, was Mexico's primary commercial investment partner and source of technology. U.S. exports to Mexico covered a broad range of manufactured goods and some agricultural products. Mexico's exports to the United States, on the other hand, consisted primarily of oil, minerals, and agricultural goods.

Following the onset of Mexico's economic crisis in 1982, the situation changed dramatically, and the gap in per capita income between the two countries widened drastically. The United States continues to be Mexico's primary trading partner, but Mexico has now fallen to fourth place among countries that trade with the United States. In addition, Mexico's trade balance with the United States now shows a surplus, largely because of the recent rapid growth of non-oil exports to the United States (Mexico increased its non-oil exports 24 percent from 1986 to 1987), but also because Mexico has had to drastically reduce its imports of capital goods and primary and intermediate products.[24]

This situation is far from optimal for either country. The decline in exports to Mexico has decreased this country's ability to satisfy domestic consumer needs and has halted investment, with serious implications for Mexico's future development. And from the U.S. perspective, U.S. sectors that are beleaguered by problems—agriculture, capital goods manufacture, and the automobile industry, for example—lose an important export market when Mexico is unable to purchase their products.

The automobile industry encapsulates the particulars of the bilateral trade relationship between Mexico and the United States. From the mid-1980s onward, Mexico's proximity to the United States and Mexico's cheap labor supply, in addition to sectoral trade policies that encouraged exports and competitive investment, generated dynamic growth in Mexico's exports and a trade balance favorable to Mexico in the amount of

[24] 1987 *Annual Report*, Banco de México (Mexico City, 1987).

approximately $13 billion in 1988. By the end of that year, the automobile and autoparts industry accounted for one-third of Mexico's manufactured exports, including nearly 200,000 vehicles and 2 million engines produced annually.

Mexico's dynamic production in this sector was a source of concern in some U.S. industrial sectors. However, what is sometimes forgotten is the fact that between 1981 and 1987, when the Mexican automobile industry declined to 60 percent of its original size, the value of Mexican imports of automobile components (most of which were imported from the United States) fell nearly $11 billion annually. The implications of this situation are clear. Mexico's recession has produced a direct negative impact on the U.S. automobile industry, in terms of both level of exports and number of jobs that this industry can provide at home.

A detailed examination of the other products could lead us to conclude that similar situations exist in other industries. The interdependence of Mexican and U.S. trade flows is obvious. When the Mexican market is restricted, U.S. industry is directly affected, and to a much greater degree than any other country's industry. Given this interdependence, surely it would be advisable in the future to consider the long-term ramifications of any economic policy decisions in terms of the policy's ability to achieve broader and more equitable trade flows among Mexico, the United States, and Canada. Taking advantage of complementarities among the three economies in an expanded and fair trade relationship would bring about improved levels of well-being in all three countries.

This consideration recalls a proposal that has been voiced repeatedly—the possibility of a North American common market encompassing the United States, Canada, and Mexico. This proposal may well tantalize Mexico, especially given current international trends toward forming economic blocs and concentrating new financial, commercial, and technological networks in the United States, and considering the many obstacles to realizing Mexico's dream of Latin American integration.

Many Mexican observers, however, question the wisdom of a North American common market. They note that, although proximity to the United States necessarily increases Mexico's interdependence with that country—where the geographic reality is so strong that it can overcome any and all artificial barriers, especially in the border zone—the United States and Canada are at similar levels of economic and technological development, while Mexico's values, institutions, and level of development are very different and would hinder Mexico's effective integration into a common market.

Mexico's asymmetry versus Canada and the United States in technological and economic development is striking, and in salary levels and social well-being even more notable. Mexico could only pursue the concept of a common market it if were able, first, to diminish these tremendous disparities and design long-term plans of action that take into account the present asymmetry in trade, finance, technology, and wages, not to mention differences in culture and institutional structure.

Unfortunately, U.S. policy in recent years has not been oriented toward recognizing such differences and agreeing to contingency protections. The United States, in fact, has been more prone to deny these differences, demanding strict reciprocity between unequal partners. And there is no hint that changes in the U.S. outlook will be soon forthcoming. Nevertheless, the promise and advantages offered by the complementary aspects of the two economies should encourage Mexico to explore perhaps less ambitious but more realistic formulas for cooperation. One such formula could be the establishment of sectoral accords in fields identified as appropriate both by recent experience and international trends. Among these are the automobile, textile, and clothing industries.

Such sectoral accords hold potential benefit for all three countries of North America. They could also pave the way for establishing more extensive and more ambitious programs at a future date.

Technology Development, Technology Transfer, and Intellectual Property

Developing countries such as Mexico can achieve sustained growth; modernize; export; and fulfill their obligations to growing national populations and outside countries only to the degree that they are able to incorporate new technologies and raise their levels of competitiveness, productivity, and product quality. As previously discussed, to achieve these goals Mexico will have to increase dramatically its national efforts. But inevitably the country will also have to seek technologies—patented and unpatented—from abroad.

Anticipated technological trends, especially the increasing protectiveness that companies display toward their own technologies, argue for a varied, flexible strategy that would allow Mexico to combine 100 percent foreign investment, joint investment, and licensing contracts in order to acquire foreign technology. Determining which route to follow for acquiring technology in a specific case would depend on the industry and product involved.

Nevertheless, there are strong indications that the major transnational companies are increasingly reluctant to license their technologies, and the United States and Japan in particular are showing increasing protectiveness toward their nationally developed technologies. A clear indicator of this tendency is the extension and strengthening of the patent system.

In recent international discussions, the dreams of technological parity formerly harbored by developing countries have often been buried along with their hopes for an international code of conduct for technology transfer or a revised Paris Agreement. Further, recent discussions within the United Nations International Development Organization (UNIDO) have attempted to eliminate the topic of technology transfer from consideration for international action, arguing that technology transfer is a matter for the individual companies owning the technology and not a concern of governments.

Not only is this attitude not cooperative, it is contrary to the interests of the developed countries themselves over the long term. Recent studies demonstrate that if the markets of the more advanced and more heavily populated of the developing countries do not grow, and if these countries are not able to incorporate modern technologies, the world economy will find recovery much more difficult and the expansion of high-technology industries in the United States will be stymied.

The developing countries need not resort to arguments of humanitarianism or international fairness in their defense, nor must they play on fears of social or political upheaval if economic and technological cooperation is not forthcoming, especially given the traditional forbearance of their populations. Their most powerful argument is much more direct. North-South economic and technological cooperation is in the economic self-interest of the industrialized countries, especially the United States. This single consideration should convince developed countries to replace their autocratic stance with a cooperative approach to technological development.

Recent difficulties in the U.S. automobile, electronics, and capital-goods industries demonstrate that the contraction of their traditional export markets in Latin America and elsewhere has had a significant impact. Policies that would help these markets to recover their dynamism and would support their future growth would stimulate both the United States and the developing countries involved. As Thyson and Castells point out, stepped-up technological change in Mexico and other developing countries would not undermine the competitive position of the United States because science-based development is a cumulative process. Given their capacity for innovation, U.S. institutions and industries would continue to hold a technological edge, assuming that industrial development kept pace with scientific advances.[25]

[25] Castells and Thyson, "High Technology Choices Ahead."

Certain measures come to mind which, if adopted, could support development in many Latin American countries. Each could be applied individually or in coordination with the World Bank, organizations of the United Nations, or regional Latin American entities. These include the following:

■ Measures that facilitate the flow of human and financial resources for technological development and the assimilation of modern technologies, especially in cutting-edge sectors.

■ Actions that support the formation of human resources, especially technical personnel, teachers, and researchers, in both the United States and Latin America.

■ Measures that strengthen the science and technology institutional infrastructure in Latin America and support regional programs for scientific and technological development in advanced technologies.

Concurrent with the implementation of these measures, government representatives, businessmen, and academics from Canada, the United States, and Mexico should examine alternative formulas for resolving the progressively worsening conflict over industrial property. No one argues against protecting intellectual property as a means of compensating its developer. In fact, developing countries such as Mexico need such protective instruments in order to encourage innovation and technological developments by national companies and researchers. However, just as there are preferential programs in the trade area that recognize different levels of development among countries, perhaps a differential and preferential treatment for technology and intellectual property could establish a basis for a more equitable international order, as well as the basis for worldwide economic expansion in the upcoming decade.

This proposal may appear idealistic, but if we do not explore it and if we fail to adapt the present formulas for negotiation, the outlook for the next few years will remain discouraging, and future trends could well thwart the interests of both developing and industrialized countries.

But there is still time.

PART V
Labor Markets and Adjustment Assistance

The Effect of Free Trade on the North American Labor Market

Morley Gunderson and Daniel S. Hamermesh

M ANY OF THE adjustments to free trade will occur in labor markets. While all markets will experience adjustments, those in the labor market are particularly visible because they often involve jobs and wages, which directly affect the well-being of people. This contrasts with benefits such as lower prices, which are often dispersed across a broader population.

The consequences of free trade for the labor market are compounded because they are occurring when the labor market is adjusting to many other changes such as deregulation; technical change; privatization; the continued influx of women; deunionization in the United States; increased world competition; plant closings; and legislative initiatives like pay equity (comparable worth or equal pay for work of equal value), employment equity (affirmative action), legislative bans on mandatory retirement, and changes in employment standards. These later legislative initiatives in the labor market have been more important recently in Canada than in the United States, since the United States has been less interventionist during the Reagan administration.

This paper discusses the possible effects of the recent Canada-U.S. Free Trade Agreement on the North American labor market. We concentrate on the Canadian labor market because the agreement obviously will have a disproportionately larger effect on that smaller, trade-dependent economy. (Thirty percent of Canada's GNP depends on trade, over 70 percent of which occurs with the United States, while exports amount to less than 10 percent of U.S. GNP.) We emphasize the range of issues that will be involved and indicate what we have and have not learned from the literature. We begin with a discussion of our rationale for focusing on the labor-market adjustment issues. Then we discuss the expected labor-market effects of freer trade and provide some limited empirical evidence for these expectations, attending especially to the reasons for the substantial wage adjustments that displaced workers will likely experience. The paper ends with a summary and some observations.

WHY ANALYZE LABOR-MARKET ADJUSTMENT ISSUES?

The reasons to be concerned about the consequences of freer trade for the labor market can be categorized under three interrelated rubrics: equity, efficiency, and political expediency.[1]

Equity

To the extent that freer trade permits scale economies and specialization according to comparative advantage, the resulting efficiency gains provide the means to make everybody better off. That trade expands the production-possibility frontier, however, does not mean that everybody will in fact be better off. The efficiency gains give winners an opportunity to compensate the losers, but there is no guarantee—certainly not through the market mechanism—that such compensation will occur.

The equity rationale for focusing on the labor-market consequences of freer trade stems from a number of interrelated facts: (1) Much of the adjustment falls on the labor market, (2) Many workers who are adversely affected may already be disadvantaged in terms of their wages, gender, industry, or region, (3) Unlike in the capital and product markets, it is more difficult for participants in the labor market to diversify against the risks of trade shocks, and (4) It corresponds to our notion of justice that losers should be compensated when they are adversely affected by policies that make the rest of society better off.

The equity arguments are particularly compelling in Canada because of its special emphasis on balanced regional development. There is also the worry, at least on some people's part, that the current free trade agreement will jeopardize Canada's system of social welfare and regional development at the very time the system will be needed most to adjust to freer trade. Certain social welfare and regional development programs may be interpreted as unfair labor-cost subsidies and hence lead to an imposition of countervailing duties on their associated exports.

Equity concerns stemming from the labor-market consequences of

---

[1] These rationales are discussed in the context of appropriate compensation for displaced workers by Daniel S. Hamermesh, Joseph J. Cordes, and Robert S. Goldfarb, "Compensating Displaced Workers—What, How Much, How?" in *Labor Market Adjustments in the Pacific Basin* (Boston, 1987).

freer trade in Canada may go deeper. Trade unionists worry that the ability of unions to protect the interests of workers will be vitiated by the "unfair competition" from the United States with its lower degree of unionization and less-stringent employment standards. (Unions represent only 16 percent of workers in the United States, less than half the Canadian rate.) Unionists and others have also expressed concern that business support for free trade is really a veiled attempt to promote deregulation and privatization, reduce the role of government in the economy, reduce income support and regional development, and generally facilitate the ascendancy of market forces aimed at promoting efficiency over distributional goals. Of course, these concerns are difficult to disentangle from rent-seeking behavior; unions understandably may be trying to protect their rents and avoid the concession bargaining that has been more characteristic of their U.S. counterparts.

Efficiency

The efficiency concerns about the labor-market consequences of free trade are more difficult to establish. In essence, they have to rest on market-failure arguments—that is, on the possible inability of the labor market to fully internalize the costs and benefits of trade-related adjustments. Although such arguments are often brought forth under various guises when dealing with any adjustment issue, they raise as many questions as answers.

Freer trade involves reallocating resources to their most valued use. The income losses that will occur, which can be substantial for some market participants, are transfers or pecuniary externalities reflecting price (wage) changes. They are not technological externalities that reflect a failure of market prices to incorporate the real resource costs and benefits of adjustment. In fact, the price changes that are occurring indicate that the market is working to reallocate resources efficiently. The reallocation may be inequitable, but it is likely to be toward improved efficiency.

There are a number of possible caveats to this general proposition. For market prices to internalize externalities, there must be a reasonable degree of information about the likelihood of events occurring. For example, for workers to demand an *ex-ante* compensating wage differential for the risk of trade-related displacement requires information on the likelihood of their particular job being at risk. Their employers may have better information on the likelihood of such events, but they obviously do not have an incentive to reveal such information, since it would imply having to pay a compensating wage premium. Such asymmetric infor-

228 MORLEY GUNDERSON AND D. S. HAMERMESH

mation may prevent market prices (compensating wage premiums) from fully internalizing the adjustment consequences of freer trade.

"Congestion externalities" may also arise in situations where free trade leads to plant closings and mass layoffs in particular communities. The externality arises when individuals who enter the job-search process fail to account for the possibility that their own search may adversely affect the search time of other unemployed workers in situations where the labor market is unable to absorb the mass unemployment.[2] Analogous congestion externalities occur when motorists enter an expressway and impose waiting-time costs on other motorists. (In the labor-market case, though, prices may be more operative, since reservation wages could adjust to the unemployment congestion.)

A different externality may arise if trade-displaced workers place extra costs on social services or transfer programs. This cost may occur directly; for example, if the workers collect unemployment insurance or receive social welfare assistance. It may occur indirectly, if the displacement leads to social problems of crime, mental instability, suicide, or ill health—all of which have been identified with mass unemployment.[3] These problems often represent pecuniary externalities emanating from the public decision to provide such social services, but they are costs that taxpayers must consider if they are to provide these services to trade-displaced workers. Perhaps it is at least globally more efficient to slow down an otherwise efficient market adjustment that could lead to adverse social consequences, which engender additional costs.

Trade-displaced workers may also lose industry- or firm-specific human capital, which has no value in the other industries or firms to which they are displaced.[4] Such human capital generates quasi-rents, as firms pay such employees a wage in excess of their next-best alternative to reduce turnover and hence the loss of the specific human capital. Obviously there will be bargaining over those rents, as firms want to pay

[2] The importance of mass layoffs on the search time of other workers, in the context of trade liberalization, is discussed in C. Michael Aho and Thomas Bayard, "Costs and Benefits of Trade Adjustment Assistance," in *The Structure and Evolution of Recent U.S. Trade Policy* (Chicago, 1984), 81, and Richard G. Harris, F. D. Lewis, and Douglas D. Purvis, "Market Adjustment and Government Policy," presented at the Second John Deutsch Roundtable on Economic Policy (Kingston, Eng., 1982). It is also emphasized in studies of plant closings in small communities. See Jeanne P. Gordus, Paul Jarley, and Louis A. Ferman, *Plant Closings and Economic Dislocation* (Kalamazoo, Mich., 1981), 81.
[3] Harvey Brenner, *Estimating the Social Costs of National Economic Policy: Implications for Mental and Physical Health and Criminal Aggression* (Washington, 1976); Gordus, Jarley, and Ferman, *Plant Closings and Economic Dislocation*; R. S. Saunders, *Aid to Workers in Declining Industries* (Toronto, 1984).
[4] Daniel S. Hamermesh, "The Costs of Worker Displacement," *Quarterly Journal of Economics* 102 (Feb. 1987), 51–76; Daniel S. Hamermesh, "Plant Closings and the Value of the Firm," *Review of Economics and Statistics* vol. 70, no. 4 (Nov. 1988), 580–86.

workers a wage equal to their next-best alternative wage, while workers try to extract a wage equal to their value to the firm, including the value of the specific human capital. Such bargaining is exacerbated by the asymmetry of information: workers may not have good information about the probability of plant closings, and employers may not have good information on the employees' next-best alternative (their reservation wage).

Once such human-capital investments are made, they should be regarded as sunk costs having a social opportunity cost of zero if they have no use. In that sense, the loss of such human capital invested in trade-displaced workers is not an efficiency loss, though it can have severe distributional consequences. Nevertheless, trade shocks may exacerbate bargaining over the quasi-rents, and this in turn could lead to efficiency losses if, for example, a plant were prematurely closed because of insufficient wage concessions. Distributional and efficiency issues become difficult to disentangle in such situations. Nevertheless, a possibility exists that efficiency losses will result as the parties bargain over the division of rents.

The possibility of efficiency losses in the labor market increases in situations where predatory pricing follows in the product market. In such circumstances, if competitors are driven out, losses of firm-specific human capital may be irreversible. That the competitors may be driven out artificially rather than by natural market forces means that the loss of firm-specific human captial was not market driven—that is, the quasi-rents did not dissipate because the investment was no longer useful. Yet once the workers go to alternative activities, it may be impossible to reinvest in training for new workers to compete later with the predatory firm.

The irreversibility argument can have broader applications. For example, the specialization induced by free trade could homogenize the skills of a country's work force. This in turn may make the country less self-sufficient (for example, in cases of national emergencies) and more vulnerable to particular trade shocks or to other changes that could affect its specialized work force (for example, technical change for a work force that has specialized in high technology, or resource price changes for a resource-based work force).

Some broader political arguments imply that certain labor-market inefficiencies may result from the FTA. Specifically, some argue that it is a mistake for Canada to become a trading partner with a nation that itself is declining as a major trading nation. (This argument ignores the fact that free trade enables specialization in declining as well as expanding markets.) Others have argued that bilateral free trade with the United States may preclude the possibility of greater gains from multinational free trade. Such arguments have seldom been precisely formulated in the literature—though theoretical work would be welcome—and hence it is difficult to judge their potential importance. However, the inefficiency arguments seem less convincing than the equity arguments. Perhaps the safest generalization is that the burden of proof lies with those who believe that free trade will lead to labor-market inefficiencies. It also lies with those who feel that the labor-market adjustments will not have distributional consequences.

Political Expediency

A policy that adversely affects the labor-market position of certain groups is not likely to attract political support unless the adjustment consequences are addressed. In fact, it is somewhat surprising that the current agreement has advanced as far as it has given that the benefits are indirect, dispersed, and spread into the future while the costs are more direct, concentrated, and current. The classic ingredients for political opposition to otherwise desirable policies could have combined to leave this agreement stillborn.

One of the strongest reasons for compensating losers in a situation such as this is to reduce their resistance to what is otherwise an efficient move. Compensation increases the likelihood of converting a potential into an actual Pareto improvement. Cynics may see this as simply bribing the losers, while others regard it as a viable way to reduce understandable resistance to growth-oriented change. Guaranteeing that gains are broadly distributed and losers are compensated ensures that the change has a broad base of support, which increases its likelihood of long-run success. Of course, this argument applies to changes such as deregulation, privatization, and technological change as well as free trade. Resistance to such change tends to be less, for example, in countries like Japan, where many workers are guaranteed lifetime employment with their firm. In North America, however, where large adjustment consequences take place in the external labor market, resistance is substantial.

THE IMPACTS OF TRADE LIBERALIZATION

Trade expansion resulting from free trade will create both winners and losers in the labor market. Even though free trade should tend toward greater global efficiency, the outcome could be negative net job creation. Even if the net job creation is positive, moving to the new equilibrium will involve labor-market adjustments. Moreover, the adjustment resulting from the expansion of the export sector can itself create problems such as specific skill shortages and retraining and relocation needs.

The effect of increased import competition on wages and employment can be illustrated by adapting the model developed by Hamermesh, which was originally used to indicate what determines the likelihood of worker displacement through plant closing.[5] Workers and firms sort themselves in a way that generates a locus of equilibria between the probability that a plant closes and excess wages (amount paid above that received by otherwise identical workers who have not accumulated firm-specific training). This model provides a useful way to analyze how free-trade legislation will affect two aspects of labor-market behavior— worker displacement and wage growth—that are of great concern to workers.

Workers acquire firm-specific human capital that raises their wage rate, W, above W^r, the reservation wage available outside the firm. This excess, $W - W^r$, can be termed "wage rents." The firm faces a known density of random prices P, $h(P, S)$, where $P \geq 0$, and S indexes exogenous shocks to product demand. A higher S shifts the distribution of product prices to the right. The capital stock is fixed at K^*. Profits are:

$$\pi = PX - WL - rK^*,$$

where output $X = F(L, K^*)$, W is the wage rate, and r is the cost of capital services.

Wages are set at the start of each period in full knowledge of the particular product-market shock S_0 that occurs. The plant draws from the density function $h(P, S_0)$ and decides whether to shut down. Let π^* be the critical level of profits that determines its continued existence. It will close if $\pi < \pi^*$. Then at π^* the product price must be:

$$P^* = \frac{\pi^* + WL + rK^*}{X}. \tag{1}$$

The probability of closing, p, is thus:

$$p = \int_0^{P^*} h(P, S^*) \, dP. \tag{2}$$

The implicit relation between p and W defined by Equation 2 shows the set of probabilities that the plant remains in operation at each particular wage rate for a given S_0. Its slope is:

$$\left(\frac{dp}{dW}\right)_{S=S_0} = h(P^*, S_0)\frac{dP^*}{dW}, \tag{3}$$

---

[5] Hamermesh, "Plant Closings."

where:

$$\frac{dP^*}{dW} = \frac{[W - P^*F_L] \, \delta L/\delta W + L}{X}.$$

dP^*/dW can be rewritten in terms of labor-demand elasticities to show that $(dp/dW)_{S-S_0} > 0$. Figure 1 presents the probabilistic shut-down frontier for $S = S_0$, with the origin at W^r. It contains all points along which probabilistic profits are at the competitive minimum π_0^* given W and S_0.

The typical worker's satisfaction depends on the wage rate earned and the probability that the plant will close (and thus the probability of being able to earn only the reservation wage W^r). Workers choose among combinations of wages and probabilities of the plant closing; hours of work are assumed constant. The typical worker's expected additional utility over W^r from staying in the plant after having acquired firm-specific training is:

$$V = [1 - p]U(W - W^r) + pU(0), \qquad U' > 0, \qquad U'' < 0. \qquad (4)$$

If W falls below W^r, the worker leaves voluntarily. Letting $U(0) = 0$, the slope of the worker's indifference curve is:

$$\left(\frac{dp}{dW}\right)_{V=V^*} = \frac{[1 - p]U'}{U} > 0. \qquad (5)$$

Typical indifference curves, showing the combinations of the probability of plant closing and the excess of wages over the wage available outside the plant, are shown in Figure 1. V_0 is preferred to V_1, for at each wage rate the risk of plant closing is lower.

Equilibrium in the internal labor market is defined by the tangency of an indifference curve to the probabilistic shutdown frontier for fixed S_0. Firm-specific investment partly insulates the average worker from random shocks to product demand. This produces an equilibrium at point A in the first quadrant of Figure 1. A negative shock that lowers S to S_1 produces a new equilibrium at point B on the new shutdown frontier $S_1 S_1$. Under reasonable assumptions (workers' risk aversion, typical production functions, and a uniform marginal density $h(P, S)$), the equilibrium locus $E_0 E_0$ has the negative slope shown in Figure 1.

How is this analysis changed by an agreement that exposes firms to increased competitive pressure from foreign sources? Such exposure is equivalent to a negative demand shock: The distribution of prices shifts leftward, resulting in a leftward *-shift in the probabilistic shutdown frontier. That by itself would just represent a shift from $S_0 S_0$ to $S_1 S_1$.

Probability of
Plant Closing

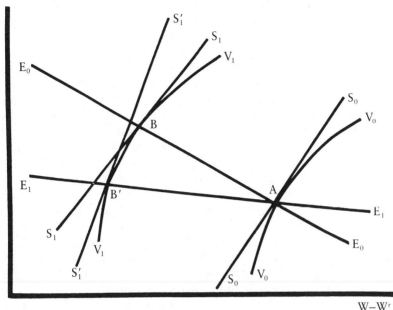

Fig. 1

Another factor intervenes to modify the analysis, though. The increase in competition facing domestic industry makes firms' shutdown frontiers more vulnerable to the wage-rate increases that the firms offer. This increased sensitivity is shown in Figure 1 by the tilt in the shutdown frontier from $S_1 S_1$ to $S_1' S_1'$. This tilt shows that labor-demand elasticities rise when an industry becomes more competitive, which follows from Marshall's laws describing determinants of labor-demand elasticities.

In the standard case of demand shocks with an unchanged industry structure, we saw that the equilibrium locus of the probability of plant closing, p, and wage rents, $[W - W^r]$, was $E_0 E_0$. With the tilt in the probabilistic shutdown frontier to $S_1' S_1'$, along with the leftward shift to $S_1 S_1$, the equilibrium locus shifts to $E_1 E_1$. The new equilibrium corresponding to the shock induced by trade liberalization is at point B'. The equilibrium locus becomes flatter as a result of opening product markets to increased foreign competition. Agreements that produce such an increase will obviously reduce the rate of wage growth in the affected industries and increase the fraction of plants that close. They will, however, make the industries' rate of plant closing less sensitive to wage increases obtained by the workers who remain employed. The structure of labor markets will change to increase plant closings; but wage increases that occur after the initial effects of the trade agreement will produce smaller increases in the rate of worker displacement.

The upshot of this analysis, focusing only on the import side, is that export competition from free trade will lead to more plant closings and job losses, and slower wage growth in the remaining jobs, but fewer job losses emanating from subsequent wage increases in the remaining jobs.

The previous analysis focused only on the import side of the equation. Increased exports from freer trade should expand job opportunities and lead to wage growth in the expanding sector. However, the general increase in competition will mean that employment will be more sensitive to subsequent wage changes—that is, the aggregate demand for labor will be more elastic. The net effect of increased imports and exports on wages and employment is ultimately an empirical proposition.

EMPIRICAL EVIDENCE

The following discussion of the empirical evidence is designed to illustrate the kinds of labor-market adjustment issues involved in analyzing the effects of free trade. A comprehensive review of the evidence is beyond the purview of this paper. In any event, there is simply insufficient evidence at this stage to provide a systematic and definitive picture.

Determinants of Labor Displacement

As discussed in Pearson and Salembier,[6] the main methodologies for estimating the employment effects of trade liberalization are (1) trade-employment balance studies, (2) decomposition studies, and (3) labor-adjustment cost studies. The trade-imbalance studies basically determine the changes expected in exports and imports from free trade and then use procedures like input-output analysis to establish the employment effect of those changes. Trade-imbalance studies can involve the use of macroeconometric models to estimate induced indirect effects, or computable general equilibrium models to incorporate other behavioral responses. The decomposition studies basically disaggregate domestic employment changes into components resulting from domestic demand, productivity, and trade. The labor-adjustment cost studies typically examine the wage and employment behavior of workers before and after labor displacement. Each approach has its strengths and weaknesses and contributes some information, but none provides a complete, comprehensive analysis of all adjustment consequences.

[6] G. Pearson and G. Salembier, *Trade, Employment, and Adjustment* (Montreal, 1983).

An alternative approach is provided by Hamermesh, who offers empirical evidence on what determines the probability of individual workers being displaced by a plant closure.[7] A bivariate probit equation (where the dependent variable was coded one if the individual was displaced because of job loss, zero otherwise) was estimated for 2,636 workers from 1977 to 1981 in the Panel Study of Income Dynamics. The results indicate that negative demand shocks lead to both wage concessions and labor displacement through plant closings, with most of the effect absorbed by wage concessions. The wage concessions are not sufficient, however, to prevent labor displacement. Specifically, a negative demand shock that led to a 1 percent reduction in real wages over the period was also associated with an approximately .0003 increase in the probability of a worker being displaced because of a plant closure. The 1 percent reduction in real wages was about 7 percent of the real wage growth over that period. The .0003 increase in the probability of labor displacement due to plant closings was about 1.3 percent of the average probability of labor displacement of 0.023 over that period.

More of the negative demand shock seems to be absorbed by slower wage growth than by labor displacement through plant closings. It does not appear likely that substantial wage concessions will reduce the risk of such displacement. Whether this generalization applies to trade-induced demand shocks, and the extent to which such shocks would lead to labor displacement through mechanisms other than plant closings, are not answerable by this empirical exercise.

Overall Employment Effects

The previous analysis focused on the wage and employment effects of increased import competition associated with free trade. A complete analysis would require comparing job losses from import competition to job gains produced by increased exports, as well as the indirect effects of changes in factors such as consumption, investment, and government spending.

The Economic Council of Canada has provided such a decomposition study based on a simulation from their macroeconomic forecasting model, CANDIDE 3.0, and the Statistics Canada Input-Output Model of the Canadian economy. Two alternative simulation scenarios result. Simulation 1 is based solely on the removal of trade barriers—tariffs, non-tariff barriers, and procurement policies. Simulation 2 adds improvements in manufacturing productivity due to scale economies and rationalization. Both simulate the effect of the likely phased reductions in tariff and nontariff barriers over the ten-year period 1989–1999.

---

[7] Hamermesh, "Plant Closings."

The results of these simulations are given in Table 1 and are listed in descending order based on the net change in employment under simulation 2. In general, the overall employment effects are positive, with 251,300 net new jobs created (a 1.8 percent increase) and productivity improvement. Much of the gain comes from the productivity improvement associated with specialization and rationalization. Without the productivity improvement, the net employment gains are only one-third as large. There is considerable variation in the gains and losses across industries, ranging from a 6.08 percent employment gain in printing and publishing to a 3.38 percent employment loss in electrical products. In general, the primary and service industries experience the greatest employment gains, while manufacturing industries have a mixed experience with a net positive impact.

Although not shown in that table, other generalizations emerge from the analysis. Provincial variation in the percentage employment gains are not substantial, ranging from a high of 2.08 percent in Alberta to a low of 1.70 in Ontario (relative to the national average of 1.80). The smaller gains in Ontario (and Quebec at 1.75 percent) reflect the concentration of manufacturing in those provinces. The net new job creation of 251,300 results form 439,100 new jobs created and 187,800 jobs lost. This implies adjustment consequences, since adjustment (in the form of training and shortages) is required on the upside as well as the downside. Nevertheless, the trade-induced adjustment is small relative to the normal turnover (less than 2 percent of permanent displacement results from freer trade). The distribution of employment changes by sex is similar to the current male-female distribution of employment.

Evidence on Income Losses of Displaced Workers

Labor-adjustment-cost studies provide information on the income losses of displaced workers and perhaps shed some light on the issue of adjustment to free trade. Studies of income loss have generally focused on workers who permanently lose their jobs because of such factors as plant closings or trade liberalization. Canadian studies in this area have been reviewed by Gunderson and Robb and U.S. studies have been reviewed by Martin and Hamermesh.[8]

[8] Morley Gunderson, "Alternative Mechanisms for Dealing with Permanent Layoffs, Dismissals and Plant Closings" in W. Craig Riddell, ed., *Adapting to Change: Labour Market Adjustment in Canada* (Toronto, University of Toronto, 1986), 111–62; Roberta Edgecombe Robb, "The Canada-U.S. Free Trade Agreement: Employment Effects and Adjustment in the Labour Market," presented at the National Conference on the Free Trade Agreement (Toronto, Osgoode Law School, 1988); Philip L. Martin, *Labor Displacement and Public Policy* (Toronto, 1983); Daniel S. Hamermesh, "What Do We Know about Worker Displacement in the U.S.?" *Industrial Relations* vol. 28, no. 1 (Winter 1989), 51–59.

TABLE I

Employment Impact of the Canada–U.S. Free Trade Agreement

Industry	Net employment change with no productivity change		Net employment change with productivity improvement	
	No. of jobs	Percent	No. of jobs	Percent
Retail trade	32,054	1.67%	59,626	3.11%
Construction	15,020	2.03	37,454	5.07
Other finance, insurance & r.e.	12,743	1.27	30,327	3.02
Accommodation & food	11,764	1.06	23,607	2.12
Business services	6,882	0.40	19,956	1.17
Wholesale trade	6,706	1.00	15,720	2.34
Other & personal services	5,104	0.33	10,281	0.67
Transportation & storage	2,991	0.61	8,753	1.77
Printing & publishing	2,585	1.87	8,422	6.08
Agriculture	1,986	0.50	7,192	1.80
Food & beverage	2,072	0.65	6,375	2.00
Education & health	2,500	1.48	5,859	3.46
Mining	1,759	0.60	4,984	1.69
Primary metals	4,636	2.73	4,971	2.93
Amusement & recreation	2,418	0.90	4,560	1.71
Wood products	974	0.82	1,963	1.64
Elec., power & other utilities	637	0.44	1,956	1.34
Clothing	−6	−0.01	1,561	1.73
Metal fabricating	−2,889	−2.09	1,396	1.01
Communications	−842	−0.31	1,163	0.43
Non-metallic minerals	−579	−0.85	1,054	1.55
Paper & allied products	−999	−0.63	981	0.61
Machinery	−2,026	−1.59	838	0.66
Forestry	112	0.09	658	0.50
Transportation equipment	−1,188	0.61	584	0.30
Furniture and fixtures	−976	−1.95	456	0.91
Fishing, hunting & trapping	120	0.39	273	0.88
Petroleum and coal	−22	−0.16	106	0.77
Tobacco products	−36	−0.42	8	0.10
Chemical and chemical products	−2,828	−2.62	−366	−0.34
Knitting mills	−1,364	−7.07	−510	−2.64
Leather products	−979	−3.66	−552	−2.06
Misc. manufacturing	−3,735	−5.82	−913	−1.42
Textiles	−3,457	−5.61	−1,266	−2.05
Rubber & plastic products	−4,468	−4.70	−1,642	−1.72
Electrical products	−10,670	−7.95	−4,535	−3.38
TOTAL	76,000	0.55%	251,300	1.80%

SOURCE: S. Magun, S. Rao, B. Lodh, L. Lavallée and J. Peirce, *Open Borders: An Assessment of the Canada–U.S. Free Trade Agreement* (Ottawa, Economic Council of Canada Discussion Paper 344, April 1988), p. 61.

While subject to numerous qualifications, the following generalizations emerge: (1) Displaced workers who are reemployed typically earn only 85 to 90 percent of their previous earnings, (2) There is considerable variability in the loss, with some workers gaining and others experiencing very large losses, (3) The losses are greatest for older, higher-paid, unionized, less-educated, blue-collar workers who have considerable seniority, and the losses are larger in recessionary periods, and (4) Considerable sociopsychological consequences have also been documented, including increased suicides, homicides, admissions to mental hospitals and prisons, as well as stress-related diseases. There is no consensus on whether the losses are greater for males or females or for blacks than for whites (though blacks and women are more likely to be displaced).

WHY INCOME LOSSES ARE OFTEN LARGE

It is puzzling that the income losses of many displaced workers are large, because it suggests that they were receiving substantial wage rents. Why are such rents so prevalent, and why do they not dissipate completely to avoid the costs of displacement? Various explanations are possible, although it has not been possible to determine the relative importance of the factors.

First, the rents may reflect premiums that firms pay to reduce the costly turnover of employees with firm-specific human capital that has no value in alternative employment. (That is why the firm-specific human capital commands a premium in the existing firm but not in alternative jobs.) Second, the rents may be pure rents generated by such factors as unionization or noncompetitive behavior. They may in fact be the reason for the plant closing or the inability to compete under trade liberalization. Third, the premiums may simply be elements of deferred compensation that are paid, for example, to deter shirking or encourage bonding. The plant closing, in fact, may be a way in which the firm avoids its deferred compensation obligations when faced with a permanent negative demand shock. Fourth, the wage premium may be an *ex-ante* compensating wage paid for the risk of displacement; the wage loss reflects that risk coming to fruition after the displacement occurs. Any or all of these factors may contribute to employees receiving wages in their current jobs that exceed those paid in their next-best alternative employment. This, in turn, may help explain the substantial income loss that occurs for many displaced workers.

It is obvious that the possibility exists for large losses to occur. The reasons why those losses occur are less clear. Consider workers' behavior from several years before displacement occurs. If workers had good information about their employer's financial situation, they would respond to the firm's reduced prospects by investing less in firm-specific human capital and more in general human capital. When the plant closed, the value of their remaining firm-specific capital would be small and their increased general investments would have raised their alternative wage so their losses would be minimal. This does not happen: There is clear evidence that workers continue to invest in firm-specific human capital at the same rate until their plant closes.[9] Workers are surprised by plant closings and lack the information to make the necessary adjustments before it happens.

When the closing becomes apparent to workers, they still do not accept the wage concessions necessary to avoid the all-or-nothing possibility of being permanently laid off. A variety of explanations are possible. When employers have better information than workers about the true nature of demand shocks, they may bluff about the shock's existence to obtain wage concessions. To avoid this scenario, employees may compel employers to adjust to negative demand shocks with employment rather than wage reductions, because employment reductions are also costly to the firm, whereas wage reductions are not. (Also, the cost of employment reductions may be somewhat offset by state support, such as unemployment insurance, which is not the case for wage reductions.) Median workers, who may determine union decisions, may not feel that they are at risk for layoffs and hence may not accept wage concessions to avoid marginal-worker layoffs. Even in declining industries, it may be sensible for workers to avoid concession bargaining because there is little threat of employers relocating their plant and capital elsewhere. Besides, there is no guarantee that wage concessions would preserve jobs rather than whet appetites for more concessions. In such circumstances, employees may rationally opt for concrete wage gains rather than a vague possibility that jobs will be preserved. Certainly, as illustrated above, they will rationally opt for a combination of an increased probability of wage and displacement concessions, rather than only wage concessions, in the event of a negative demand shock.

CONCLUSION

Although this discussion highlighted the importance of the labor-market consequences of free trade, it raised as many questions as it did answers. Who precisely are the gainers and losers in the labor market, in terms of characteristics like sex, wages, and region—all of which have important equity implications? Are the losses permanent or temporary,

[9] Daniel S. Hamermesh, "Costs of Worker Displacement."

and what is the relative importance of different components like unemployment, wage reductions, and hours reduction? How do we attach a monetary equivalent to the nonwage aspects of jobs? What are the adjustment problems that may be associated with such factors as shortages and training needs? What barriers, if any, may prevent market mechanisms such as compensating wages from fully internalizing the consequences of trade-induced labor displacement? What barriers, if any, prevent collective bargaining from handling the adjustment consequences? If the market mechanisms and collective bargaining fail to handle the labor-market adjustment effects properly, what is the appropriate role of the government—what is the optimal mix of these alternative mechanisms (labor market, collective bargaining, government intervention) for dealing with the labor-market consequences of free trade? Should trade-displaced workers be eligible for special adjustment assistance or simply the usual adjustment assistance? Should assistance be directed toward firms or workers? To what extent can marginal adjustments through such factors as quits, turnover, hours reduction, worksharing, and early retirements reduce the need for nonmarginal adjustments such as plant closings and permanent job losses? To what extent can wage concessions preserve jobs? To what extent will reduced restrictions on flows of goods and services affect immigration and emigration? How important will trade-induced adjustments be relative to other types of labor-market adjustments, and how can we determine these relative magnitudes? Many of these questions have been addressed in the literature on adjustment issues. Nevertheless, they illustrate the sorts of questions for which we need more precise answers to deal properly with the labor-market consequences of free trade.

Labor Market Interdependence Between Mexico and the United States

Saúl Trejo Reyes

L ABOR MARKET interdependence on a North American scale has now
become a fact of life. By and large, such interdependence involves
movement of labor from Canada and Mexico into the United States, le-
gally or otherwise. Whether penalized by discriminatory legislation as in
the case of Mexico, or disguised by cultural and racial similarity in the
case of Canada, this movement will likely have profound effects in coming years. Of course, this phenomenon cannot be analyzed by itself, or in
a purely North American context. In fact, the global nature of trade,
production, and financial flows means that adjustment possibilities as
well as policy responses will be directly influenced by the global context.
At the same time, a close interdependence between labor flows, trade,
and debt exists (particularly for relations between the United States and
Mexico), which has no doubt depressed conditions in the Mexican
economy. Although recognized by Mexico, this relationship seems particularly difficult for U.S. policymakers to accept. By and large, they have
preferred until now to ignore the existence of the relationship and to
pressure Mexico for fuller "cooperation" at election times on issues important to particular U.S. constituencies.

LONG-RUN CONTEXT

Whether explicitly recognized in policy discussions, policy responses
in all three countries will depend to a large extent on how each fares in
the new world division of labor. If the United States has favorable growth
and labor demand prospects, it will be inclined to take a more accom-
modating attitude toward labor immigration from both Mexico and Canada. Of course in the long run, the problem is not the labor market but

how each country sees its role in the world economy (in particular its relationship to the other two North American countries), and what each perceives its role to imply for domestic welfare levels. A main policy concern in the United States is the loss of high-income manufacturing jobs, which are replaced, at best, by low-skill, low-income service jobs. This loss gives rise to protectionist pressures, as well as pressure to close off the domestic labor market.

To a large extent, the Mexican economic recovery is not only an important policy problem for the United States, but also a problem of joint maximization. To the extent that Mexico's economy remains stagnant, pressures for labor migration to the United States, legal or otherwise, will continue unabated, and might increase. But the problem of Mexican economic recovery also brings up debt and trade-policy issues. Currently, the high burden of debt service and its expected effect on tax rates for domestic factors of production discourage investment and hamper the growth of its domestic market by depressing internal economic activity.

Naturally, the United States, as the strongest country, would like to impose the brunt of the cost of adjusting to drastically changing world conditions on the other countries. In fact, since 1982 Mexico, like most debtor countries, has been forced to take extreme policy measures. It has faced an unprecedented recession as a result of the adjustment effort required to service its foreign debt. Thus, it has faced strong internal criticism, while being criticized abroad (especially in the United States) for its domestic policies, which lower incomes for poorer groups of the Mexican population! It should be pointed out, of course, that satisfying social and political demands more successfully than before is hardly possible when the economy has been in a recession for six years. This fact is never considered in U.S. discussions of Mexican policies.

Although compression of domestic demand and drastic devaluation of the exchange rate have resulted in a large trade surplus for Mexico, a return to a positive growth trajectory is nowhere in sight. The export sector still accounts for less than 20 percent of GDP. The trade surplus at best covers debt-service payments; since 1982 it has not always done so. At the same time, protectionist sentiment has become stronger in the United States among groups that would be affected by a radically higher Mexican trade surplus. There is growing talk of "fair"—not free—trade, and of restricting imports from countries that have a trade surplus with the United States. Such a view, which separates trade from debt, may not be logical; more important, it is dangerous for long-run U.S.-Mexican relations.

Basically, each of the three countries at present sees the outcome of its participation in the international economy as independent of the other two, as it in fact is in the short run. Alternatively, however, the problem could be posed by all three as one joint maximization. In this case, the region's output would be the objective function to maximize. Of course, allocating gains both between countries and internally is too difficult at present. However, this difficulty does not rule out all forms of cooperation. In order to make any short-run sense, these cooperative efforts must be based on the principle that the region may gain at the expense of the rest of the world. In the longer run, of course, this need not be the case.

Each country faces, in principle, two paths. The first is not to consider the others in the region in any special way. Thus, the United States might continue to strengthen trade and investment relations with countries in the Far East, which have low labor costs. Mexico would continue the path of trade liberalization it has recently initiated, also without considering the United States in any special way. And Canada would continue to integrate with the U.S. economy. The problems that would emerge in this scenario are easy to foresee.

For Mexico, this scenario would mean that even under the most favorable conditions the employment problem would continue to worsen. Given the high rate of growth of the labor force from now until 2000, the high burden of the debt service would make it very difficult for the Mexican economy to grow as it did from the 1950s to the 1970s. Even assuming complete success of the liberalization process, growth could not create enough jobs. Thus, migration would continue, both from the countryside to the cities, and from urban and rural areas to the United States. Whether such migration is permanent or temporary is not the point; the fact is that wage and salary differentials between Mexico and the United States could continue to widen, as they have since 1982. This disparity in wages would constitute a powerful incentive for workers to migrate.

If the United States continued on its current path, pressures for protectionism would become progressively greater. However, it is unlikely that these pressures would stop the trend toward displacing many firms' activities to other countries. Unless this trend is offset by a strong emphasis on developing new technologies and raising the overall productivity level, labor-management conflicts over moving industries in search of better conditions would become ever more common. Much of this protectionist sentiment would probably be turned not only toward Japan and Germany—countries with high structural trade surpluses—but toward Mexico, which (1) must generate a sizeable trade surplus simply to try to service its foreign debt, and (2) is conveniently close by.

Thus, the stage seems to be set either for greater cooperation or for a growing conflict between the United States and Mexico. What might

Canada's role be? It is evident from recent developments, in particular, the U.S.-Canada Free Trade Agreement, that Canada has decided on a course of growing economic integration with the United States. This move has been interpreted by some quarters in Mexico as a warning that unless Mexico does likewise, it will somehow be "left out." But more directly, it means that Canada, perhaps at some cost in economic independence, will assure permanent access to the U.S. market. It already has easy, effective access to the U.S. labor market; it has clearly insured itself against U.S. protectionism. Whether the cost will prove politically acceptable to Canada in the long run is open to question; however, current evidence indicates it will. Thus Mexico faces what at first seems a difficult choice: to speed its economic integration with the United States, or sacrifice important output and employment growth opportunities. Obviously, a number of options exist.

GROWTH OF MEXICO'S LABOR FORCE: PAST AND FUTURE TRENDS

Although labor flows between Mexico and the United States are a historical phenomenon, and not the exclusive results of economic "push-pull" factors, the fact remains that a long-run recession in the Mexican economy will influence the degree of labor flow. Although there are no clear data, Mexican migration to the United States has clearly risen in the last few years.

Mexico's labor force, as Table 1 shows, has grown at an accelerated pace over the last two decades, from 11.3 to about 22 million persons in only 20 years. It is expected that by 2000 the labor force will include 40 to 42 million persons. Such growth has been accompanied by a rapid growth in urban population. Although Mexico's rural population is not entirely employed in agriculture, the agricultural labor force remained almost constant during the same period (increasing at most from 5 to 6 million persons, if an allowance is made for errors in the 1980 population census). Thus, the nonagricultural labor force rose from 3 to roughly 23 million persons between 1950 and the present. It is not known with certainty where this labor force is employed or how many persons are in the United States.

A conservative estimate of GDP growth requirements claims that in order to maintain the approximate employment mix of 1985, the GDP would have to increase 5.3 percent annually between 1985 and 2000, to compensate for the foreseeable increase in the labor force.[1] This increase

[1] See Saúl Trejo Reyes, *Empleo para Todos: El Reto y los Caminos* (Mexico City, 1988). Most of the data for future employment growth referred to in this paper come from this book. A model applied by Michio Morishima et al. to Great Britain has been adapted to

TABLE 1

The Structure of Mexico's Labor Force, 1960–2000

(*thousands of persons*)

	1960	1970	1980	Projected 2000	Growth rates 1970–80
Population	36,046	48,225	66,846	100,039	3.3%
Labor force	11,332	12,955	22,066	41,870	5.5[a]
Activity					
Agriculture	6,143	5,145	4,901	6,005	0.5
Mining	142	180	240	840	3.1
Manufacturing	1,556	2,363[b]	2,417	8,941	3.2
Construction	408	571	1,687	3,944	6.6
Electricity	41	53	63	177	3.1
Transport	357	391	907	2,560	5.0
Commerce	1,075	3,097	2,637	3,233	–
Services	–	–	–	–	–
Government	1,609	407	5,913	10,350	6.7
Other	–	747	–	–	–
Not specif.	–	–	4,366	5,820	–

SOURCES: *Population Censuses*, 1950, 1960, 1970, 1980; and Saúl Trejo Reyes, *Empleo para Todos: El Reto y los Caminos*, (Mexico City, Fondo de Cultura Económica, 1988).

[a]The higher rate for 1970–80 results if 1980 census figures for the labor force are used. If a correction is made to account for the differences in census definitions between 1970 and 1980, then a lower growth rate results.

[b]Includes repair activities, which in previous years were classified as services.

in GDP does not seem possible, especially in view of the burden of debt service payments. Thus, it is likely that the pressure for Mexican immigration to the United States, and in a minor way to Canada, will continue unabated.

A great deal of recent discussion concerns the size and characteristics of the so-called informal sector, or "underground economy," in the Mexican economy. To the extent that such types of employment can grow, the pressure on the job market will of course be reduced. However, even under the most optimistic assumptions, the potential for these types of activities is also limited by the evolution of key macroeconomic policy variables.

The evolution of wage and salary levels is also an important determinant of labor flows. The sizeable drop in real wages and salaries in 1982–1988 has probably run its course, as further reductions would probably lead to strong protest from the labor sector. At the same time,

evaluate the possible employment impact of alternative growth paths for the period 1986 to 2000. See also Michio Morishima et al., *The Working of Econometric Models* (Cambridge, 1972).

to the extent that the Pacto de Solidaridad Económica succeeds in reducing inflation, real wages are more likely to remain stable, and may even rise again in the short run.

However, for the medium run, the problem of emphasizing "best sectors" for economic development is important.[2] A number of activities are promising for employment creation in Mexico, and in principle promoting them would seem sensible. Key among these are tourism, assembly plants, and labor-intensive agriculture, especially fruits and vegetables, whether for domestic or export markets. These are export-oriented activities, so their promotion would make it easier to reconcile employment, export, and growth objectives. At the same time, their development would most likely occur outside the central area, so that it would help decentralize economic growth. The costs and the policies required for promoting these activities, however, are significant; a number of obstacles must be overcome.

Perhaps the first obstacle to promoting these activities lies in the nature of the economic policy instruments that the Mexican government has developed until now. These policies have tended to favor physical investment in import-substituting activities and inefficient resource use. Even in recent years, when exports have become a much more important policy objective, macroeconomic policies—exchange rate, interest rates, aggregate demand, fiscal policies, and low-wage policies—have been emphasized. By and large, development of modern organizations and new knowledge, as well as the application of technology to productive processes, have been neglected in government policies, although they are the most profitable activities. However, objectives such as these are very difficult to attain using traditional policy instruments; a policy change implies effecting a radical transformation of the public sector in Mexico.

The second major point regarding the development of an export- and employment-oriented policy encompasses Mexico's need to transform its relationship with the United States, its international economic policies, and its ability to participate in the world economy. Greater interaction with the United States is undoubtedly necessary, but this interaction is politically difficult. It would require that the United States invest in a way likely to have a favorable long-term impact on Mexico's development. And it would also imply that Mexico must develop policies to guarantee certain minimum standards of living to the whole population, in order to maintain social stability and make rapid modernization possible. Although foreign investment would be more welcome than in the past, the terms would have to be stricter: fiscal policy would be important, and firms would be expected to make a lasting contribution not only to em-

[2] I do not favor emphasizing specific industries.

ployment—the fact that they do is obvious—but also to long-term social objectives and the financing of the economic and social infrastructure they require. Until now, foreign investors have not always paid the full cost of the externalities they impose on Mexican society.

But problems also exist in the international sphere. It is highly unlikely that the North American free trade zone, about which so much has been said, would be acceptable to the United States if it included the labor market. It is equally unlikely that it would be acceptable to Mexico, or in its best interests, if it included only trade in goods and services. What is needed, and what may be easier to achieve, is a change in policies and attitudes in both countries. Just as Mexico might implement policies that would make it possible to advance more rapidly toward employment and growth objectives and a more open economy, the United States would have to implement more open policies toward Mexican exports and adopt a more long-term view of Mexican foreign debt. This might appear a wish list, and indeed it is. But it is also one way in which Mexico's employment performance might break from foreseeable trends. It is also a means for resolving potentially greater conflicts between Mexico and the United States over labor and trade issues, given that population and employment trends augur such unfavorable developments for Mexico.

MEXICO'S DEBT-SERVICE BURDEN AND GROWTH PROSPECTS

Mexico's reported GDP has not grown since 1981, while its labor force apparently has increased by roughly 5 to 6 million persons—that is, around 25 percent. Table 2 shows GDP for the period, expressed in constant pesos.

Analysis of the relationship between debt service burden and GNP is complex. At first, during the initial phase of adjustment (around

TABLE 2

Evolution of Gross Domestic Product

Year	GDP index	GDP deflator	Percent increase
1980	100.0	100.0	28.7%
1981	108.8	126.0	26.0
1982	108.1	202.8	61.0
1983	103.6	386.1	90.4
1984	107.3	614.4	59.1
1985	110.1	963.1	56.8
1986	105.7	1679.5	74.4
1987	107.2	4082.2	143.1

SOURCE: Banco de México, *Informe Anual*, 1987 (Mexico City, 1988).

1983), it was optimistically expected by some governments and by international institution and creditor banks that a period of perhaps two years might be sufficient to effect required changes in debtor economies. Such changes, it was thought, would make debtors creditworthy again, so that credit flows would be resumed. However, as has become evident, the size of the required transfer has not only been highly inflationary, it has so distorted relative prices and wages that an equilibrium compatible with growth seems more distant than ever.

For Mexico, transfers abroad in 1987 were approximately 6.6 percent of GDP. Although this percentage is expected to drop in 1988, a resumption of growth is nowhere in sight under current foreign-debt-payment conditions. Mexico cannot grow under the restrictive policies necessitated by its debt service. This inability to grow, of course, has direct repercussions for its employment prospects, and for the size of the potential labor flow to the United States. Thus, as Mexican politicians have repeatedly stated, it is not possible to pay service on debt if the country cannot grow.

THE NEW INTERNATIONAL DIVISION OF LABOR
AND THE NORTH AMERICAN REGION

It is evident that offshore assembly plants will likely be a permanent and growing characteristic of the world economy. Their relative importance will certainly vary among industries; however, the worldwide search for lower labor and natural-resource costs will probably continue, because it is both profitable and technologically feasible. Only very extreme social and political changes in industrialized countries—changes that would severely limit firms' decisions—could cause the relative importance of foreign assembly plants to drop off sharply.

A country's bargaining position and the results of its participation in the new international division of labor depend on that country' characteristics, resource base, and size and nature of its corporations. In Mexico's case, such increased participation in the new division of labor has had a greater effect on employment than on net export income. The figure for net export income in 1987, the highest to date, was only $1.5 billion. At the same time, however, the social costs that foreign companies impose are not fully paid by their actual out-of-pocket costs in Mexico. The taxes foreign firms pay are low, and the needed infrastructure is often subsidized by the government, which hopes to attract more such firms. Local interest groups, in a self-serving manner, proclaim that any attempt to charge *maquiladoras* the full costs they impose on society, or to raise wages, will simply result in their relocating elsewhere. Opponents of such firms, most often from the far left of the political spectrum, argue that such firms are highly unstable, since at any time they may go elsewhere, leaving in their wake unemployment and more demands on government. Such "*maquiladora*-chasing" policies have a limit considering the government's bleak finances. It is equally clear, however, that such plants, as a whole, are no more unstable than other industrial activities.

The United States has benefited as much as, or perhaps more than, any other country from the new international division of labor. Over the last two decades, U.S. firms have gained new sources of cheap labor; thus, even if the resulting trade deficit is of great concern to policymakers in the United States and other nations, profits of U.S. firms have not suffered as a result of the import boom of the last decade. The U.S. labor force, however, has suffered the loss of thousands of highly-paid industrial jobs, not only from production moving abroad, but also from technical change. The change to a "service economy" means that many new U.S. jobs are low-wage jobs.

Mexico, on the other hand, has attracted a significant number of new manufacturing facilities (often referred to as 'assembly plants," although they are much more than assembly operations). As of September 1989, 440,000 workers,[3] almost 15 percent of manufacturing employment, are in such firms, located mostly along the northern border. Although highly visible, especially to the U.S. labor movement, such firms are not simply a U.S.-Mexico phenomenon, but rather a result of global changes in the way productive processes are organized. Such changes result from advances in transportation, communications, and management technology—advances that made it possible for firms to seek the best cost conditions worldwide and plan output and distribution on an international scale. Of course, the wage disparity between Mexican and U.S. workers (the firms pay Mexican workers only 10 to 15 percent of what they were paying U.S. workers) does not result in comparable income transfer to Mexican labor, but primarily a shift of income from wages to profits.

Some appraisals of the relative costs paid by assembly industries in Mexico argue that these industries have been subsidized by both the United States and Mexico, the United States through favorable tariff provisions and a favorable tax law definition, which actually underestimates foreign value added, and Mexico by providing cheap labor and more secure access to the U.S. market than offshore assembly operations located elsewhere could offer.[4] Such security in fact has been obtained free by assembly plants, but the bargain has also included cheap labor.

[3] INEGI-SPP, *Industria Maquiladora de Exportación* (Mexico City, October 1989).
[4] See George Baker, "The Competitive Advantage of the *Maquiladora* for United States and Japanese Firms," preliminary draft, October 9, 1987 (Las Cruces, New Mexico State University, 1987).

In the last few years, Mexico's export-promotion policy brought about a substantial increase in export earnings, and thus a sort of recovery. An alternative interpretation, however, credits the export boom to the debt crisis, so that to the extent that no debt relief is forthcoming, debtors will continue their attempts to raise their exports. In this view, the debt crisis had two immediate effects: drastic devaluation of the domestic currency, and extreme contradiction of domestic demand. The resulting change in relative prices and expected profitability of different activities deflected resources to exports while discouraging imports.

The effects that the Mexican debt crisis has had on advanced industrial economies, and particularly on the U.S. economy and U.S. exports, have been well documented.[5] Substantial export volumes have been lost, affecting jobs in export industries. At the same time, at least part of the labor flow from Mexico is explained by its low salaries and scarcity of good job opportunities. In recent years, the flow of educated and skilled people from Mexico to the United States has increased. This large loss of human capital concerns Mexican authorities, because such a loss could adversely affect prospects for long-term recovery. Thus, present trade and financial policies of advanced industrial countries hinder Mexican efforts to recover a satisfactory growth and employment path. We can no longer expect recovery to occur and conditions similar to those on the eve of the crisis to reappear somehow. Rather, we must now concentrate on averting further damage to the domestic economy, and preventing permanent disequilibrium in North American labor markets.

TECHNOLOGICAL CHANGE, GROWTH, AND EMPLOYMENT IN MEXICO

The future relationship between technological change and employment growth in Mexico will likely be rather complex: several forces are at work. First, as a result of adjustment policies undertaken during the last five years, relative factor prices have changed dramatically; labor of all types is now considerably cheaper than it was prior to the 1982 debt crisis. Labor will probably be used more intensively.

Second, accession to GATT means that Mexican producers will face increased competitive pressures at home and must compete abroad in order to survive. By itself, such pressure might lead to a faster rate of technological change, as Mexican firms strive to catch up to international quality levels and efficiency standards. The effect of such pressure on capital-labor rations cannot be determined a priori.

---

[5] "The Impact of the Latin American Debt Crisis on the U.S. Economy: A Staff Study," prepared for the use of the Joint Economic Committee, Congress of the United States (Washington, 1986).

Third, world technological change, especially in high-tech industries, will likely have profound effects on the whole productive structure. Technologically weak countries, such as Mexico today, will find it ever more difficult not to copy leading countries' use of productive techniques. Thus, unless Mexico is able to raise its level of internal technological activity, it might simply have to follow foreign production techniques. The absence of such internal activity would cause productive employment growth to fall far short of job creation requirements, since investment for production capacity would continue to rely heavily either on imported capital goods or on capital goods incorporating foreign technology.

Under any reasonable assumption about the growth of the Mexican economy, the labor force will greatly exceed labor demand for the foreseeable future. Growth of different sectors of the economy will not be sufficient to absorb the growth of the labor force. Table 3 projects the evolution of the population of labor force age for 2000, as well as the estimated labor force (assuming that age-specific participation rates remain at their 1980 levels). As may be seen from Table 3, the largest increase in the labor force will be observed in persons aged 20–39. This group will almost double in size, from 11.8 to 22.8 million persons.

TABLE 3

Population and Labor Force Estimates by Age, 1980 and 2000

Age	Population		Labor Force		Pct. employed, 1980
	1980	2000 (est.)	1980	2000 (est.)	
0–4	10,605,491	9,590,813			–
5–9	10,768,060	9,325,195			–
10–14	9,435,740	9,788,904	833,365	864,556	8.8%
15–19	7,823,891	10,004,442	3,217,966	4,114,827	41.1
20–24	6,378,869	10,020,615	3,799,892	5,969,280	59.6
25–29	5,059,985	10,257,418	3,216,632	6,520,641	63.6
30–34	4,192,164	8,920,844	2,672,505	5,687,038	63.8
35–39	3,393,221	7,346,105	3,137,390	4,627,312	63.0
40–44	2,769,025	5,987,973	1,737,563	3,757,453	62.8
45–49	2,313,013	4,722,374	1,423,428	2,906,149	61.5
50–54	1,913,739	3,856,034	1,148,052	2,313,235	60.0
55–59	1,541,296	3,034,339	903,199	1,778,123	58.6
60–64	1,148,704	2,363,313	620,185	1,275,953	54.0
65–69	853,944	1,827,264	413,224	884,213	48.4
70–74	651,630	1,332,202	290,171	593,230	44.5
75–79	429,904	882,118	149,736	307,242	34.8
80–84	254,806	481,237	88,749	167,615	34.8
85+	121,625	297,818	42,362	103,730	34.8
TOTAL	69,655,107	100,039,008	22,694,419	41,870,595	32.6

SOURCES: For 1980, *IX Censo General de Poblacion* (Mexico City, 1985). For 2000, *Proyecciones de la Población de México y de las Entidades Federativas: 1980–2000, INEGI-CONAPO* (Secretaría de Programación y Presupuesto, Mexico City, 1985).

CONCLUSION

Whether it will be possible to advance toward the kind of North American negotiation necessary to assure long-run growth and social stability in all three countries is unknown. At present, prospects do not seem very favorable. Negotiating mechanisms and institutional arrangements are set up for a kind of piecemeal approach that no longer applies to the types of problems North American countries face now, and will likely face in the future. A regional outlook is necessary, yet each country's government sees itself as very different, and worse, far from the other two. This outlook makes it very difficult for them to exploit the opportunities inherent in their geographical proximity.

It seems very likely that Mexico will persevere in modernization. But there are clear limits to what internal measures can achieve. These limits are all too evident after almost six years of unprecedented austerity policies. Whether the Mexican economy can resume growth and labor absorption in the next year will depend to a large extent on what happens to its foreign-debt-service payments. Medium-term employment performance will depend on whether the kind of North American labor-trade agreement implied in this paper can be achieved, and on whether each of the three countries can fully understand the economic restructuring and policy formulation this agreement would require.

PART VI
Bilateral Trade Agreements and the Future of North American Economic Relations

The Canada-U.S. Free Trade Agreement and Future North American Trade Relations

Richard G. Harris

I WAS ASKED to address the ambitious and highly speculative subject of where North American economic relations might be in twenty years. This is an intensely interesting question but one over which I hardly have any particular advantage here. I would, however, like to address a more narrowly defined but equally speculative question that bears directly on the broader question of economic relations between Canada, Mexico, and the United States and the role the recent Canada-U.S. Free Trade Agreement might play in these future relations.

The agreement contains features characteristic of a free-trade area and a common market. I wish to address what incentives will exist for harmonizing trade policy between Canada and the United States. Since the agreement maintains both countries' sovereignty with respect to barriers regarding third countries (taking appropriate account of GATT obligations), ostensibly trade policy in both countries will be different. However, there are a number of economic forces that will tend to produce long-term incentives to move toward common external barriers. In the second part of the paper I will review these arguments.

At the same time, questions regarding mobility of factors, both labor and capital, have occupied a good part of the free trade debate. It has been argued that the agreement will increase the incentive to harmonize tax, fiscal, and social policies to facilitate mobility of factors. In the third part of the paper these arguments are considered. In general it will be shown that with respect to Canada and the United States, the agreement will reduce incentives to harmonize policies and facilitate factor movements. In the last section, I will take up the issue of global trade alliances and North American economic relations.

THE CANADA-U.S. FREE TRADE AGREEMENT
AND TRADE-POLICY HARMONIZATION

The FTA reduces tariffs and a variety of nontariff barriers to Canada-U.S. trade. In this respect, it qualifies as a classic free-trade area agreement. The rules of origin in the agreement are intended to contend with the traditional trade deflection problem associated with different external tariffs in the two countries. Although much of the relevant discussion in the customs-union literature pertains to tariffs, external barriers will most likely continue to be in the form of permanent protection through quotas, voluntary export-restraint agreements, and so on, or in the form of contingent protection facilitated by administrative trade laws covering antidumping and countervail. These instruments produce effects similar to trade diversion and trade creation, although the analysis in this case is not conclusive.

There will be a number of pressures placed on Canada-U.S. relations by the FTA that may lead to harmonization with third countries in both permanent and contingent protection mechanisms. The first argument for harmonization concerns the difficulties involved in administering rules of origin. Defining North American content in many manufactured products may be nearly impossible in many cases. Parts produced in the United States and put into a subcomponent that is then reintroduced as part of a machine assembled in Canada will raise difficult measurement issues for the administration of the rules of origin. Both customs services can look forward to increased employment opportunities; situations like this will provide ample demand for their talents. The costs, however, of administering the system could become quite high, and the administrative rules that evolve will inevitably be arbitrary and in many cases lead to tensions. Administering the rules of origin will also create its own distortions. Producers will manufacture products to just meet the rules-of-origin requirement, departing from the least-cost production method. This scenario will be more prevalent the more significant the external tariff. Thus a producer in the United States wishing to export duty-free to Canada may use much more expensive North American-produced components, rather than pay the duty necessary to export to Canada using foreign-produced parts. This type of trade diversion will induce deadweight losses approximately equal to the foregone tariff revenues on the cheaper imported foreign parts.

Many of the permanent barriers will be quotas, or voluntary restraint arrangements with their countries. One argument in favor of a free trade agreement over a common market posits that a free trade agreement is less harmful to broader free trade given the absence of harmonized barriers against third parties. The usual argument is that the terms-of-trade gains to each partner in the agreement from their own protection is smaller than potential terms-of-trade gains to the joint union under a common market arrangement. This argument seems a bit dated given that most quota rents accrue to foreigners, thereby eliminating terms-of-trade gains through home-market protection.

What does it mean to talk about harmonized quotas? The basic idea is that an importer to North America would face a restriction on total sales to North America independent of whether these sales would ultimately occur in Canada or the United States. (In the present system, quotas are administered separately in each country.) This raises an interesting issue. Because Canada is the smaller of the two countries, quotas put in place by the United States will raise the U.S. producer price. Under the FTA, Canadian producers will have the benefit of exporting to the United States and enjoying U.S. protection against the third country. Canadian consumers, however, need not pay for this protection, as the benefits to protecting the Canadian producers through a similar scheme will not be as great. Thus, as the smaller partner in the area, Canada has a strong incentive to free ride on U.S. protectionism.

Could such a situation persist? Quite possibly it could for some time, but it seems inevitable that given the benefits being conferred on Canadian producers, inevitably there would be a strong demand that Canada pay its fair share for the benefits of the protection. Thus Canada would be required to protect its market to the same degree, or alternatively a harmonized quota system would be needed to replace the existing system of independently determined quotas. An obvious example would be the negotiation of the next round of voluntary restraints on Japanese automobile imports. It will be interesting to see whether the demand for such restraints comes first from Canada or the United States.

Quotas, unlike tariffs, generate rents that may accrue domestically or to foreigners. In oligopolistic high-entry barrier industries, they also generate collusive prices and outputs.[1] A harmonized quota system would, in principle, have a neutral collusive effect on the North American industry structure. That is, the North American industry as a whole would have its pricing, output, and plant location decisions affected. Using protection to affect profitability of plant location may become an important indirect goal of protection policy. A firm that produces for both the Canadian and U.S. markets but competes in both countries with imports

---

[1] See Richard Harris, "Why Voluntary Export Restraints Are 'Voluntary'," *Canadian Journal of Economics* vol. 23., no. 4 (1985).

from a third country may locate production where profitability is highest and market share is more secure. This effect will not necessarily dominate least-cost production-location choices, but it will certainly be an important consideration. If the United States were to become protectionist, then low barriers in Canada for industries with high degrees of entry barriers would tend to induce location in the U.S. market. On the other hand, if Canada were to become protectionist in these industries, it would not necessarily attract a great deal of new investment. Those already producing from the United States could continue to export duty-free into Canada under the FTA and enjoy rents generated in Canada. In such a situation Canada, the smaller country, would be induced to offer similar degrees of protection afforded in the larger country rather than risk losing Canadian production.

A fourth reason for harmonizing external trade barriers is the reserve adjustment problem. The same issue was raised in discussing the merits of sectoral versus complete free trade.[2] If each of the two countries in a free trade agreement adjusts its industrial structure to facilitate existing external protection in both countries, then contemplates changing the pattern of external protection, a reverse adjustment could occur. Consider an industry that expands under the free trade agreement in country A. Country B then lowers protection on a crucial input to its domestic industry competing with the same industry in country A. The industry in country A would now be forced to contract. Harmonizing the cost of imported inputs in both countries would reduce this problem.

One could argue that prior to the Canada-U.S. Free Trade Agreement the same thing could happen. In the absence of an agreement, however, country A could respond by raising barriers against country B imports, thus reducing the need for adjustment. The desire to reduce reverse adjustment after the FTA is in place will inevitably raise pressures to harmonize the cost of imported inputs. Common external-trade barriers accomplish harmonization most efficiently.

A prominent feature of the new protectionism is export-promotion policies. The literature on strategic trade policy suggests that export promotion is used to shift rents in favor of domestic producers in high entry-barrier industries.[3] It may also be an expedient way to make transfers to export industries when these transfers appear politically necessary. The latter argument seems more relevant than the profit-shifting argument in

[2] David Cox and Richard Harris, "A Quantitative Assessment of the Economic Impact on Canada of Sectoral Free Trade with the United States," *Canadian Journal of Economics* (August 1986).

[3] J. Brander and B. Spencer, "Export Subsidies and International Market Share Rivalry," *Journal of International Economics* 18 (1985), 83–100.

industries such as agriculture. In addition to external protection policies, one can imagine harmonizing export promotion to third countries.

There is one very good economic reason to harmonize export promotion: in general, cooperative choice of export subsidies leads to superior national welfare relative to noncooperative policies. For concentrated oligopolistic industries, the country that fails to promote exports may lose the industry. Competitive subsidization of exports may occur not because of a desire to raise economic welfare, but rather from the desire to retain domestic production; Harry Johnson's argument about the positive benefits of industrialization comes to mind.[4] With large-scale footloose production, subsidy competition between countries may be self-defeating. Harmonization of export subsidies may be a sensible political solution. Note that harmonizing export promotion would not be necessary nor likely in those cases where competition between countries in a third market was unlikely.

The argument for harmonization thus far has not really depended upon the existence of the FTA. I now wish to argue that the existence of the FTA makes harmonization of export promotion more likely. The first argument simply repeats the plant-mobility argument; in some industries large asymmetries in export-promotion policies between Canada and the United States could effect plant location (in that both countries would want to take advantage of these policies), while the benefits of free access to both markets in the agreement would be retained independent of location. With truly open borders in a free trade agreement, export subsidies offered by one country but not the other would attract a sort of welfare-reducing trade creation. Goods that normally would be exported directly from the nonsubsidizing country would be diverted to the subsidizing country in partially finished form so as to qualify for the export-subsidy program. This strategy would of course put additional pressure on the treasury of the subsidizing countries, and require modified rules of origin for administering export-subsidy programs.

Under the Canada-U.S. Free Trade Agreement, there is an understanding to look at subsidies, anti-dumping, and countervail over the five-year period after the agreement takes effect. It is extremely difficult to know whether harmonization is likely with respect to these policies. Domestic and trade policies are intertwined at this level, and both countries have difficulty establishing jurisdiction over relevant offending practices. Similar remarks could be made about anti-trust and combines policy. To the

[4] Harry G. Johnson, "An Economic Theory of Protectionism, Tariff Bargaining, and the Formation of Customs Unions," *Journal of Political Economy* vol. 73, no. 3 (1965), 256–83.

extent that the FTA fosters an increase in the trade volume between the two countries, one would expect there to be higher returns to harmonizing, or at least reducing, the harmful effects of contingent protection laws. Hopefully this will occur. The potential results of applying these policies or laws against third countries are not clear. In general, the administrative nature of the process governing application of this protection and the cyclical nature of the demand for this protection will continue to be the dominant factors at work.

FACTOR MOBILITY AND THE CANADA-U.S. FREE TRADE AGREEMENT

The Canada-U.S. Free Trade Agreement contains a number of elements that enhance factor mobility, particularly capital mobility. These elements include the right of national treatment in both countries, the reduction in investment-review procedures for acquisitions in both countries, and the right of establishment in the service industries. Labor mobility is more or less unchanged except for improved temporary bilateral access for the purpose of servicing customers.

A long-standing question in economic theory is whether trade in goods substitutes or complements trade in factors. In the traditional Hecksher-Ohlin model of trade based on endowment differences, trade in goods and trade in factor services are perfect substitutes under free trade. Historically, it is well known that investment flows are often caused by tariff jumping; investment comes in instead of the goods themselves in the presence of the tariff. Such investment may be employment creating in the short run, but it is welfare reducing in terms of long-run efficiency.[5]

If the latter view is true, the FTA should reduce incentives for harmonizing the treatment of investment, including tax treatment. The basic argument is that with free trade in goods, trade in factors is no longer necessary. Investment flows between Canada and the United States would be reduced over the longer term and most of the benefits of free trade would come from flows of goods. However, this argument only works if there are truly prohibitive barriers to capital movements and if factor-price equalization tends to exist in the absence of factor mobility. Both of these seem unlikely in the Canada-U.S. context.

My own view, consistent with the early work I did with David Cox, is that the increased trade volume accompanying the FTA will be accompanied by an increased volume of two-way investment flows. This will occur because in most complex service and manufacturing activities ex-

[5] For an excellent discussion, see James R. Markusen and James R. Melvin, *The Theory of International Trade* (New York, 1988), chap. 19.

porting tends to be accompanied by direct investment in both production and distribution. Second, in footloose industries national, state, provincial, and local jurisdictions will be constrained in their choice of tax instruments and policies by their need to create horizontal equity of investment across both countries.

A major economic effect of the free trade agreement will be to raise real wages in Canada relative to those in the United States. This will raise the capital intensity of production in Canada and ultimately cause a period of increased capital inflows, unless Canadian savings rates rise significantly; however, there is no reason the capital will come from the United States. Current macro imbalances suggest that the capital might more naturally originate in Japan if the real rate of return to investing in Canada were to rise. Over the longer term, however, it is reasonable to expect a significant level of direct investment by both countries in each other's jurisdiction. In these circumstances, national treatment becomes a principle worth a great deal to both countries' interests.

What of labor mobility? There is little in the agreement that pertains directly to labor mobility. Indeed the immobility of labor is the principal practical feature of a free trade area that distinguishes it from complete economic integration. A basic question is whether over the longer term the FTA will create forces that will increase labor movements across borders. One fear often voiced in the free trade debate within Canada is that investment will leave Canada, wages will fall, and skilled workers will leave Canada for higher-paying jobs in the United States. Let's look at this argument and others in more detail.

The FTA has two major effects on Canadian labor markets. First, an increase in the general level of real wages—probably 10 to 12 percent over the long run according to my estimates. Second, an increase in the level of specialization within the manufacturing sectors; this may in turn lead to an increase in the level of specialization required across the occupational-skill spectrum. Two observations follow from these assumed impacts. In general, there will be less incentive for labor to move from Canada to the United States for higher wages; thus incipient pressures to immigrate to the United States will be reduced for many workers. When one takes into account the tax-public goods package offered in different state and provincial jurisdictions, it may well turn out that more U.S. residents will come to Canada. This latter statement is entirely speculative, but has some validity if the urban environment of Canada remains the same and U.S. cities show little sign of improvement.

There will, however, be emigration from Canada by skilled workers when Canadian firms do not need the skills they offer. The rationalization process accompanying free trade may create some excess supplies of certain types of industry-specific labor. It is unclear how acute this problem will be in the long term. Once the industrial structure has settled down, education and retraining of general skills will continue and flexible manufacturing systems may actually reduce demand for traditional product-specific skills.

Thus on balance it would seems that the FTA may actually reduce incipient economic pressures for labor to move from Canada to the United States. Resource booms will of course require labor to move between the countries and regions as it has in the past; the agreement will do little to change this. A more fundamental question is whether labor-market and social policies will necessarily be forced to harmonize as a result of the FTA. Given the relative size of the two countries, this is almost entirely a Canadian issue. Certainly if these policies are forced to harmonize, one could reasonably expect considerable friction in future economic relations between the United States and Canada. Indeed one could predict with some certainty that the agreement would be terminated by Canada if its basic social policies became seriously threatened.

Defenders of the Canada-U.S. Free Trade Agreement have argued, and correctly so, that in the presence of labor immobility across the U.S.-Canada border, broad social policy differences will be under little threat from the agreement. The exchange rate or nominal wages will adjust to account for the mix of pecuniary and social-policy benefits offered in Canada and the United States. If an industry is to produce in both Canada and the United States with capital mobility and identical technologies, the cost of labor services to business must be the same in both locations. If Canadians demand a higher level of social services than in the United States, however, then these services will have to be paid for with a lower after-tax take-home pay. Nevertheless, gross wages to labor in Canada will be higher with the agreement. It is entirely possible that the 10 percent real wage gains in Canada will be spent on social policies.

Having described the positive scenario, let me turn now to a potential problem that may accompany future economic relations between Canada and the United States. In a transition period, perceptions and lags in adjustment can have long-run effects. Witness the effect on U.S. manufacturing of the overvalued U.S. dollar from 1981 to 1985. Canadian business and capital owners will take the self-interested position that any labor-market or social policy that appears as a direct cost to them should be eliminated in order for them to be competitive with the counterpart U.S. firm.

There has already been some indication that Canadian companies will demand that these policies be eliminated. With the implementation of the FTA, we will no doubt hear a great deal more of this argument. To give an analogy, when the Canadian dollar appreciates against the U.S. dollar, one often hears companies arguing that their wage costs are too high. Of course, the argument is completely fallacious; the dollar could be appreciating for many reasons. In the long term, the demand for the companies' products could fall and necessitate either a reduction in labor costs within the firm, or, if the firm's activities are noneconomic at the new exchange rate, it could shut down or go bankrupt.

Canadians should resist changing broad social or labor-market policies because of claims by business that their costs are too high. The company should be forced to make whatever changes necessary to be competitive within the existing policy environment. The macroeconomics of trade and investment flows will set the Canadian exchange rate appropriately given the mix of policies undertaken. This is not to defend any particular existing social policy, but merely to point out that the FTA itself provides no cause for change in social or labor-market policy, nor should it impinge on any desired future changes in these policies.

The arguments made in the preceding paragraph are just as valid in the absence of the FTA. There is a worry, however, that now that the FTA has been set in place, arguments in favor of policy harmonization will be given more credit than they deserve. If a major social policy within Canada were eliminated, and if this act were linked in the minds of the public with the FTA, inestimatable damage would occur to future Canadian economic relations with the United States and the rest of the world. In particular, abandonment of a major social policy would, in many peoples' minds, raise a permanent doubt about the benefits of a liberalized trading system that has served Canada so well over the past four decades.

It is somewhat ironic that the United States would inadvertently be drawn into a major Canadian domestic policy debate. The U.S. Congress and U.S. trade officials should restrain their calls for the infamous "level playing field" when the perceived differences are based on variations across countries in broad social and labor-market policies. These types of claims do little to advance the cause of trade liberalization and leave the serious misrepresentation that political integration is necessary for countries to benefit from freer multilateral and bilateral trade.

At the same time, however, economic relations between Canada and the United States will inevitably be affected by regional economic policies undertaken. In Canada, it is questionable whether the provinces can be restrained from undertaking policies that seriously distort both interprovincial and interregional trade. The same can be said with respect to states' policies on taxes and subsidies in a variety of areas. I am not terribly optimistic that much cooperation will be achieved between the regional governments. Indeed, I suspect that we are in for a long period of learning in which countervail will be used in both countries with some frequency. It is conceivable that ultimately a subsidies code covering this type of regional competition will be developed, but at the moment the constraints on regional governments that would be implicit in such a code are unacceptable. It seems the best that can be hoped for is a reduced level of regional competition in which the tendency to protect regional industry and subsidize exports is attenuated by fiscal constraints on these governments. Certainly in a freer trade environment the ability of one region to shift the costs of its own protectionist activity onto other regions is significantly reduced. By isolating locally the costs and benefits of policies, more rational political decision making may occur. Inevitably this will be more important for provinces than for states. Under the FTA, Canadian provincial trade will orient toward north-south flows more than it has in the past. This means, for example, that Ontario will have to respond fairly quickly to the costs of attempting to subsidize exports to the United States, either with higher taxes on Ontario residents, or more dramatically with a countervail case in the United States.

GLOBAL TRADING ARRANGEMENTS
AND NORTH AMERICAN ECONOMIC RELATIONS

There has been some discussion over the years about Mexico-United States free trade and even of a Canada-Mexico-U.S. free trade area.[6] This is quite a complex issue with many questions that go beyond those raised in the Canada-U.S. debate. A central question for future economic relations between the three countries, and indeed for the success Mexico will have at raising income levels under any economic strategy, is the extent to which the world trading system becomes balkanized into large regional trading blocs. It is possible to imagine a situation in which the non-Communist industrialized world roughly divides up into three blocs—Europe, North America, and the Pacific Rim countries.[7] The failure of GATT to make significant progress on nontariff barriers and the continued international macroeconomic imbalances make this a highly

---

[6] Sidney Weintraub, *Free Trade Between Mexico and the United States?* (Washington, 1984); Gerardo Bueno, "A Mexican View," in *Bilateralism, Multilateralism, and Canada in U.S. Trade Policy* (New York, 1988).

[7] Note that this chapter was written before the dramatic events in Eastern Europe during 1989–90. I think the basic point remains valid.

plausible scenario. With the FTA, and 1992 arriving for the European Community, some think it inevitable.

In the event this scenario occurs, what would happen to economic relations between the three countries? First, I think Mexico would achieve much greater importance in the relationship as the low-cost labor country for manufacturing. Currently this position is being met largely by the far east newly industrializing countries. Should these Pacific Rim countries (and possibly China) align regionally with Japan, then barriers by the United States and Canada against the bloc's exports to North America would make Mexico an attractive site for plant location. Second, there would be a great deal of trade diversion toward either domestic sources or other member countries as sources of supply. In general, trade between the North American region and the rest of the world would decline and that within the region would expand. Within the United States, this shift in economic flows would effectively place much greater emphasis on the trade relations between Canada and Mexico than has heretofore occurred, and probably a greater sensitivity to the domestic policy concerns of those countries. Third, in the event of regional trade balkanization, both Mexico and Canada would take on greater strategic significance as sources of oil and gas for the United States. This significance would not automatically occur since OPEC might not be aligned within any particular regional industrial trading bloc, but the possibility would certainly weigh considerably in a period of increased international trade frictions.

Finally, in the event that such trading blocs would exist, we would certainly see most basic industries revitalized in North America, although many of these would end up in Mexico. The trend toward deindustrialization would diminish, supported by protection against manufactures of non-North American countries. The general tendency would be toward greater internal harmonization of the North American market, with greater economic clout afforded both Canada and Mexico.

This scenario is hardly to be hoped for. The accompanying reduction of international trade would be a great loss to the world economy. Clearly the liberal hope is for increased reduction of barriers internationally with as little balkanization of trade as possible. What of North American economic relations in this optimistic case? I think the FTA would likely emerge as but a transition measure to greater world trade liberalization, particularly along Europe-North America-Pacific Rim lines. Truly successful negotiations to deal with services, agriculture, and nontariff barriers would reduce substantially the need for the FTA. Indeed North American trade would inevitably take on an east-west character, with

Canada, for example, becoming a resource exporter to Japan, China, and the United States. Similarly, manufactured exports in North American countries would be sold in all regions. This diversification of trade would tend to reduce the one-sided nature of both Mexican and Canadian trade. The United States would become less significant to both countries as a source of trade volume. Nevertheless, the United States by sheer physical proximity will continue to be the most important trading relationship for both countries. On the other hand, it is conceivable that the international globalization of markets could harmonize individual countries' national economic policies far more than would the balkanization of trade. For example, the Canadian identity may be threatened much more by a sort of monolithic international culture than it ever was by U.S. culture. The global village may become a fact. National political interests will be second to the interests of the global economy.

It probably goes without saying that the Canada-U.S. Free Trade Agreement will eventually be rolled over into a broader multilateral trade agreement should the trend toward internationalized markets continue. However, it may be a very long time before we get to that situation. In the interim, the FTA will have to be a flexible arrangement that can adjust to changing circumstances of domestic situations and the positions of Canada and the United States toward other countries. Significant changes could occur in a number of areas, which will call for renegotiation of substantial portions of the agreement. Services and agriculture certainly come to mind as future trouble spots. Politically, it may be difficult to deal with continued shifts in power toward the Canadian provinces—shifts that require significant amending to the agreement. Many of the problems of the European Community will no doubt haunt this particular arrangement. Yet the critics of the agreement are probably right about one thing: there is no doubt that having done the deal, it will be much more difficult to undo it than might be imagined. Economic interests of the North American regions will become even more closely linked than before and the continentalist vision will be one step closer to reality.

Trade Policy in North America: Where Do We Go from Here?

Sidney Weintraub

THERE HAVE BEEN some remarkable developments in trade policy in North America during the past few years. Canada and the United States reached agreement on a free trade area, something that had eluded them for more than one hundred years. Mexico and the United States signed a number of agreements, one on subsidies and countervailing duties and several others, potentially more significant, establishing a framework for trade negotiations between the two countries. For Mexico, these developments came after a fundamental shift to trade opening, or *apertura*, from half a century of protecting just about everything produced, or that conceivably could be produced, within the country. The attitude in the United States, fueled by trade deficits approximating $150 billion (U.S.) a year, moved increasingly toward market protection. This tendency has yet to run its full course.

For all three countries, bilateralism now shares the policy focus with multilateralism. This emphasis has not yet run its course either and, until it does, its implications for the multilateral system will not be known.

The Canada-U.S. Free Trade Agreement is now mostly taken for granted as part of the normal landscape. The longer it endures, the more irreversible it will become even if the Conservatives are replaced as the governing party. This assumption is based on the calculation that abrogation of the agreement would be so costly in terms of relations with the United States that a Liberal government would reconsider earlier rhetoric. For the United States, even if protectionism increases (which I anticipate), Canada would be exempt from its worst manifestations because of the FTA. For Mexico, two assumptions are made, (1) that the apertura will continue, thereby institutionalizing it, and (2) that interest in the

Canada-U.S. Free Trade Agreement will grow as Mexico's apertura covers more of its import structure and deeply alters the composition of its trade.

I will now discuss trade issues in the three countries based on this set of assumptions and speculate about future trade policy in North America.

COUNTRY ISSUES

There is always tension in U.S. trade policy between liberalization and restrictionism. For most of the period since World War 2, the general policy has been openness accompanied by specific acts of protection. The counterpart positions are well illustrated by the simultaneous successive rounds of liberalization in the General Agreement on Tariffs and Trade (GATT) negotiations and restrictions on imports of textiles, steel, automobiles, agricultural commodities, and other products. The openness was represented by tariff reductions; the protectionism by the use of a variety of nontariff barriers.

The cumulative effect of large trade and current-account deficits has shifted the balance today. It is now unclear whether the scale has tilted definitively in favor of protection. The overwhelming support in the U.S. Congress for a trade bill in 1988 that many of its advocates describe as one that "could have been worse" evidences this assessment. Protection, usually phrased as fairness, has become the politically popular position.

It may be that the protectionist sentiment will diminish if U.S. trade surpluses decline, but by then a new set of protectionist realities may have been set in place. The situation would then be similar to the 1930s, when the reciprocal-trade-agreements program was used to diminish the restrictionism of Smoot-Hawley.

My own judgment is that the drive for protectionism is now so powerful that it will steamroll over efforts to change direction. I predict that protectionism will become more serious—by how much, I do not know. Regardless of the accuracy of this prediction, however, it would be foolhardy for vulnerable countries like Mexico and Canada not to factor this worst-case scenario into their policy formulation. As Table 1 shows, between 65 and 75 percent of these countries' exports go to the United States.

Canada has already made this calculation. The FTA has two rationales, one positive to stimulate Canadian productivity, and the other negative to forestall the worst manifestations of U.S. nontariff protectionism. After making a similar assessment, in its fashion, Mexico concluded the agreements with the United States noted above.

TABLE I

Exports by U.S., Canada, and Mexico, 1986

(billions of U.S. dollars)

Exports from	Exports to			Total
	U.S.	Canada	Mexico	
U.S.	—	44.8 (21%)	12.4 (6%)	217.3 (100%)
Canada	65.0 (74%)	—	0.3[a]	87.3 (100%)
Mexico	10.7 (67%)	0.2[a]	—	16.0 (100%)

SOURCES: U.S. exports: Department of Commerce, *1986 U.S. Foreign Trade Highlights*; Canadian exports: Statistics Canada, *Exports, Merchandise Trade* (Canadian dollars converted at average exchange rate for year from IMF, *International Financial Statistics*); Mexican exports: Banco de México, *Indicadores Económicos*.

NOTE: Each country's import data differs from the export data shown in the table above. For example, Mexican trade data give 1986 imports from the United States as $7.4 billion, not the $12.4 billion provided in U.S. statistics of exports to Mexico. Imports from Mexico in 1986 are calculated by the U.S. Department of Commerce as $17.1 billion, which is substantially higher than the Mexican export figure of $12.4 billion. The differences result from the timing when transactions are recorded, varying definitions of what should be included in the merchandise trade account, and sheer inaccuracies.

[a]Less than 1 percent.

U.S. protectionism, whatever its attributes, promotes a North American trading bloc. This is not necessarily what the U.S. Congress has in mind, but it has unwittingly set these integrative forces in motion.

The other main tendency in U.S. trade policy is toward bilateralism. This is best exemplified, of course, in the Canada-U.S. agreement, but there are other examples: the Israel-U.S. Free Trade Agreement, and suggestions by U.S. officials about full-fledged or partial free trade agreements with countries in the Pacific. Bilateralism can be a route to trade liberalization, as it was for the United States in the 1930s; but it can also be a path to restriction when the starting point, unlike the 1930s, is a relatively open trading system. The purpose of the FTA for both Canada and the United States is to open the market to the other country, but not to all other countries. The traditional static analysis of trade-creation versus trade-diversion for customs unions and free-trade areas does not really capture the parties' motivations for these arrangements.

The consequences for GATT of the Canada-U.S. Free Trade Agreement—or of further U.S. bilateralism—are still uncertain. The FTA will likely produce dynamic effects beneficial to third countries, although possibly not for Mexico. Despite its shortcomings, the agreement opens as much trade as the regional integration schemes in Europe.[1] But the agree-

[1]I do not wish here to discuss the protective elements that will remain in Canada-U.S. trade. Jeffrey J. Schott, "The Free Trade Agreement: A U.S. Assessment," in *The Canada-U.S. Free Trade Agreement: The Global Impact* (Washington and Ottawa, 1988), 3–4 refers to the agreement's suboptimal results in five main areas: subsidies, investment in

ment with Canada further shifts U.S. policy away from the unconditional most-favored-nation (MFN) goal that it held up as the cornerstone of GATT. This shift comes on top of other derogations from MFN in non-tariff import restrictions and government procurement.

MFN was never fully unconditional despite article 1 of GATT; many areas of discrimination existed (and many countries were excluded from receiving MFN tariff treatment from the United States). However, as with the general countervailing tendencies between openness and restriction in U.S. trade policy, there is now a fierce contest between conditional and unconditional MFN. The pendulum in the United States (as in Europe) is swinging toward conditionality. Over time, this may require profound alterations in the operation of the international system.

In summary, the dominant elements in current thinking on U.S. trade policy are the growing salience of protectionism, the increasing influence of bilateralism, and the diminishing importance of the unconditional MFN clause. When taken together, these elements signal a clearly more aggressive approach to trade relations with other countries. Multilateralism still has force, as evidenced by the negotiations in the Uruguay Round of GATT. But the balance has definitely shifted away from the earlier overwhelming emphasis on multilateralism, which is now but one of many competing philosophies. The process described here has yet to play itself out.

The tension between liberalization and protection that always exists in the United States is obviously present in Canada as well. But there is a difference; the United States is a cause of Canada's tension, whereas the reverse is not true. The history of Canadian thinking about its trade relations with the United States is an often-told story.[2] What is more interesting now that a free trade agreement with the United States is in effect are the issues raised by the agreement.

Interplay between bilateralism and multilateralism, now so much a part of the U.S. trade policy process, occurs in Canada as well. Canada, while long a participant in GATT negotiations, approached the degree of trade liberalization of the United States and the countries of Western Europe only during the last decade, largely as a result of its participation in the Tokyo Round.[3] Because of Canada's recent conversion, its statements

---

energy, government procurement, transportation, and intellectual property rights. Free trade agreements in Europe do not always address all these areas, and even the European Community has not yet received optimal results in all of them.

[2] Some examples are Murray G. Smith, "The Free-Trade Agreement in Context: A Canadian Perspective," in *Global Impact*, 37–64; and Simon S. Reisman, "The Issue of Free Trade," in *U.S.-Canadian Economic Relations: Next Steps?* (Washington, 1984), 35–51.

[3] Because GATT negotiations have successfully reduced tariffs, Canada's lesser participation in these negotiations results in its nominal tariffs on imports being still higher than

now tend to be even stronger on the importance of the multilateral system than those from official U.S. sources. One should expect this; strength in numbers is more significant for Canada than for the United States. Yet, when the moment of truth came, Canada opted for bilateralism. Free trade with the overwhelmingly dominant partner, yes; free trade with everybody, not yet. The decision to negotiate an agreement with the United States was based on pragmatic, not ideological, considerations.[4]

Nevertheless, to an outsider the debate in Canada about the ratification of the FTA had a marked ideological tone, especially when dealing with the agreement's nontrade implications. The issue of Canadian identity became more salient than the economic consequences of free trade. The weaker partner in a bilateral free trade agreement naturally has nontrade concerns relating to sovereignty, identity, and dependence that do not arise in the stronger partner.

The dominant trade issues in Canada today relate to the FTA. There is still debate as to whether the agreement will increase Canadian productivity in manufacturing and service industries to the degree necessary for a successful outcome. Some fear exists that the FTA will lead to trade diversion in favor of imports from the United States at an increased cost to Canada because of Canada's relatively high tariffs. There is concern whether arrangements for dealing with contingent U.S. protection (countervail and antidumping petitions) can be improved during the five to seven-year negotiation period called for in the FTA.[5] Finally, the continuing Canadian debate includes many specific issues about the workings of the agreement in practice. This issue will dominate thinking on trade in Canada for the indefinite future.

The Mexican *apertura* involves a more profound change for that country than the FTA demands from either Canada or the United States, although it clearly does not have the same systemic implications. A half century of internal development as the only engine of growth is being jettisoned. The process still has a long way to go until Mexico can be classified as an open economy, but it has come very far. Few imports now require prior licenses. Tariffs, at a maximum of 20 percent, are still mod-

those of the United States. A comparison of tariff rates for manufacturing industries in Canada and the United States can be found in Economic Council of Canada, *Reaching Outward* (Ottawa, 1987), 28.

[4]This is evident from reading the Royal Commission on the Economic Union and Development Prospects for Canada, *Report* (Ottawa, 1985). The practical aspects are also clear in Richard G. Lipsey and Murray G. Smith, *Taking the Initiative: Canada's Trade Options in a Turbulent World* (Toronto, 1985), which influenced the decision to take the initiative.

[5]Even if the arrangements are not improved, Canada will be treated more favorably than third countries.

estly higher than in either Canada or the United States, but import protection is now based mostly on tariffs and not licensing, putting a premium on the exchange rate.[6] The longer the Mexican market remains
open, the more established the vested interests will become in this new
market-dominated system and the harder it will be to reverse the process.

The trade debate in Mexico focuses on the apertura, whether it is going
too fast and endangering many previously protected industries. Attention
in Mexico to the Canada-U.S. Free Trade Agreement is growing.[7] Two
concerns emerge in the discussion of the FTA, (1) whether it will lead to
diversion of exports away from Mexico, and (2) how it will affect the
GATT, which Mexico only recently joined. Sectors where Canadian
products might replace those from Mexico in the U.S. market are machinery, petrochemicals, and textile and apparel products.

The dilemmas that Mexico faces in its trade relations with the United
States are more acute than those of Canada. Mexico is certainly less prepared to compete in most areas of manufactures than is Canada; its
productivity is far lower. Mexico's tariffs are still higher than Canada's,
making a phased movement to zero more traumatic. It is just as dependent as Canada on the U.S. market, and even more dependent for manufactures—at least 80 percent of Mexico's manufacturing exports goes to
the United States. Mexico does not want to be left out of a North American trading bloc, but it does not feel ready to join. Consequently, it can
do little more than analyze the situation.

Nontrade dependencies on the United States are both more and less
severe in Mexico than in Canada. They are less severe in that the discussions one hears in Canada about cultural identity are not prevalent in
Mexico. They are more severe in that U.S. invasions of Mexico are more
recent and Mexico's loss of territory in the last century is learned by every
Mexican child. Mexico trades predominantly with the United States, but
it still looks to the rest of Latin America for its spiritual allies.

For these two reasons—economic unpreparedness and political sensitivity—Mexico is not yet ready to join a North American free trade
agreement. Mexico could not now accept many of the provisions of the
Canada-U.S. agreement, such as the liberalization of energy exports, na-

[6] I mention the exchange rate because Mexico, under its anti-inflation program, has limited peso depreciation. Mexico has a history of overvaluing the peso, but overevaluation is
especially dangerous now that the exchange rate helps to protect imports and promote
exports.
[7] See Gerardo Bueno, "El tratado de libre comercio entre Estados Unidos y Canada,"
Comercio Exterior vol. 37, no. 11 (Nov. 1987), 926–35; and Gustavo Vega Canovas, "El
acuerdo de libre comercio entre Canada y Estados Unidos: Implicaciones para México y
los paises en desarrollo," Comercio Exterior vol. 38, no. 3 (Mar. 1988), 212–18.

tional treatment for services trade, and national treatment for all but the largest foreign direct-investment takeovers.

Yet it is worth keeping in mind that trade policy is changing rapidly in Mexico. The rapid *apertura* of the Mexican economy, unthinkable less than a decade ago, is taking place. The Mexican economy is now becoming export-led, based not merely on its petroleum, but on its manufactures as well. What is today unacceptable in trade policy may become acceptable in not too many years.

LOOKING AHEAD

I want to speculate in this section, keeping in mind the assumptions set forth at the outset of the paper.

Adjustment pressures of free trade in Western Europe were not severe.[8] I expect the same to be true for the United States and Canada.[9] Investing and trading in one large, mostly open market will likely become routine. There will still be protectionists, but more powerful interests will seek to expand the scope of free trade. As for the two polar pressures—reversion to protection or loosening of protective measures not removed in the FTA—the second will likely be more powerful.

As Canadians learn that neither sovereignty nor identity is fundamentally compromised from free trade with the United States, the concerns that were so great when the FTA was debated in 1988 will dissipate. I would also expect that the United States, as it gains experience under the FTA, will be prepared to grant more than its original concession on the settlement of contingent-protection disputes.

One should not expect free trade between Canada and the United States to lead to much more than free trade, but if free trade becomes routine or boring, the agreement will have been an important accomplishment. Free trade will also likely lead to efforts toward greater stability between the two exchange rates.

Mexico's thinking about its response to the FTA is still unclear, necessarily so considering the economic and political dilemmas noted before. Mexico's best strategy would be to undertake to study in great detail, by sector and product, what trade diversion is likely from the FTA. Indeed, Mexico may find a receptive audience in Canada and the United States if it can demonstrate that the FTA will damage it in specific areas.

[8] Smith, "Free Trade Agreement in Context."
[9] Sunder Magun et al., "Open Borders: An Assessment of the Canada-U.S. Free Trade Agreement," discussion paper 344 (Ottawa, Economic Council of Canada, Apr. 1988) projects increased output, employment, and income in Canada under most simulations undertaken.

SIDNEY WEINTRAUB

Beyond that, the evolution of Mexican trade policy will depend on the success of the current experiment with *apertura*.[10] If nonpetroleum exports continue to grow as they have during the past four years, then Mexican fears about North American free trade will diminish. The opposite outcome is also possible—export growth could diminish (especially if the exchange rate becomes overvalued), and Mexico could revert to looking inward. My opinion is that Mexico should begin to position itself for free-trade negotiations with the United States and Canada because the opportunity may arise in the not-too-distant future.

[10] In my view, the government is playing with fire by having allowed the peso to appreciate, in the name of fighting inflation, as much as it did in 1988. [Ed. note: The peso has continued to appreciate slowly, relative to the dollar, as of the date of publication.]

Index

Index

Library of Congress Cataloging-in-Publication Data

The Dynamics of North American trade and investment : Canada, Mexico,
    and the United States / Edited by Clark W. Reynolds, Leonard Waverman,
    and Gerardo Bueno.
    p.   cm.
Includes index.
ISBN 0-8047-1864-4 (cloth)
    1. North America—Commerce.   2. Investments—North America.
3. North America—Foreign economic relations.   4. Free trade—North
America.   I. Reynolds, Clark Winton.   II. Waverman, Leonard.
III. Bueno, Gerardo M.
HF3211.D96   1991   90-41907
382'.097—dc20   CIP

 ⊗ This book is printed on acid-free paper.